THE AUSTRALIAN ROAD TO SINGAPORE

THE AUSTRALIAN ROAD TO SINGAPORE
THE MYTH OF BRITISH BETRAYAL

AUGUSTINE MEAHER IV

Australian Scholarly

First published 2010, reprinted 2021
Australian Scholarly Publishing Pty Ltd
7 Lt Lothian St Nth, North Melbourne, Vic 3051
TEL: 03 9329 6963
EMAIL: enquiry@scholarly.info
WEB: scholarly.info

ISBN 978-1-921509-95-7

Copyediting by Ally Cheah
Design and typesetting by Sarah Anderson
Cover illustration from the Bulletin, 14 January 1942

This book is dedicated to my grandfathers George W. Booker, who served in the South Pacific in the Second World War, and Augustine Meaher Jr., who always encouraged me to read and never found a book on military history he did not share with his grandson.

CONTENTS

ACKNOWLEDGEMENTS

The assistance and support I received from many people all over the world was crucial to writing the thesis upon which this book is based. No one helped more or offered more valuable assistance than Professor John Lack, my supervisor, who shared his insights, thoughts and immense library with me. John's Australians at War course first interested me in Australian military history and attracted me to the University of Melbourne as an undergraduate in 1995. John's support and insight have been invaluable and have been offered around the world. I hope that I am as understanding and useful a supervisor as he has been. I am grateful also to Sue Lack for proofreading this book.

Dr Charles Schencking my co-supervisor has also been a crucial source of insight and has offered invaluable advice especially on Japan. The experience I gained as a tutor for his Total War in Asia and the Pacific was invaluable.

I would also like to thank Carl Bridge and John Hirst, who agreed to serve as examiners and provided many useful comments and insights which have been included in this book; and Paul Nicholls and Robert Murray, who by approaching the thesis from different backgrounds offered valuable suggestions on several chapters.

Archivists in five countries and countless institutions were crucial. Graeme Powell and his staff at the National Library of Australia's Manuscript Room were especially helpful and set a standard to which all archives should aspire. Staff at the Basil Liddell Hart Centre for Military Archives at King's College London made me feel at home while I was in London, and the staff of the Public Records Office (London) were a great help as I tried to master the British Archival system and willingly provided dozens of documents a day.

Two personal friends also deserve a special acknowledgement for finding and translating some particularly obscure documents: Karin Kruesi in Zug Switzerland and Vera Shepel of Kiev Ukraine, now living in Adelaide. They had most certainly thought that living in Europe would spare them from my PhD research, as both had endured my MA at Tulane University. Nonetheless they assisted without complaint in spite of their own busy lives.

A special thanks must also go to all the people at Newman College, especially College Rector Father Bill Uren SJ and Deputy Rector Sean Burke. Both were there to cheer me up when the thesis hit a particularly rough spot and cheerfully tolerated my long absences, necessitated through frequent trips to archives and conferences. Newman provided me with a wonderful environment and I will be eternally grateful that I was invited to join the Senior Common Room. In particular, I wish to thank Jenny McMillan, Sarah Nicole, Marita O'Callaghan and Monika Skubisz, four terrific friends, who have all learned more about Australian defence and foreign policy than they ever wanted to know.

A very special thanks must also go to the great people at Australian Scholarly Publishing especially Nick and Teryn without whose hard work this manuscript would have remained in limbo between the United States, Australia, and Estonia. I'd also like to thank Andrea Slater a great friend who provided a much needed outsider's perspective and always cheered me up when the writing seemed to be going nowhere.

No one has been more supportive of me in my PhD than my family, who have always encouraged me to study History and without whose support I could never have gone to Australia.

ABBREVIATIONS AND ACRONYMS

AAP	Australian Associated Press
AB	Army Board (Australia)
ABC	Australian Broadcasting Commission
AFV	Armoured Fighting Vehicle
AIF	Australian Imperial Force
ALP	Australian Labor Party
ASIGS	Australian Section of the Imperial General Staff
AWM	Australian War Memorial
BHP	Broken Hill Propriety Company (Australia)
CAC	Commonwealth Aircraft Corporation (Australia)
CAF	Citizen Air Force (Australia)
CID	Committee of Imperial Defence
CMF	Citizen Military Forces (Australia)
COL	Column
COS	Chiefs of Staff
CP	Country Party (Australia)
GMH	General Motors Holden
HC	House of Commons (United Kingdom)
HMAS	His Majesty's Australian Ship
HMS	His Majesty's Ship
HR	House of Representatives (Australia)
IDC	Imperial Defence College (United Kingdom)
IJA	Imperial Japanese Army
IJN	Imperial Japanese Navy
LNU	League of Nations Union
MSB	Munitions Supply Board (Australia)
NAA	National Archives of Australia
NAT	Nationalist Party (Australia)
NLA	National Library of Australia

NLA MFM	National Library of Australia Microfilm
NLA MS	National Library of Australia Manuscript
NSW	New South Wales, Australia
NT	Northern Territory, Australia
PRO	Public Records Office, United Kingdom
PRO ADM	Public Records Office, Admiralty
PRO CAB	Public Records Office, Cabinet
PRO CO	Public Records Office, Colonial Office
PRO DO	Public Records Office, Dominion Office
PRO FO	Public Records Office, Foreign Office
PRO PREM	Public Records Office, Prime Minister's Office
PRO WO	Public Records Office, War Office
Qld	Queensland, Australia
RAAF	Royal Australian Air Force
RAF	Royal Air Force (United Kingdom)
RAN	Royal Australian Navy
RMC	Royal Military College (Australia)
RN	Royal Navy (United Kingdom)
RSL	Returned and Services League (Australia)
SA	South Australia
Tas	Tasmania, Australia
UAP	United Australia Party
Vic	Victoria, Australia
VSP	Victorian Socialist Party
WA	Western Australia
WILPF	Women's International League for Peace and Freedom

TIMELINE OF MAJOR AUSTRALIAN, IMPERIAL AND INTERNATIONAL EVENTS, 1919–42

Year	Domestic	Imperial	International
1919	Nationalist Government re-elected, Hughes PM	Jellicoe's Dominion Tour	Treaty of Versailles officially ends Great War; US Senate votes not to join League of Nations
1920	Swinburne Committee reports on defence; Country Party formed		League of Nations first meets; Warren Harding elected US President
1921	Munitions Supply Board established; RAAF established	British Cabinet agrees to build Singapore navy base; Imperial Conference London	Washington Naval Conference begins
1922	Nationalists and Country Party win majority at federal elections	Conservative Government elected, Bonar Law PM	Washington Naval Conference concludes; Chanak Crisis; Mussolini seizes power in Italy
1923	Bruce–Page Coalition Government formed, Bruce (NAT) becomes PM	Bonar Law retires, Stanley Baldwin PM; Minority Labour Government elected with Ramsay MacDonald PM; Imperial Conference London, defines Imperial defence	France and Belgium occupy Ruhr; Anglo–Japanese Alliance terminated; US President Warren Harding dies, replaced by Calvin Coolidge; Tokyo earthquake
1924	ALP expels Communists; HMAS *Sydney* scuttled	Singapore navy base cancelled; Conservative Government elected, Stanley Baldwin PM; Singapore navy base construction resumes	
1925	Bruce–Page Coalition Government re-elected	CID applies Ten-Year Rule to Japan	
1926		Imperial Conference, London; Balfour Declaration issued	General Strike in Britain
1927	Federal Parliament opens in Canberra		

1928	Salmond Report on RAAF; Bruce–Page Coalition Government re-elected		Kellogg–Briand Pact outlaws war; Herbert Hoover elected US President; Hirohito becomes Emperor of Japan
1929	Scullin Government (ALP) elected; Plan of Concentration written; CMF made voluntary	Labour Government elected, Ramsay MacDonald PM	US stock market crash
1930		Imperial Conference in London	
1931	Langites expelled from ALP; Joseph Lyons leaves ALP and leads UAP to victory	National Government elected (Labour and Conservatives) Ramsay MacDonald PM; Statute of Westminster enacted	Japan occupies Manchuria
1932	ABC established	Ottawa Conference establishes Imperial Preference; Ten-Year Rule rescinded	Shanghai Crisis; Franklin Roosevelt elected US President
1933	Defence budget lowest of inter-war period		Hitler appointed Chancellor; Germany leaves League of Nations; Japan leaves League of Nations
1934	Latham leads Australian Eastern Mission; UAP re-elected, Lyons PM; Victorian centenary	Hankey's Dominion Tour	Hitler becomes Fuhrer; Japan renounces Washington Naval treaties
1935	Lyons visits Washington; Curtin becomes leader of ALP	National Government re-elected in UK, Stanley Baldwin PM	Italy invades Abyssinia
1936	Langites re-admitted to ALP; Commonwealth Aircraft Corporation established; Australia enacts trade diversion against Japan and United States	Abdication Crisis	Hitler remilitarises Rhineland; Spanish Civil War begins; Franklin Roosevelt re-elected US President
1937	UAP Government re-elected, Lyons PM	Neville Chamberlain replaces Stanley Baldwin as PM; Imperial Conference London	Sino–Japanese War begins
1938	Ellington Report on RAAF		Anschluss; Munich crisis; Germany occupies Sudetenland
1939	Lyons dies in office; Menzies becomes PM; Australia declares war on Germany; 2nd AIF formed	Britain declares war on Germany; Empire Air Training Scheme established	Germany occupies all of Czechoslovakia; Nationalists win Spanish Civil War; Germany invades Poland

1940	AIF sent to Middle East; Communist Party of Australia declared illegal; air crash kills three ministers and Chief of Australian General Staff; Fadden replaces Cameron as leader of Country Party	Winston Churchill replaces Neville Chamberlain as PM	Germany invades Denmark and Norway; Germany invades France, Belgium Luxembourg and the Netherlands; Italy declares war on Britain and France; Franklin Roosevelt re-elected US President
1941	8th Division of AIF sent to Singapore; Tobruk Falls; Australian forces arrive in Greece; Fadden replaces Menzies as PM; Curtin replaces Fadden as PM; Australia declares war on Japan; Curtin announces 'Australia looks to America'	Allies invade Syria and Lebanon; HMS *Prince of Wales* and HMS *Repulse* sunk off Malaya; British and Imperial troops retreat down Malay peninsula	Germany invades Greece and Yugoslavia; Germany invades Soviet Union; Japan occupies French Indochina; Japan attacks Pearl Harbor; Hong Kong falls; Manilla occupied by Japanese troops
1942	Rabaul falls to Japanese forces; Darwin bombed 19 February 1942	Fall of Singapore 15 February 1942	Kuala Lumpur falls to Japan; Japanese landings in Dutch East Indies

PREFACE

AUSTRALIA, THE EMPIRE AND THE WORLD: AN OVERVIEW

Britain entered the Great War to prevent Germany from dominating continental Europe and challenging British global supremacy as the world's largest empire and naval and trading power. To do this it drew on the manpower and material resources of its dominions and colonies, forged alliances with old enemies and incurred substantial debts to the rising powers of Japan and the United States. Peace in 1919 was a victory for Britain and her Empire, but the cost in lives (nearly a million dead) and war debt ($4 billion to the United States) was enormous.[1] Australia had lost approximately 59,000 men.[2] In June 1927 Australia's wartime expenditures were estimated at A£657 million, of which over half came from loans.[3] The bulk of this money was borrowed from Great Britain to be repaid over 35 years. Of the A£54 owed per head of population, A£16 per head was owed abroad, predominantly to the United States.[4] In part to help service Australia's war debt, the Commonwealth's taxation almost tripled to A£9 10s per head.

Australia was heavily influenced by the losses of the Great War and would struggle through the inter-war period to adjust to the altered balance of power in the Pacific. Other nations were less constrained with the United States consolidating its position as the world's pre-eminent power for its greater sacrifices and Japan acquiring former German colonies and with them a sea frontier with Australian territories. Nevertheless, the British Empire and Australia's place in it continued to condition Australia's foreign and defence policies and domestic politics at the expense of broader strategic alliances.

First developed as a concept in the 1870s, Imperial defence needed to reflect the changed strategic and political situation following the Great War. Aware of this, Australia asked Admiral Viscount John Rushworth Jellicoe to formulate an Imperial naval strategy during his 1919 Dominion tour. While Singapore had been mooted as a suitable site for a naval base prior to the First World War, Rushworth's proposal for a Pacific fleet based at Singapore was swiftly rejected by London and Australia as too expensive. However, the ability of the Royal Navy to operate in the Pacific out of Singapore was attractive, and in 1921 the British Cabinet relented and informed the Dominions at the 1921 Imperial Conference that it would construct the base.

Imperial Conferences allowed Dominion Prime Ministers to meet with their British counterparts. Although Imperial defence was a major issue at most Imperial Conferences, the primary issue of debate during the 1920s was the status of the Dominions. Thus while the 1921 Conference declared that there would be a common Imperial foreign policy which the Dominions would help craft, there was no attempt to establish frequent and regular consultation and no Dominion argued for it. Contrary to Australian wishes, Imperial policy was neither decided nor substantially influenced by the Dominions. Hence when the British Government decided to cancel—and then resume—construction of the base in 1924 it did so without consulting Australia. By this time Singapore had become a crucial component in Australian defence planning and the lack of consultation by Great Britain presented Australia with a significant dilemma.

The Chanak crisis of 1922 made it clear that consultation was impossible and that Canada and South Africa had no desire to follow British foreign policy. They demanded a formalisation of their status at the 1926 Imperial Conference and were rewarded with the Balfour Declaration which declared that the Dominions were 'Autonomous

Communities' and were 'in no way subordinate to one another in any aspect of their domestic or external affairs'.[5] Five years later the Statute of Westminster was enacted freeing the Dominions from external control. Australia's Prime Minister James Scullin, however, chose not to enact the Statute and thereby assert Australian independence. By choosing not to enact the Statute consultation was now out of the question and Australia was committed to following British policy.

Subscribing to British defence policy seemed wise in 1919 when the Royal Navy's supremacy was unchallenged and Japan was still an ally. A reduction in the size of the Australian military was inevitable following postwar demobilisation, and cuts were reasonable in the immediate postwar world. Europe was at peace, the German High Seas Fleet had been interned in Scotland and Japan was an ally and liberal in its international outlook. These defence reductions predated the Washington Conference of 1921–22. Prime Minister William (Billy) Hughes was gambling that the upcoming Imperial Conference in London would reach an agreement that allowed the renewal of the Anglo-Japanese Alliance, thereby avoiding an arms race.[6] Hughes had presented his 1920 defence policy as one based on the premise that a nation could not allow its war insurance to lapse.[7] The Royal Australian Navy, however, was reduced to only 4,500 sailors and its flagship, HMAS *Australia*, was 'mothballed'.[8] This removed Australia's only capital ship from service at a time when the Anglo-Japanese Alliance was uncertain and both the United States and Japan had embarked on massive naval buildups.[9]

The Hughes Government knew that Australia's defence policy needed to be re-evaluated. Defence Minister George Foster Pearce established the Swinburne Committee, comprising General James Gordon Legge, General Sir James McCay and former Victorian Minister for Agriculture George Swinburne to discuss Australia's postwar army policy. The Committee's terms of reference stated that 'finances were straitened' and therefore any recommendations must be 'within reason'.[10] Pearce firmly stated that 'practicability' or economy was the most important factor to consider.[11]

Historian David Horner claims correctly that the Swinburne Report, the Army's major study of Australian defence during the inter-war period, was the basis of Army planning for the next two decades.[12] The Swinburne Committee reported that Japan was the only possible foe. They believed it could field an army of over half a million men and easily transport an invasion force of 100,000.[13] To give Australia 'a sporting chance' the Committee proposed that a Central Training Depot be created along with 130,000 peacetime troops, most of whom would be in the part-time militia, the Citizen Military Forces (CMF).[14] The Swinburne Committee assumed that only these soldiers would be available to defend Australia. In ignoring the Government's preference for a blue water strategy, and failing to propose a policy that complemented it, the Committee's recommendations were utterly unrealistic and largely ignored. Indeed, the Central Training Depot was in existence for just six months before it was closed by the Hughes government.[15] However, the Army clung to the Swinburne Report determinedly and Army inflexibility ensured that the Army was attractive to budget cutters.

Although the Washington Naval Treaties provided 'breathing space for discussion and reflection',[16] they did not warrant further disarmament measures. As the historian Malcolm Murfett has written, 'by appeasing the Americans in this way, the British were making themselves potentially more strategically vulnerable'.[17] Australia was thus even more vulnerable, for the Imperial Japanese Navy was a one-ocean navy with newer ships.[18] The Hughes Government instituted massive defence cuts following the Washington Treaties when budget cuts should have been conservative in view of the reductions made prior to the Conference. Australia could hardly afford to wait until attack was imminent before preparing for conflict.

For most of the inter-war period Conservative parties governed Australia, the electorate only once opting for an ALP government. In 1929 the election of the ALP under James Scullin, 'a sincere pacifist',[19] put the ALP in charge of Australia's defence policy for the first time since Labor split over conscription in 1916. Scullin's government not only 'failed completely to carry out any reorientation of Australian defence policy',[20] but further weakened Australia's defences. Admittedly this ministry had the Depression and a hostile

Senate to contend with but the Prime Minister's views on defence were hardly realistic. Scullin's prescription for the Manchurian crisis was to 'refrain from making statements that might aggravate the present strained relations between China and Japan'.[21] He abolished compulsory military training, thereby robbing Australia of a trained body of men for defence.[22] At the 1930 Imperial Conference Scullin did not ask questions about defence and refused to pressure Britain to expedite construction at Singapore in spite of advice from his own defence department to do so.[23] In 1934 he stated to Parliament:

> Australia should concentrate upon purely defensive, non-aggressive equipment that will not be provocative, but will emphasize Australia's desire to live at peace with the rest of the world.[24]

Unfortunately, Australia's policy had to take account of the desires of other nations. As his biographer, J.H. Robertson attests, Scullin viewed international affairs through the 'simple ready-made framework of the immediate postwar years'.[25] The idea that war was the fault of warring capitalists was the dominant view in the federal parliamentary ALP.

When the conservatives returned to government in 1931 under Joseph Lyons and the newly-formed UAP, they found Australia's defences in a deplorable condition. However, Lyons had no experience in foreign affairs and his government's first priority was dealing domestically with the Depression. Developing a comprehensive defence policy was therefore of secondary importance, and both the ALP's isolationism and lack of a comprehensive defence policy ensured foreign policy was rarely debated in Parliament.

Lyons continued to lead Australia until his death in April 1939 when he was succeeded by Robert Menzies. It fell to Menzies to lead Australia into the Second World War in September 1939, a decision at least tacitly supported by the Labor Opposition. Menzies was re-elected in 1940 but his majority was small, and by August 1941 he had lost the confidence of his colleagues and resigned from office. Menzies was succeeded by Country Party (CP) leader Arthur Fadden who governed for just over a month before losing the support of independent MPs, who held the balance of power. This brought the ALP under John Curtin into office.

PROLOGUE

> We Australians are faced with a war for survival. The enemy thunders at our very gates.[1]
> Prime Minister John Curtin, 24 January 1942

The Pacific War began with almost simultaneous attacks by Japanese forces on American, British and Dutch territories on 7 and 8 December 1941. The speed of the Japanese assault was unexpected. Hong Kong fell on 25 December, Manila just five days later and Kuala Lumpur on 11 January 1942. Less than two weeks later on 23 January Rabaul, the capital of New Guinea and an Australian territory, was taken. On 15 February 1942 the fall of Singapore with its mighty naval base marked the end of any chance of a swift Japanese defeat by the British Royal Navy and sealed Australia's fate in Pacific events. Australia could call only on its own forces and resources. 'We know the constant threat of invasion', declared Australia's Prime Minister John Curtin on 27 December 1941, observing with a sense of abandonment that 'Australia can go and Britain can still hold on'.[2]

Australia's fear of Japan had been mounting steadily since Japan's defeat of Russia in 1905. Curtin was convinced that Japan was determined both on territorial conquest and destruction of the White Australia Policy, and implied this influenced Japan's decision to turn to the south.[3] Given this state of affairs, one might reasonably have expected not only an air of anxiety but preparedness and confidence that the nation's defences would ensure the containment if not immediate repulse of that threat. Unfortunately for Australia, however, defence policy throughout the inter-war period was dominated by wishful thinking and a failure to acknowledge the threats the nation faced.[4] Consequently, panic and unpreparedness dominated Australia's reaction to the onset of the Pacific War.

Curtin's response to the start of the Pacific War was in marked contrast to Prime Minister Robert Menzies' declaration of war on Nazi Germany in 1939. Menzies' speech had been marked by resignation at the outbreak of another European war: 'It is my melancholy duty', he began, 'to inform you officially that, in consequence of a persistence by Germany in her invasion of Poland, Great Britain has declared war upon her and that, as a result Australia is also at war'.[5] There was, at that time, no sense of panic or anything that hinted at unpreparedness. However, by 1941 the world situation was very different. The Japanese advance threatened numerous European possessions, including Britain's. The Australian government and public, for their part, reacted as though the Commonwealth and its island territories were Japan's main target. This fear underpinned the Curtin Government's belief that Australia deserved American and British protection first and foremost.

As the Japanese swept down the Malay Peninsula and into the Dutch East Indies in early 1942 the Australian Government became rattled. Curtin's famous Melbourne *Herald* article on 31 December 1942 declared:

> Without any inhibitions of any kind, I make it quite clear that Australia looks to America, free of any pangs as to our traditional links of kinship with the United Kingdom.[6]

Curtin was soon forced to disavow any intention of making a bold change of foreign policy: 'nothing in his statement was to be taken as meaning a weakening of Australia's ties with the British Empire'.[7] But his statement stood as a desperate plea for help and clear admission that Australia's inter-war foreign and defence policies had been outpaced by events. His plea also attempted to disabuse the United States of any notion that an 'Invasion of Australia and New Zealand or India is beyond the present resources of Japan',[8] and that 'the Atlantic and European area [should be] considered to be the decisive theatre'.[9] As 1941 gave way to 1942, the panic motivating the pleas for help became increasingly evident. On New Year's Eve the *Australian Worker* declared: 'Everyone in Australia expects invasion of our soil'.[10]

Japanese landings in the Dutch East Indies and New Guinea in January 1942 prompted the Minister for Supply John (Jack) Beasley to declare that the Japanese were 'on the threshold of Australia' and that with 'the battle of the Pacific lost, the Japanese Navy is ready for service in the Atlantic'.[11] The idea that Japanese naval vessels would ever operate in the Atlantic was ludicrous. Beasley's statements were an admission that Australian territories were defended insufficiently to delay, much less deter, the Japanese advance. His statements—a desperate plea for American assistance—betrayed a widely held fear that a Japanese victory was at hand. They also displayed a misguided assumption that Australia was Japan's primary target.

On 24 January 1942 John Curtin declared that the enemy 'thunders at our very gates'.[12] Instead of turning to America, the lapsed Catholic turned rationalist now turned to God: 'This Australia is for Australians; it is a White Australia, [and] with God's blessing we shall keep it so'.[13] Three days later Francis Forde, Minister for the Army, claimed: 'The advantage to Japan of a successful invasion is so obvious that we must gravely assume that an attempt may be made'.[14] For a nation accustomed to 'the constant threat of invasion' this should hardly have come as a surprise.

On 23 January 1942 the Australian War Cabinet had cabled British Prime Minister Winston Churchill concerning the fast-deteriorating situation in Malaya:

> After all the assurance we have been given, the evacuation of Singapore would be regarded here and elsewhere as *an inexcusable betrayal.* Singapore is a central fortress in the system of Empire and local defence.

Singapore was neither abandoned nor defended to the last man, but surrendered by the British on 15 February 1942. Curtin regarded Japanese invasion as imminent, even inevitable.

> The fall of Singapore [he declared] opens the Battle for Australia. On its issue depends not merely the fate of this Commonwealth but the frontier of the United States of

America and, indeed, all the Americas, and therefore, in large measure, the fate of the British speaking world.[15]

This was yet another ambit attempt to link the fate of Australia with that of the United States. American pre-war plans, which had never accorded Australia a prominent role, gave priority to the protection of the 'Latin American Republics on the West Coast of South America against invasion'.[16] This strategy did not necessitate securing Australia. American logic was sound. The Monroe Doctrine of 1823 had firmly established American opposition to territorial acquisitions in the Americas by outside powers. Two days later Curtin, still lacking a concrete American commitment, warned that 'No one can know at this minute the precise target in this vast Commonwealth that the enemy has selected for his first impact; of his offensive against us'.[17]

On 19 February 1942 the Japanese threat to Australia was realised with the bombing of Darwin. Beasley rushed into an Advisory War Council meeting yelling: 'The Japs have bombed Darwin! That settles it [the destination of Australian troops returning from the Middle East]'.[18] Sir Frederick Shedden remembered that the Advisory War Cabinet behaved 'like a lot of startled chooks'.[19] In Darwin there was 'mass panic in the town's small civilian population and within the ranks of its uniformed defenders'.[20] Widespread looting occurred and many defence personnel deserted. Curtin attempted to calm the nation:

> The government regards the attacks as most grave and makes it quite clear that a severe blow has been struck on Australian soil. In this first [sic] battle on Australian soil it will be a source of pride to the public to know that the armed forces and civilians comported themselves with the gallantry that is traditional in the people of our stock.[21]

Far from heralding a full-scale Japanese invasion, however, the raid on Darwin was intended to prevent Allied counterattacks on recently captured Japanese territories and was 'Japan's southernmost and last major territorial bombardment'.[22] However, the raid led to a further panic-stricken plea to America for assistance. Broadcasting to the

United States, Curtin begged Americans to realise that 'Australia is *the last bastion* between the West Coast of America and the Japanese. If Australia goes the Americas are wide open'.[23] He struck a ludicrous, even insulting, note when he urged that 'the saving of Australia is the saving of America's west coast. If you believe anything to the contrary then you delude yourselves'.[24]

The belief both that the Japanese military were obsessed with Australia and that the defence of Australia was crucial to that of the United States continued throughout 1942. Even after the Battle of Midway in June 1942, which saw the destruction of the only possible Japanese invasion fleet, Curtin agonised that Australia could be conquered leaving the United States vulnerable: 'if that [Australia's capture] happens, then Hawaii and the whole North American coast, from Alaska to Canada down to Mexico will be open to Japanese attack'.[25] Such delusions were purely Australian.

The rhetoric of Australia's frantic leaders in the summer of 1941–42 as the Japanese war machine rolled southwards, seemingly inexorably, towards the Australian mainland incorporated two Australian certitudes that have so dominated popular writing about Australia in the Second World War as to deserve the title of 'national myths'. The first of these was a myth that issued from Australia's longstanding suspicion, now hardened into conviction, that Japan both intended and planned to invade the continent with a view to incorporating it into the Japanese Asian–Pacific Empire.

The second myth asserted that Britain had allowed Singapore and its great naval base—the base intended to warn off Japan against depredations in Southeast Asia and Oceania—to fall into Japanese hands. After pouring her troops and airmen into the European, Mediterranean and Middle Eastern theatres of war, Australia had been abandoned to her fate at the hands of her most despised and feared enemy. Consequently, continued the myth, unless America intervened Australia faced the near certainty of Japanese occupation, rapine, subjugation and racial contamination.

A third national myth—misconception, rather than myth perhaps, being of more recent invention though related to the hoary legend of Australia's central role in wining the Pacific War—asserts that far from discovering herself unarmed and defenceless in 1941–42, Australia was in fact armed and ready for war. This version of history asserts that it was Australian battle-readiness that dissuaded the Japanese in 1941 and 1942 from mounting an invasion of the mainland. Japan intended to invade but thought better of it.

Let us briefly consider each of these myths and their current status in Australian historical writing. Although seriously challenged in the early 1990s and thoroughly discredited more recently, the myth of an intended Japanese invasion simply will not go away. So evocative is this myth of old Anglo-Australian racial fears and hatred, and so soothing is it to notions of national honour humiliated and then salvaged by Australia's military performance in the Pacific War, that it is embedded in the national psyche. Over a period of almost 40 years Japan's rise as a treaty partner, war ally and naval power in a range of theatres steadily ratcheted up Australian invasion anxieties. It was the speed, rather than the direction, of Japan's southern lightning strikes in 1941–42 that surprised and alarmed Australians and their novice Labor government.

Most Australian observers in the summer of 1941–42 and later shared the view that Australia was a target for invasion. Historians such as Lionel Wigmore (1957), John McCarthy (1976) and David Day (1988), describing Australia's perilous position as the European War developed into a world war, assumed that a Japanese invasion was possible, even probable. This certitude about invasion became a media staple, especially on military anniversaries, and the nation's leading playwright David Williamson even scripted a version for television. His wife, Kristin Williamson, published a book-of-the-film, *The Last Bastion,* in 1984.

The invasion myth persists despite Henry Frei stating categorically in his important monograph on the issue, *Japan's Southward Advance and Australia* (1991), that Australia 'did not figure on the list of war objectives prepared for the [Japanese] General Staff on the eve of the outbreak of the Pacific War'.[26] Frei notes that while the Japanese Navy entertained thoughts in December 1941 of attacking strategically important points on the northern and north-eastern coasts, these raids were intended to secure maritime and air supremacy for Japanese gains in Southeast Asia. Furthermore, the Japanese Army, overstretched in China and shortly to be involved heavily in Malaya, the Dutch East Indies, Papua New Guinea and Melanesia, was reluctant to assume extensive Australian garrison duties.

Frei's research seeped into academic writing but not into popular writing and popular consciousness. In October 2002 Peter Stanley, then Principal Historian of the Australian War Memorial, extended this analysis to 1942, pronouncing 'the invasion myth … one of the more persistent furphies' of that year.[27] 'The Invasion that wasn't' placed Stanley at the centre of an acrimonious debate about Japanese war intentions and the probity of the wartime Curtin Labor government. The article argued that while officers of the Japanese Army and Navy debated their options early in 1942, neither troops nor ships could be spared as Japan consolidated her gains in Southeast Asia, maintained her presence in China and nervously studied Soviet intentions in Manchuria.

Stanley's main assailant in print was Bob Wurth, notably in *1942: Australia's Greatest Peril* (2008), a book endorsed by academic historian David Day. Almost conterminously, Stanley published his extensively documented argument as the persuasive monograph *Invading Australia: Japan and the Battle for Australia, 1942*. Undoubtedly Stanley has had the better of the argument and his undermining of the invasion myth has also dented the myth of British betrayal. In Australia's worst hour, the myth of British perfidy would have us believe Britain betrayed Australia by failing to ensure that Singapore was strong enough to survive the Japanese assault and ensure Australian safety. After all, had that not been Britain's guarantee to her Pacific Dominion? Failure to honour that guarantee amounted, in the words of the Australian War Cabinet, to 'an inexcusable betrayal'. By implication, Australia had escaped Japanese invasion and occupation by the skin of its teeth thanks to the intervention of the United States and the splendid resistance of the Australian Imperial Forces (AIF) to the Japanese in New Guinea and nearby islands.

This book seeks to debunk each of these myths through a thoroughgoing analysis both of the academic literature and historical evidence around the fall of Singapore and Australia's understanding and execution of its responsibilities—and those of Britain—under Imperial defence. If in fact it can be established, and I argue that it can be established beyond doubt, that Japan's interest in Australia was limited to isolating the continent from her American ally and preventing its conversion to an American base—a more limited objective that Japan failed, signally, to achieve—then the Australian certitude of Japanese invasion in 1941–42 is no more than a myth. This conclusion alone must remove much of the force from the charge of British betrayal in the Pacific. Similarly, if it can be established that Australia misunderstood the nature of Imperial defence then this must deliver a grievous body blow to Australia's second most cherished myth: that of British betrayal. Australia obstinately refused to discharge its responsibilities for local defence and attempted to oblige a Britain *in extremis* in 1941–42 to provide an ironclad guarantee against Japanese attack and invasion. Singapore and its mighty naval base were never intended alone to render Australia inviolate to enemy attack and to suggest otherwise is a misrepresentation of the facts. And finally, despite Japan's relatively limited assault on Australia, Australia's defences proved to be weak and ineffectual. The assertion of Australia being armed and ready for war as Day and others assert is simply not supported in military or historical terms by the evidence.

While historians such as Jeffrey Grey (1990), Paul Burns (1998) and David Horner (1998) give little credence to the notion of British betrayal in their monographs and general histories, the myth has lasted a lot longer in popular history writing thanks to numerous reprints of David Day's *The Great Betrayal* (1988)—perhaps the best known book on Australia in the war—and Day's many articles in the media. Labor Prime Minister Paul Keating gave British betrayal a popular currency for his own political purposes in 1992, but Day has done the most to prolong the life of the myth of British perfidy and it is time that his contributions were subjected to thoroughgoing analysis. Graham Freudenberg has recently furthered this myth by claiming 'Charles Bean's accusation that "Churchill's excess of imagination" caused disaster at Gallipoli in 1915 rings true for Singapore in 1942'.[28]

In 1995, when Australians were celebrating the jubilee of the ending of the Pacific war ('Australia Remembers'), there was an attempt to add a third and face-saving myth to the story of how Australian defences saved the situation in 1941–42. Contrary to the accepted account of Australia defenceless and vulnerability before the Japanese threat, A.T. Ross' book *Armed and Ready*—adjudged scholarly and convincing enough to warrant the imprimatur-by-subsidy of the 'Australia Remembers' authorities in 1995—asserted that by 1942 sufficient trained men and stockpiled materiel existed to repulse any Japanese invasion. Furthermore, Ross argued, Japan's understanding of Australian preparedness made the enemy have second thoughts. While established historians have been dismissive of Ross' claims,[29] his book has largely escaped serious scholarly scrutiny.

The Road to Singapore argues that while Australia did not face a full-scale invasion in 1941–42, it was neither armed nor ready for the limited Japanese attacks that did occur. The Curtin Labor government privately blamed British betrayal for Australian vulnerability, but the situation revealed a basic misunderstanding of the nature of Imperial defence: that being the necessity for an adequate home defence to complement the role of the British navy. Britain could not and did not give Australia an ironclad guarantee of inviolability against coastal and air attack. The real question is why Australia persisted in believing that it had an entitlement to such complete protection and had enjoyed that protection in the past.

The first chapter of *The Road to Singapore* demonstrates that Australia was not armed or ready either for the European War in 1939 or for the Pacific war in 1941, which converted the European War into a truly global conflict. Australia lacked sufficient trained troops and weapons of all types, possessed a miniscule air force and lacked the infrastructure to transport troops and equipment around the continent.

In truth, during the inter-war years Australians and their governments misunderstood Imperial defence and especially the Singapore strategy component of it. Imperial defence did not mean that the Royal Navy (RN) would protect Australia come what may and the Singapore naval base was never intended, despite Curtin's claims, to be a key component of Australia's local defence.[30] Not only did Australia's armed services fail to reach a consensus on the meaning of Imperial defence or develop a coordinated defence policy, but armed service rivalries ensured that inter-war governments received a variety of often contradictory opinions on an appropriate defence strategy. This confusion, combined with a failure on both sides of politics to appreciate the dangers revealed by inter-war crises, allowed successive Australian governments to minimise defence spending and exacerbated, rather than strengthened, Australia's local defence weaknesses.

The inability of Australian governments to agree on what sort of attack Australia was likely to face sprang, at least in part, from a failure to appreciate the significance of the rise of fascism in Italy and Spain, Nazism in Germany and Japanese militarism—all of which threatened to precipitate European and Asian wars. In spite of numerous attempts by concerned citizens, Australian governments and the public did not appreciate the national implications of these major inter-war international crises. The class-based and highly partisan nature of inter-war domestic politics undermined national comprehension.

But domestic politics alone cannot explain Australia's unpreparedness. Australia's industrial, military and political elites played a critical role in shaping Australian foreign and defence policy. Historians have only cursorily examined these elites and never in relation to their role in conditioning Australian foreign and defence policies.[31] Well-integrated elites might have generated and assimilated progressive thinking on Australia's place in the world and the need for appropriate foreign and defence policies during years of deteriorating international order. But Australian elites, deeply divided as they were by education, occupation and religious sectarianism, were not well integrated. The weakness in leadership was critical in the 1930s when Australia faced an increasingly hostile world with limited resources and minimal defence forces. Rectifying these problems required from these elites urgent and coordinated responses. The inadequacies of Australia's elites offer the ultimate reason why Australia was so unprepared for the outbreak of war first in Europe and later in the Pacific.

The Australian Road to Singapore examines key elements of Australia's defence position and policy in the pre-war and inter-war periods. Chapter 1 investigates Australia's preparedness for invasions including large-scale occupations or raids in 1941–42. It argues that both United Australia Party (UAP) and Australian Labor Party (ALP) policies proved inadequate to Australian needs and that Australia consequently was incapable of producing sufficient arms, aircraft or vehicles quickly enough to meet the threat it feared after the fall of Singapore. Additional aspects of Australian defence policy and its underpinnings are examined in subsequent chapters.

Chapter 2 examines the historiography of Australian inter-war defence policy, broadly divided into early accounts and histories both of foreign policy and the armed forces and popular historical works. Historians who have researched the inter-war period have done so largely with reference to specific services, people or policies. The chapter argues that in order to answer why Australia was and felt so vulnerable in 1941–42, it is necessary to consider Australian defence and foreign policies together. Further, research must be focused on Australian decisions in the context of Imperial policies as Australians chose to understand and interpret them.

Chapter 3 examines the concept of Imperial defence and the nature of Anglo-Australian relations in regard to Australian defence policy. It contends that Imperial defence, the cornerstone of Australian defence, was fundamentally misunderstood by Australian armed services and politicians and that Australian governments ignored the Imperial defence requirement that a nation provide for its own local defence. Properly understood, Imperial defence would have allowed Australia to weather the turmoil of early 1942 much better. But Australian politicians failed to realise the need to articulate and implement more detailed and unified local defence policies.

Chapter 4 examines Australian political and public responses to the international crises of the 1930s. It argues that the significance of Abyssinia, the Spanish Civil War, the Anschluss and the Sino-Japanese conflicts was not appreciated by successive Australian governments, which failed to enact effective policies in response to an increasingly dangerous world. Additionally, although Australian governments tried repeatedly to improve relations with the United States, these efforts were hindered by a fundamental misunderstanding of the United States at the political and public level.

Chapter 5 demonstrates that numerous attempts were made within Australia to alert the Australian government, military and public that war was imminent. Many publications by politicians, public servants, soldiers and ordinary citizens highlighted the dangers Australia faced. However, radio was a new medium and few warnings reached a large audience or had a noticeable effect on public thinking, military planning or government policy making.

Chapter 6 explores why the warnings of Australia's peril were ignored. A failure to agree on the nature of the threat, debate over raids or invasion and an Opposition seemingly incapable of challenging the government on defence allowed the government to remain committed to a naval-centred strategy at the expense of a stronger local defence.

Chapter 7 provides a brief historical overview of inter-war politics. It argues that neither major political party critically examined Imperial defence nor its underlying assumptions, and each, in opposition, failed to hold the government accountable for its policies. Particular weight is given to the ALP's role in opposition and focus on a defence policy designed to keep the party from splitting rather than addressing Australia's needs. Additional attention is given to the influence of pacifist organisations and advocates of collective security, who further discouraged the development of realistic defence policies.

Chapter 8 argues that one of the main reasons repeated warnings fell on deaf ears was a failure of Australian leadership owing to an inability of the various elites—political, military and industrial—to communicate effectively with each other. An analysis of the socio-economic background of members of the elites demonstrates significant differences which no doubt contributed to their often insular operations. The failure of members of the industrial elite to communicate their concerns effectively to others or to the political elite ensured that alternate opinions and policies were not available to government.

CHAPTER 1

UNARMED AND UNREADY

In his seminal work *Armed and Ready* (1995), historian A.T. Ross contends that Australia was fully aware of its responsibilities under Imperial defence and that both Nationalist and UAP governments had embarked on a bold programme of industrial development which provided Australia with the industrial capacity to arm itself.[1] Hence, by June 1942 the Department of Munitions had produced enough armaments to equip an anti-invasion force,[2] and Australia was 'armed and ready' for what lay ahead. Forthright and persuasively detailed, Ross's thesis is convincing until examined more closely. As this chapter will show, and contrary to Ross's thesis, industrial development during the inter-war period was driven overwhelmingly by *economic* rather than strategic concerns. Rearmament was not a profitable enterprise for most of the inter-war period because of the small size of the Australian market and had little attraction to an industrial elite focused on profit.

Australia's panic following the outbreak of war in the Pacific was demonstrated in the desperation of Prime Minister Curtin's appeal to the United States late in December 1941. There were good reasons for this panic. It was not just that the nation lacked the forces and equipment to defeat the much feared total invasion—enemy raids and small scale invasions aimed at securing Southeast

Asia would have also succeeded. Curtin's call for help demonstrated a realisation that Australia's determined dependence on Britain was both misplaced and foolhardy, and was an acknowledgement that the nation simply could not defend itself. Former Munitions Secretary J.K. Jensen, whom Ross cites extensively, had no doubt of Australia's situation, noting in the concluding sentence of his memoirs: 'It is obvious that invasion of this country was only stopped by the Battle of the Coral Sea'.[3]

Australia's 'unpreparedness' was systemic and the result of an apparent lack of capacity within its political, military and industrial elites over many decades to agree on the nature of the threats facing Australia and to develop a strategy to counter those threats. Australia's small industrial base necessitated a long-term approach to rearmament and the failure of the elites to reach consensus meant that in early 1942 Australia's defence capability was technologically behind Japan and the nation lacked the ability to assert local command of the air or sea. The situation was compounded by a lack of transport infrastructure which meant that the Australian forces would have struggled to protect the nation's northern and north-eastern coastlines.

THE INVASION THREAT

In considering Australia's position in 1941–42 it is important to understand Japanese intentions and capabilities in the inter-war period and the early phases of the Pacific War. At the start of the Pacific War the Imperial Japanese Navy had 10 aircraft carriers, 11 battleships and 49 cruisers which, with their support vessels, were divided into six fleets.[4] The arrival of any one of Japan's six fleets in Australian waters with their support vessels would have wreaked havoc.[5] Australia, wrote American visitor and commentator C. Harley Grattan shortly after the outbreak of the Pacific War, 'cannot hope to fend off her enemies standing alone'.[6] Additionally, as the historian Henry Frei observed in 1991, 'The southern continent did not figure on the list of war objectives prepared for the General Staff on the eve of the outbreak of the Pacific War' and Australia's vulnerability in the Pacific was largely overlooked by the Imperial forces.[7] In reality, the

Japanese were not interested in conquering Australia in 1941–42 as 'Southeast Asia already offered everything Japan needed'.[8] Within this context David Horner's observation that 'Capabilities and intentions are very often confused in the minds of those making assessments' is well noted.[9]

In December 1941 the Imperial Japanese Navy proposed invading 'the strategically most important points on the northern and northeastern coasts of Australia' to secure Japan's southern flank.[10] Such an incursion, Frei argues, would almost certainly have succeeded for it would have allowed Japan to 'annihilate the enemy's maritime forces, cut the American–Australian line of communication, and thereby deal the entire Australian nation a thorough blow'.[11] An invasion aimed at securing Southeast Asia threatened northern Australia, an area not protected by the Plan of Concentration, the Army's Sydney-centred plan for protecting Australian territory. In practice this would have meant that 'northern Australia would have suffered the same fate as Rabaul and Ambon'.[12]

The threat of invasion was a crucial factor in determining an appropriate defence strategy. The different services took dramatically different views as to the size of that threat. The Australian Army was the most anti-Japanese in its views throughout the inter-war period warning, as early as 1920, that 'Australia is exposed to the danger of invasion' and cautioning that Japan could transport an invasion force of 100,000 fully armed men in one convoy.[13] The Army, however, did not have a strategy to defeat such an invasion. Its first contingency plan in the inter-war period was for expeditionary warfare, not home defence. Prepared in response to the 1922 Chanak crisis, Plan 401 was to be implemented 'when the Australian territory is not threatened but the forces of the Empire are engaged or are likely to be engaged in operations outside Australia'.[14]

The fear of Japanese invasion predated federation and continued in spite of the Anglo-Japanese Alliance (1902–23). Japan's acquisition of Germany's colonies north of the Equator following the Great War temporarily exacerbated Australian fears, but the Washington Naval Conference somewhat soothed them. Henry Frei observed that following the Washington Naval Conference 'Australia slipped back into the same old kind of Nipponese ignorance that she had suffered before the war'.[15] However, ignorance did not translate into comfort and by 1928 the Army was again warning of a potential Japanese invasion. The predicted invasion was smaller now, at three divisions or less, but nevertheless an early attack on Australia in the event of war was forecast—possibly, warned the Army, on the first day of hostilities.[16] The threat of an attack coinciding with the commencement of hostilities made local defence all important. Even the most optimistic of Royal Navy plans warned of a month-long period before the navy could arrive at Singapore,[17] during which Australia would be dependent totally on its own resources.

A year later the Army developed a plan to counter a Japanese invasion: the 'Plan of Concentration'. The plan assumed that 'The most likely forms of land attack against Australia would be raids on certain important centres and/or invasion by a force of, or equivalent to about three divisions'.[18] The Army acknowledged that Japanese troops would 'probably be more highly trained and more completely equipped than any force that Australia could put into the field in the first three months of a war'.[19] Furthermore, cautioned the Army, a quick initial victory 'might place him [the enemy] in a position from which it would be difficult to eject him'.[20] The Army assumed that Japan must 'seize some area in Australia which is vital to the continuance of our economic life, and the loss of which would cripple our war effort'.[21] It concluded that Japan's objective would be Sydney or the Newcastle–Maitland area because the region contained one-fifth of Australia's population and the navy's only major repair facility, chief port and largest industrial area. Indeed, Lieutenant-Colonel Vernon Ashton Hobart Sturdee feared that 'The moral effect alone of its [Sydney's] capture by an enemy may well be sufficient to force the Commonwealth Government to sue for peace'.[22]

However, as David Horner observed, 'There were, of course, many weaknesses in this plan' and in the absence of necessary resources 'the plans were quite unrealistic'.[23] Nonetheless, the Plan of Concentration was the basis for numerous staff exercises in the 1930s although 'No corps headquarters were formed and until 1938 the divisions had no opportunity to exercise as formations'.[24] Paul Burns (1998) observes that the vulnerability of rail lines to the area of concentration meant transport would be a 'combination of horsed and motorized units' of restricted manoeuvrability.[25] Indeed the Army had noted that between Sydney and Newcastle the Hawkesbury was spanned by only one railway bridge and that 'all road crossings are by ferry'. It observed that 'this forms a very serious hindrance to north-south movement which hampers the defender far more than the attacker'.[26] Troops could not travel from one area of concentration to the other let alone to other regions of Australia. Indeed, Lieutenant-Colonel Sturdee's lecture on the plan exposed the lack of adequate roads throughout the Sydney–Newcastle region.[27]

Two years later in 1931 the Army predicted that the three divisions would land in Sydney or the Newcastle–Maitland area.[28] This was the area the Army felt best able to protect with Australia's resources, though in reality was unlikely to be invaded by an enemy protecting its southern flank in Southeast Asia. A year later the Committee of Imperial Defence (CID) warned Australia that 'the Japanese could despatch a force between 60,000 and 100,000 men'.[29] Four years later the CID warned that Japan could transport in one convoy 120,000 to 170,000 men and their equipment to Australia in a month.[30] This was a much larger threat and more difficult to repel. In the same year, however, the Chief of the Australian General Staff, Major-General Sir Julius Bruche, predicted a Japanese invasion force half that size in the order of 60,000 to 100,000 troops.[31] Horace Robertson, an Army Staff Officer, believed that Australia needed to be able to defeat an invasion of 60,000.[32] The smaller the potential invasion, the more probable it was that the Army could counter the threat.

The Royal Australian Navy (RAN), on the other hand, predicted that an invasion by Japan would require an invasion force of over a quarter of a million, which Japan could not transport to Australia. It also believed that if such a force were landed it could not be defeated.[33] However, the RAN astutely observed that 'The actual military gain or effect on the major war strategy (of an invasion) is slight'.[34] By this reckoning the Army was preparing for a nonexistent threat and the most expensive one to counter. By ruling out the possibility of an invasion the RAN was shrewdly asserting the irrelevance of the Army to Australia's defence.

The RAN believed that the greatest risk Australia faced was interdiction of trade and coastal raids—i.e., naval bombardment or small landing parties. Both threats could best be countered by naval forces preventing Japanese warships from approaching the Australian coast and protecting Australian trade. By 1937, however, the RAN accepted that Japan could mount an invasion too strong for the Army to defeat:

> [T]he force which Japan could eventually land from her conscript army of over a million backed by a population of 70,000,000, with an ample supply of munitions and air forces, and with complete freedom as to where to strike, leaves no reasonable doubt as to the final outcome.[35]

The RAN therefore felt that Australia's defence should be focused on assisting the Royal Navy to ensure that the Imperial Japanese Navy never gained naval supremacy, a requirement for invasion. As only the RAN could play a part in denying Japan naval supremacy, the navy should therefore receive the lion's share of the budget. The RAN also believed that if Japan were ever able to mount an invasion the Army could never muster the men or equipment necessary to protect Australia even if they received most of the defence budget. The events following the fall of Singapore would prove that the RAN's fears about Australia's ability to raise adequate land forces for Australia's protection were correct. However, the RAN still maintained that 'It is logical to conclude that even if Australia were her sole objective, an attempt at invasion is a very unlikely course for Japan to take'.[36]

Faced with contradictory advice the Australian delegation to the 1937 Imperial Conference asked the CID for its view on the form an invasion or raid might take, and suggestions as to how best defend Australia. Defining 'invasion' as

> an attack by a force which is landed with the intention of prolonged or even permanent occupation of the territory invaded, and which is dependent for success on the maintenance of a line of communications.

the CID concluded:

> We, therefore, assume that the invasion of Australia by Japan implies the establishment and maintenance of Japanese military forces in Australia on a scale sufficient to enable them to undertake operations with the object of eventually overcoming all Australian resistance and forcing Australia to sue for peace.[37]

The CID had therefore defined an invasion aimed at securing Australia rather than the southern flank of an advance into Southeast Asia. A definition of 'raid' was more problematic because raids could be aimed at destroying or damaging coastal fortifications, creating a diversion for a larger raid or invasion, or simply creating alarm.[38] The CID advised, however, that

> The essential characteristic of a sea-borne land raid is that it is carried out by forces that are self-contained and do not depend on a line of communication for maintenance during their operations.[39]

It additionally warned that raiding troops 'would be landed with a specific task' and 'the loss of the raiding party might be accepted'.[40] This was a more severe though vague threat than the light raid scenario, which the Government continued to believe was the most likely form of attack. The CID refused, however, to tender advice on appropriate defence preparations because

> Numerous factors may govern the scale of land attack to be expected at a given port; the chances of attack and its possible strength will be influenced by the naval situation at the moment, the strategic importance attached to the success of the particular raid, the enemy's information about the defences and many other factors.[41]

'It is therefore of little value', the CID warned, 'to attempt an accurate forecast of the maximum and scales of sea-borne land attack to be expected at a particular port'.[42] In short, Australia needed to prepare for attacks of varying scale around the continent.

WARTIME ASSESSMENTS

It is telling that as late as 1937 there was still no definition of 'invasion' other than in general terms, in spite of the Army planning for 'invasion' for nearly a decade. The outbreak of the Pacific War in December 1941 and subsequent fall of Singapore forced the military elites to radically alter their views of probable Japanese strategy and Australia's defence requirements. The inaction of inter-war governments and the failure to appreciate the danger Australia faced led to panic. Even the most pessimistic predictions of Japanese intentions and capabilities seemed too conservative. Invasion novels such as *Japan Must Fight Britain*,[43] which described a Japanese attack on Darwin, and the Japanese Prime Minister's declaration that 'The southward advance is the irrevocable destiny of the Japanese Race',[44] seemed portentous rather than the fanciful product of overactive imaginations.

The Chiefs of Staff Appreciation of 11 December 1941 warned that 'This [Japan's attack on Malaya] might well be a first step in the Japanese plan for a major attack on Australia' and that the 'most probable form of attack on the mainland of Australia was naval and air bombardment of important objectives'.[45] The usually reserved Secretary of the Department of Defence, Frederick Shedden, who had previously agreed with the RAN about the appropriate defence strategy,[46] now believed that the military was not taking the threat seriously enough. Shedden wrote to the Prime Minister: 'I was very disappointed with the showing of the Chiefs of Staff at this morning's War Cabinet meeting'.[47] He suggested the Government 'press it right home that this is a new war which entails an entire review of our position and the extent and direction of our efforts'.[48]

The resultant review of Australia's position did not lead to the realisation that invasion remained improbable for the reasons that the RAN and CID had repeatedly stated. The rapid advance of the Japanese down the Malay peninsula and into the Dutch East Indies led to increased fear, and in some cases panic, within the Australian Government. Minister for Supply Jack Beasley warned on 23 January 1942 that '[t]he Japanese are in New Guinea. In New Guinea they are on the threshold of Australia'.[49] The fall of Singapore strengthened the Government's conviction that invasion was imminent. A mere 10 days after Singapore fell the Minister for External Affairs H.V. Evatt claimed:

> when the invader comes, he will be fought here by a people who know that they are not only defending their homes, but that they are standing on one of the critical battlegrounds in the history of mankind.[50]

Gone was any suggestion that an invasion was beyond Japan's capability. It was now believed that Japan intended to and would invade Australia. That Japan had no intention of invading Australia was unknown to Australian politicians or to military leaders. They therefore had to assume the worst for which they were not prepared.

Peter Stanley's assertion that Prime Minister Curtin was 'banging the invasion drum' for electoral advantage and to maintain secrecy about Allied intelligence capabilities is probably correct after mid-1942.[51] However, in early 1942 it was not only the Government that believed invasion was a serious possibility and probability. The Chiefs of Staff reported two days after Evatt's speech that 'Japan is now at liberty to attempt the invasion of Australia' and warned that 'The forces are everywhere inadequate to meet the scale of attack that may be brought against them'.[52] A Japanese invasion force would have been composed of battle-hardened troops with several years of combat experience. Further, the Imperial Japanese Army (IJA) had considerable experience at combined operations, which gave the IJA a significant psychological advantage over the Australian forces. Additionally, the permanent Australian military was quite small. The Australian Army estimated in December 1941 that 25 divisions (approximately 375,000 men) were necessary to protect Australia. The Army had only 12.[53]

Another issue facing the Australian military was that by early 1942 the vast majority of professional and trained soldiers were either in the Middle East with the 2nd AIF or scattered throughout Australia's northern island territories. Australian local defence was primarily the responsibility of the Citizen Military Forces (CMF), commonly referred to as the 'Militia'. The CMF originally provided compulsory universal military training and had its origins in the colonial militias but in 1922 was restricted to cities and large towns.[54] In 1929 the CMF became voluntary and by 1935 was down to 26,000 men reliant on World War I vintage equipment and private vehicles for transport.[55] The CMF declined in strength again the following year.[56] In 1935 Army Staff Officer Horace Robertson warned in the *Army Quarterly* that 'militiamen cannot spare the time to deal with the increasingly technical side of war'.[57] In the same year a British report described the CMF's efficiency as 'below that of our own Territorial Force' and questioned its ability to defend Australia.[58] The Australian Government, aware of the lack of public confidence in the CMF who were commonly derided as 'Chocolate Soldiers' (likely to melt in the sun) or 'Koalas' (protected native species),[59] attempted to camouflage the CMF's weaknesses with statements such as 'Every man being trained for the AIF while still in Australia is a powerful unit in local defence'.[60]

The Lyons Government was aware of the need to strengthen the CMF, but it remained a low priority because the CMF could not be sent overseas. It appears that it did not occur either to Australian politicians or the Australian Army that a strong militia would have ensured that Australia could meet its local defence commitments. Many in the UAP favoured making CMF service compulsory, but Prime Minister Lyons believed this was 'morally repugnant, and refused to permit the existing voluntary training system to be replaced by compulsion'.[61] The Government was thus forced to focus on encouraging citizens to volunteer for the Militia in spite of 'the results of recruiting for the volunteer militia forces [being] recognised to be disappointing'.[62] Defence Minister Pearce called on businesses to support the Militia by encouraging their employees to enlist and by giving preference to militiamen in employment.[63]

Lyons finally did authorise a major campaign to bolster Militia enlistment, but only in 1938. William Morris 'Billy' Hughes embraced this role energetically and toured the nation calling for volunteers.[64] Even though the Militia could not be sent overseas (a condition consistent with ALP's isolationist defence policies), Labor in opposition was opposed to plans to increase the Militia's strength for it believed that strengthening the Militia in any form would eventually lead to conscription. The choice of Hughes to head the enlistment campaign certainly heightened the ALP's fears. Hughes as Prime Minister had split the Labor Party and the nation with his two attempts during the Great War to secure by plebiscite conscription for overseas service. Now, as Minister for External Affairs in the Lyons Conservative UAP government, he sparked much Labor and trade union distrust. An *Australian Worker* cartoon portrayed him banging a drum labelled 'Voluntary Enlistment' which had chains hanging from it labelled 'conscription'.[65] Indeed, the ALP's opposition to the Government's entire defence programme was grounded in its staunchly anti-conscriptionist views.[66]

Despite fierce ALP opposition Hughes' campaign was a success. By 1939 there were 77,000 men in the Militia[67] and by the outbreak of the Pacific War 132,000 men in the CMF.[68] Yet it is unlikely that the CMF could have repulsed a major Japanese landing even if they had been called out and strategically located, for it was easier to call up troops than equip them. The CMF was equipped with three-quarters the number of the rifles it needed and less than a third of the grenades.[69] It also lacked adequate transportation, having less than half of the medium and light trucks required and only 13% of heavy transport.[70] The Australian Army Unit Training Assessment of July 1942 revealed that of the 31 major combat units in the Australian Army, only 4 had reached A-level, none had reached B-level and 26 received the lowest possible score.[71] This evaluation omitted the recently returned AIF, whose troops were the best equipped and trained in Australia. They could not be everywhere, however, and their return, though providing a significant boost to morale, left Australia still well below the 25 divisions that the Army and Government reasoned were necessary for Australia's defence.

Transportation and artillery remained a significant issue throughout the inter-war and early war years and ultimately resulted in an ill-equipped and landlocked army incapable of quickly amassing or defending its troops in response to an immediate threat. Australia lacked the ability to transport troops long distances by air—the fastest method. The reliance on a complex limited rail network for the transport of troops meant the vast regions of Australia were left effectively unprotected and vulnerable to assault from the Pacific.

As early as 1920 the Army requested over 200 pieces of heavy and light artillery, but owing to 'financial constraints, the Government failed to approve any of the proposals for new equipment or for an arsenal'.[72] In 1933 the Army still possessed only six anti-aircraft guns.[73] In June 1940 it complained to the War Cabinet that 16 pounder and 4.5 inch howitzers were 'not held in great quantities' and that there were only 'a few' 60-pounder and 6-inch guns and anti-tank rifles and no anti-tank guns or 25-pounder guns.[74] As David Horner observes in his history of Australian artillery, 'By the outbreak of the Second World War, in terms of numbers of equipment and units training, the Australian artillery had fallen well behind its British counterparts'.[75] The situation was somewhat improved by the outbreak of the Pacific War. Five infantry divisions were training with their quota of artillery units and 'there were sufficient field guns for each regiment to be issued with sixteen rather than 24 guns' and 'anti-tank regiments [to be] issued with 24 rather than 48 guns'.[76] Nonetheless, Australia's defenders would be scattered to cover multiple locations and a depletion of artillery forces was a serious weakness.

Scant attention had been paid to the possibility that Australia might need to arm itself against an assault by a superior Japanese air force on its northern frontier. An enemy landing force would be able to concentrate all its firepower at its beachhead and would be supported by naval and air power. Horner observes that as late as 1939 'there had been little alteration to the order of battle of the coast artillery since 1924',[77] which 'called for 678 anti-aircraft guns while only 114 were available'.[78] Anti-aircraft units had not even calibrated their guns before the Japanese attacked Darwin and '[m]any of the gunners had never actually heard an anti-aircraft gun fire until the first raid' because 'headquarters would not allow the expense of ammunition being fired—even for calibration'.[79] Prime

"Mr. Hughes will repeat the activities that made him famous in the war years in his appeal for voluntary enlistment."—Daily paper.

Will Donald, *Australian Worker,* 16 November 1938

Minister Scullin claimed in 1934 that 'shore batteries to repel an invader and aircraft to prevent approach to our shores, would adequately safeguard Australia'.[80] In reality, neither the coastal artillery nor the RAAF could have defeated an invading enemy force. An over-reliance on the Singapore strategy meant that Australian planners had installed only 9.2-inch calibre guns in most places as coastal artillery.[81] These were incapable of engaging the capital ships, which could shell Australian positions from a range of 7,000 yards beyond that of the coastal artillery.[82]

The RAAF did not suffer the same range limitations as coastal artillery but was also poorly equipped to engage an attacking fleet and certainly could not achieve air superiority. At the outbreak of the European War the RAAF had only 246 planes, in spite of Admiral Viscount Jellicoe and the Air Board recommending an air force of nearly 1,000[83] or 644[84] aircraft, respectively, in 1920. When it came to defending Australia in 1941 the RAAF had 'hardly a feather to fly with', according to the Chief of Air Staff.[85] Two days after the Pacific War began the RAAF possessed 101 Wirraways, 53 Hudsons, 12 Catalinas, 9 Sea Gulls, 72 Battles and a further 108 Wirraways subject to 'armament deficiencies'.[86] This constituted 15 of the 64 squadrons the RAAF needed to protect Australia.[87]

Australia needed not only more aircraft but better aircraft. The Wirraway had been designed as a trainer and was not expected to engage anything but seaplanes.[88] The Japanese Zero could travel more than 100 miles per hour faster than the Wirraway and had two 20-millimetre cannons and two 7.7-millimetre machine guns,[89] while the Wirraway had only three .303-calibre machine guns.[90] An engagement between Wirraways and Zeros over Rabaul was described thus:

> The engagement was brave but hopeless and the end came soon when the Wirraways, completely outclassed in speed, manoeuverability and fire power, were shot down in flames.[91]

Even if the RAAF had located the attacking fleet and penetrated its combat air patrols, Australia's ability to inflict meaningful damage on the enemy would have been minimal. Most of the RAAF's bombs were more than 20 years old[92] and the RAAF needed another 46,000 bombs to protect Australia adequately.[93]

AUSTRALIA FAILS THE TEST

If evidence were needed of Australia's vulnerability and lack of preparedness in the event of attack, one need only review local responses to the bombing of Darwin and mini-submarine attack on Sydney in the first six months of 1942. In 1924 the Australian Government approved plans to develop Darwin as a naval base in support of Singapore.[94] The CID supported this decision in 1925, stating that 'In a war with Japan, Port Darwin will be of considerable importance as an operational base'.[95] Yet 'Darwin was as unprepared as ever' when nearly 200 Japanese aircraft attacked on 19 February 1942, heavily damaging the military and civilian airfields and sinking or severely damaging half the vessels in the harbour at the expense of only seven aircraft.[96] The port ceased to be a staging-post for the allies and the raid 'caused widespread panic among Royal Australian Air Force personnel'.[97] Historian Douglas Gillison observes that radar was not operating at Darwin prior to the first attack on 19 February and attributes Japanese success to a 'lack of effective aerodrome defence measures', noting that 'the air force was "gravely at fault"'.[98]

However, while Darwin in 1942 was an exposed outpost on the fringe of Australia, geographically closer to Japan's bases than to Australia's population centres, Sydney was the nation's premier city and one which for over a decade the Army had predicted would be a target. John Robertson points out that 'Throughout early 1942 there always was a heavy numerical preponderance of Allied over Japanese soldiers within a radius of 3200 kilometres of Sydney'.[99] Sydney was defended by shore guns, searchlights, patrol boats and a modest number of fighters.[100] Yet there were clearly 'serious weaknesses in Sydney's defences'.[101] Between 31 May and 1 June 1942 three Japanese mini-submarines managed to enter Sydney Harbour under darkness and sink the naval depot vessel (a converted ferry) HMAS *Kuttabul*. Grose notes that '[t]here was wild shooting from all directions':

> Some ships fired aimlessly into the air, believing this was an air raid and they might as well be seen to be doing something. Others felt obliged to sound off with klaxon horns or sirens, adding to the mindless pandemonium.[102]

The shelling of Sydney by a full-size Japanese submarine a week later again caused panic. The submarine remained undetected prior to firing and 'The first anybody knew was the characteristic whistling of inbound shells'.[103] Indeed Grose maintains that the shelling 'caused more alarm among the civilian population' than did the mini-submarine raid.[104] So unprepared was the city that throughout the shelling the Sydney and Manly ferries continued to cross the harbour.[105] It appeared that the nation's anticipation of an attack was insufficient impetus to produce a city on a war footing: 'Sydney remained a party town'.[106]

Nonetheless, the impact of what amounted to two very small raids on the nation's premier city had a dramatic and disproportionate impact, serving to reinforce national assumptions that invasion was indeed imminent. In reality, the battle of Midway, which coincided with the shelling of Sydney, removed any chance that Japan would acquire the necessary naval supremacy to mount a full-scale invasion of the Australian continent.

REARMAMENT IS A LONG PROCESS

The poor response to the Darwin and Sydney raids served to underscore deficiencies in Australia's inter-war rearmament programme. Lyons' warning in 1938 that 'Rearmament is a long process'[107] was an accurate assessment but delivered far too late. Imperial defence, the Government's policy, mandated self-sufficiency 'in terms of materiel at all levels except for the heaviest equipment' as early as 1923.[108] This was a difficult goal to achieve considering Australia's small industrial base and could only have been accomplished if a long-term programme had been developed. Once the Pacific War began Australia was incapable of producing the arms, ammunition or support equipment necessary to equip the 25 divisions the Government believed necessary.

Australia's rearmament programme had its origins in the immediate aftermath of the Great War. In 1919 Arthur Leighton, chairman of the Board of Management of the Commonwealth Government Factories and Defence Research Laboratories, urged the Government to establish a policy of 'self containment of munitions production within Australia', by which he meant 'self-sufficiency'.[109] Self-sufficiency would further be enshrined in policy at the 1923 Imperial Conference, which established the foundation of Imperial defence. Hence in 1921 the various Commonwealth munitions factories were unified under Prime Minister 'Billy' Hughes to create the Munitions Supply Board (MSB), which became the main instrument of rearmament.[110] The MSB's most important function was to 'manufacture and arrange for local production of arms, armaments, ammunition, supplies and stores of all types'.[111] It was also to provide facilities for scientific research, inspect and examine armaments, ensure that Australia continued to follow British service specifications, design the factories, machines and tools necessary to produce arms and ammunition and train men in the manufacturing of munitions.[112] It was too much to ask.

The Depression certainly inhibited Australia's rearmament, but it was not the only factor. The MSB's budget was always small, receiving less than 9% of the defence budget throughout the inter-war period and no funding between 1922–24.[113] Its divergent objectives meant that the MSB was effectively prevented from mastering any task and as a government entity was affected, often detrimentally, by every political vagary of the inter-war period. Additionally, Australia lacked the population and industrial base to produce the wide variety of weapons and ammunition required to arm 25 divisions. Once war began materiel was consumed quickly, exacerbating existing shortages, and 'there emerged a tendency to spread production plans over too wide a range of weapons and equipment'.[114]

The MSB could not hope to undertake the research and development necessary to maintain an armaments industry under such conditions. In 1940 Australia produced nearly 21,000 rifles and 846 machine guns, but no Bren guns, anti-tank guns, submachine guns or mortars.[115] At the start of the Pacific War the Army reported that it possessed 178,000 rifles, 7,729 pistols, 4,320 submachine guns, 3,694 light machine guns, 1,905 heavy machine guns, 906 three inch mortars and only 64 anti-tank rifles.[116] The Army lacked even the requisite number of steel helmets for 25 divisions, and had only 46 heavy lorries for transport.[117] Australian industry would struggle to make up this shortfall and certainly could not do it quickly. Unable to develop a self-sustaining armaments industry, the MSB instead focused (as Ross concedes) on maintaining 'a nucleus basis—i.e. the lowest level of production compatible with maintaining knowledge of production technique'.[118] It was a rearmament strategy based on capacity and potential rather than actual arms and was of limited value as a deterrent. Yet as Coulthard-Clark (1999) observes in his history of the post-war Australian Defence Industries, by 1929 the MSB 'faced the prospect of mutilation, if not extinction'.[119]

The MSB's development strategy pre-supposed sufficient lead-time to any outbreak of war to counter Australia's limited industrial potential, which was insufficient to allow rapid expansion in wartime. The Army had reported in 1935 that it was dissatisfied with the MSB's production capacity,[120] and after June 1940 realised that 'the current war was producing wastage rates in rifles which far exceeded the assumptions made in 1937'.[121] Since the MSB could only hope to preserve the knowledge necessary to produce munitions, Australia was still producing fewer munitions in 1939 than it had produced in 1920.[122] The reason for the lack of production capacity was that preserving knowledge did not resolve crucial issues such as the lack of precision machinery. In 1941 the 'majority of Australian engineering shops were still not set up for mass production of articles of moderate to fine precision such as guns, fuses and shells'.[123] Indeed, the industrialist Essington Lewis had warned Frederick Shedden in 1938 that 'it is not practicable to undertake with anything like efficiency the manufacture of shells, bombs, etc. in existing commercial engineering shops'.[124] Further, there were only three lead presses, crucial for the manufacture of small arms ammunitions and, until Dunkirk (June 1940), one was dedicated to civilian production.[125] This ensured that when war broke out Australia could not produce the armaments necessary to equip its 25 divisions.

The MSB's establishment in 1921 did not prevent a general decline in Australian defence. Throughout the 1920s Australia repeatedly cut its defence budget in spite of Europe becoming increasingly unstable and the days of a peaceful liberal Japan and international disarmament policies being clearly over. By 1933 Australian defence was at its lowest point since the Great War, the budget being a mere A£3 million pounds with only A£180,000 (6% of the Defence budget) allocated to the MSB.[126] Australia's industrial capacity was severely limited and incapable of ensuring the nation's safety. During the Manchurian crisis of 1931 the Army had attempted to develop an alternate market through the export of surplus arms to China but was vetoed by the Australian Government.[127] The MSB was therefore forced to compete for civilian contracts, even producing lipstick containers, pencil sharpeners and bottle openers.[128]

Given Australia's small industrial base and inability to re-arm swiftly, the Japanese invasion of Manchuria should have sounded an immediate warning to those in government and led to a large-scale investment in defence. In October 1933, Prime Minister Lyons announced:

> The government recognizes that the provision made for defence has been inadequate for some years and that there is urgent need for certain extensions of our defence activities.[129]

By then Defence Minister Pearce's defence budget was barely over A£4 million (spread over three years), which was grossly inadequate in the context of reductions in defence spending over previous years.[130] Four million pounds was, however, the largest possible budget in view of the Depression which Australia was then experiencing and the Government's refusal to countenance deficit spending. If Australia was to provide for its own local defence and defeat a Japanese raid without British assistance, it needed to commence a massive rearmament program immediately.

Some members of government recognised the need for a stronger Australian defence. Eric Harrison (UAP, Bendigo, Victoria) noted in 1933 that 'Japan has increased her navy personnel by 29,000 or 75 per cent'.[131] Harrison also presciently observed that

> it behoves us more than ever not to rely too much upon what the Mother Country may do for us, but to help, so far as our finances will permit, to ease the load which Great Britain is bearing.[132]

Easing Great Britain's load was the best Australia could hope to manage, but in doing so its value as an ally increased. Improving Australia's value to would-be allies increased the odds both that a great power would come to Australia's aid and that Australia could hold out until that happened. Harrison went on to observe that the RAAF was much smaller than Japan's and even smaller than the air force of Siam.[133]

THE ALP AND REARMAMENT

Rearmament required bipartisan agreement, but Labor and the conservatives shared little common ground and lacked a common understanding of international events and Australia's place in the world. The Labor Opposition vehemently opposed even the small increase in the 1933 defence budget, in spite of Japan's ongoing operations in Manchuria. Eddie Ward (ALP, East Sydney, NSW) asked, 'Why should the cost of arms, armament and ammunition be increased by A£6,000?', and charged that the Government was 'actively preparing to participate in warlike operations'.[134] The ALP argued that no country had 'evil designs on Australia' and presented Switzerland, Denmark and Sweden as models for Australia to follow.[135] The ALP either did not know or chose to forget that both Switzerland and Sweden had compulsory national service and that the armaments industries of both countries consequently had a large domestic market.

The idea that Australia was preparing to undertake warlike operations was laughable, but the ALP's opposition to increased defence spending further hindered the rearmament programme because it made the Government cautious. Unless the build-up had bipartisan support, no government was going to undertake a massive defence programme while the nation was still recovering from Depression. UAP ministers would have remembered the ALP's decidedly negative effect on defence politics at the time of the conscription plebiscites during the Great War. They were well aware of the ALP's ability to tap into anti-military sentiment to wreak political havoc and were unwilling to concede that advantage. Defence spending was thus increased incrementally. In 1935 Australian defence forces returned to their pre-Depression strength—at least on paper.[136] But the pre-Depression military reflected a period when Japan was peaceful and Hitler had yet to come to power.

The situation was no different in 1937 when the defence budget increase of nearly a million pounds was strongly attacked by the leader of the Opposition. Curtin argued that 'Australia is making much more elaborate provision for defence than is being made by any other Dominion'.[137] While this was true, such facts gave a false sense of security as other Dominions faced different and arguably lesser strategic threats by virtue of their geography. Curtin seemed unable to grasp the key point that a nation's defence spending should be compared to that of its adversaries rather than to the budgets of minor allies. When Thomas White (UAP, Balaclava, Victoria) asked Curtin how much Great Britain was spending, Curtin again took refuge behind the other Dominions, replying: 'I am at the moment talking not about Great Britain's expenditure, but about the expenditure of each Dominion'.[138] Canadian, New Zealand and South African defence spending had little bearing on the defence of Australia, but British defence spending did. Australia was dependent on British military aid and if Great Britain believed the world situation demanded increased defence spending it was prudent for Australia to follow suit. In 1936, for example, the RAF ordered 900 Hurricanes and Spitfires while the RAAF ordered 10 obsolete Demons—in spite of intelligence that Japan was developing advanced monoplanes.[139] While the British orders were a clear call to arms, Curtin resolutely maintained that Australia's strategic position was the same as South Africa's.[140]

TOO LITTLE TOO LATE

Pearce's defence programme fell short of ensuring Australia's preparedness for a major war and did not greatly alleviate the

"There is not the slightest likelihood of conscription being introduced in Australia."—Minister for Defence Parkhill.

AUSTRALIA: "Glad to hear you say so, for if I have to bury conscription again, IT'S NOT THE ONLY THING THAT WILL BE BURIED!"

Will Donald, *Australian Worker,* 16 October 1935

dominion's reliance on the United Kingdom. In 1938 further increases in expenditure were introduced by the new federal Treasurer Richard Casey in a three-year A£25 million defence programme.[141] The UAP ordered two new cruisers from the United Kingdom and two locally produced sloops for the RAN, and authorised an increase in strength of 1,500 sailors.[142] The Army was allocated an additional A£5.5 million to improve coastal defences and increase its troops by 1,300 men, and the RAAF nearly A£9 million—the bulk of the 1937–38 defence budget—to create nine new squadrons and recruit an additional 2,500 airmen.[143]

The new defence budget included the 1937 defence estimates, which had been greatly modified following warnings at the 1937 Imperial Conference of a two-theatre war and caution against reliance on the United States. The Czechoslovakian crisis of 1938 led to more rapid expenditure of A£10 million.[144] It is important to remember that budgetary figures do not reflect the actual sums spent. Indeed, that the A£3,750,000 allocated for capital defence expenditure in 1933–37 had not been spent in full[145] demonstrates that defence could not be dealt with by massive expenditures at a time of crisis but required a long-term approach to planning and rearmament. As such, Australian defence capacity was restricted not just by available funds but by the ability to spend them. By 1939 the defence budget was over A£14.5 million, the greatest ever peacetime defence expansion.[146] However, this defence build-up had not enjoyed bipartisan support. The ALP was still highly suspicious of the Government and declared following the 1938 increases that the Government's new slogan was 'Bombs before bread',[147] arguing that its defence programme would lead to increased unemployment.

THE COMMONWEALTH AIRCRAFT CORPORATION

In the early to mid-twentieth century weapons had one primary market—governments. But rearmament required more than weapons. Aircraft and vehicles critical to 'modern' warfare could be produced by civilian manufacturers only if there existed an established civilian industry. Neither civilian demand nor military necessity, however, was sufficient to support an Australian domestic aviation industry in the 1920s. Although the 1928 Salmond Report concluded that the RAAF's aircraft were unsuitable for defence, the RAAF had little chance of securing the funds necessary to purchase new frontline aircraft.[148] There existed no potential threat from an air force of any note in 1928, and until the mid-1930s the RAAF was an effective deterrent against Japan since the Japanese air force was also lacking in modern aircraft.[149] However, the situation changed once the Japanese air force began a massive build-up—which Australia needed to match immediately. When it became apparent that the Japanese air force was modernising, the catalyst for the development of a domestic aviation industry in Australia was finally realised. In May 1936 Archdale Parkhill announced that the Government would support an aircraft industry: the Commonwealth Aircraft Corporation (CAC).[150] An impressive industrial–governmental accomplishment, the CAC established a domestic aviation industry in Australia where previous attempts had failed.

Defence Minister Archdale Parkhill had warned his government in 1935 that '[m]uch of the material required was not at present produced in Australia',[151] which included the vast majority of tools and jigs necessary for aircraft production.[152] However, government patronage immediately secured the support of the major corporations General Motors Holden (GMH) and Broken Hill Proprietary (BHP), the latter demanding a 10-year monopoly before it would embark on aircraft production.[153] The UAP boasted in 1937 that in one year 'the CAC has been capitalised and is preparing to lay down its plant at Fishermen's Bend'.[154] The first aircraft produced was a licensed copy of the North American 16 trainer, 'a comparatively small two-seater using an engine which would not tax too heavily the manufacturing resources of the company [BHP]'.[155] It was only natural that the first Australian-built aircraft was simple to construct as an aviation industry would take time to develop. BHP described the first flight of an Australian-built North American 16, renamed the Wirraway, thus: 'the nation progresses to a greater peak of industrial self-containment and security'.[156] It was too late.

The CAC remained a relatively small organisation until the Pacific War, where it increased from 1,000 to 7,000 employees

A further £3,500,000, to be raised by taxation, will be needed for defence purposes.

THE MAN WHO CARRIES THE DRUM.

Will Donald, *Australian Worker*, 7 September 1938

almost overnight as it struggled to produce a 'Panic fighter'—the Boomerang—a modified Wirraway.[157] Because the Wirraway was never intended as a frontline fighter, 49 variants of the Boomerang were produced as the CAC desperately sought to make the Wirraway something it was not. Only 250 Boomerangs were produced, many of these never seeing active service.[158] The Beaufighter, the best known of Australia's domestically produced aircraft, did not enter active service until 1944 by which time it was obsolete.[159] To have defeated a Japanese invasion the RAAF would have needed not only frontline fighters but fighter bombers, medium bombers, support aircraft and pilots. The CAC had neither the time nor the resources to do the job.

The requirement for a wartime aviation industry and increased local air defence presupposed that in the event of an invasion or imminent threat ground forces could be assembled quickly and in sufficient strength to protect RAAF bases and prevent the enemy gaining a foothold. Yet as previously demonstrated, Australia's transport infrastructure was severely deficient and the nation lacked the industrial capability to redress this. L.J. Hartnett, managing director of General Motors Holden, later painted a grim view of the Australian automotive industry because of 'the immaturity of the interrelated industries on which we [the automotive industry] would have had to lean. Many of these industries were young, small and inexperienced'.[160] Australian automotive policy was directed by revenue-raising considerations and led by tariff rather than defence policy.

The historian Robert Conlon (2001) records that it was only immediately prior to the outbreak of the war that the Government began to 'promote complete motor car manufacture'.[161] Ross disagrees with Hartnett's view because 'except for the engine, chassis and gearbox, all components used were now from local sources'.[162] He is right. The Australian automotive manufacturing industry focused on 'replacement parts' which were produced 'with relatively basic equipment' by more than 3,000 companies, each averaging only 11 employees.[163] But a vehicle without a chassis, engine or gearbox is of no use to an army, nor is it much of a vehicle. Even if Australia had managed to produce gearboxes, engines and chassis, the vehicles would have needed tyres and Australia's rubber industry was not focused on military demands and no plans existed for it to convert to wartime production. Indeed, the industry had only enough rubber to meet eight months' demand following the fall of Singapore.[164] The rubber industry effectively ceased during the Pacific War and a plan to create synthetic rubber was considered too expensive and subsequently cancelled.[165]

In spite of the shortcomings of the Australian automotive industry, the Australian Government decided to engage in the development of Armoured Fighting Vehicles (AFVs) such as machine gun carriers and tanks. The Army considered this at the time to be 'the biggest area of failure in the Department of Munitions'.[166] John Robertson observes that 'a lot of effort was wasted on attempts to make a tank'.[167] The machine gun carriers did not 'represent what the Army wanted for suitable battlefield survivability'.[168] It is true, however, that they were available in early 1942, but survivability was far more important than availability. The Australian tank was never intended for local defence but to serve with Australian troops in the Middle East. Australia was wasting valuable resources on a complex machine not developed for Australian conditions which, regardless of purpose, could not be produced quickly enough.

***

Australian military and political elites panicked following the fall of Singapore, reinforcing a broader, populist view that invasion of the continent was imminent. No attempt was made to allay those fears by referring to self-containment or self-sufficiency, or to question Japanese intentions and capabilities in the Pacific. The conduct of Australian service personnel in Darwin following its bombing in February 1942, and the confusion that again abounded in Sydney following the raids of May/June 1942, was indicative both of a military psychologically unprepared for combat and a broader population gripped by invasion hysteria.[169]

In 1940 Prime Minister Menzies had been in no doubt that Australia was incapable of defending itself. In a June 1940 radio broadcast he conceded: 'The munitions side of our effort is less spectacular and more difficult'.[170] He went on to identify munitions production as a 'key problem' and announced that the Government was 'urgently re-examining the industrial resources of Australia with [a] view to having them more and more effectively marshalled for the war effort'.[171] But it was too little, too late. Two months later Menzies felt compelled to make another broadcast. He admitted: 'You cannot in a few months provide modern weapons and munitions',[172] acknowledging both the inability of the MSB to meet wartime production requirements and the lack of 'adequate supplies of precision plant, of skilled managers, of competent and industrious workmen, of an almost infinite variety of materials'.[173]

In spite of a belated attempt by the political, military and industrial elites to implement a strategy for Australia's defence, nearly two years after the onset of war Australia lacked the resources, manpower and infrastructure to arm and defend itself. However, Australia had done all it could do. Hampered by a small industrial base and an Opposition fiercely opposed to every attempt at rearmament, Australia's unpreparedness at the commencement of the Pacific War was the product not of British perfidy but of an internal failure to recognise and address the nation's vulnerabilities.

CHAPTER 2

THE HISTORIOGRAPHY OF AUSTRALIAN INTER-WAR DEFENCE AND FOREIGN POLICY

The state of Australian defence preparedness at the outbreak of the Second World War has been observed by historians primarily in discussions on foreign policy and defence within broader military histories. Australian reactions to international events, the development of Australian foreign policy and shifts in Imperial relations have attracted far less interest in their own right.

One of the earliest works to provide an overview of changes in Imperial relations,[1] and a useful framework for their study, was Canadian R. MacGregor Dawson's *The Development of Dominion Status, 1900–1936* published in 1937. Dawson's work treated Australia primarily as a contrary example to the other Dominions and, in particular, Canada. Although Dawson did not explore the rationale behind Australia's more cautious foreign policy, he demonstrated that Australia could have initiated a more independent foreign policy by more quickly embracing the Balfour Declaration and Statute of Westminster, as had other Dominions.

Serious Australian examination of Australia's inter-war foreign policy began only with E.M. Andrews in the 1960s. Consequently, the best of the short histories of Australia by Ernest Scott (revised by Herbert Burton in 1947), A.G.L. Shaw (1955) and Manning Clark (1963) confined themselves to brief, general observations on foreign policy and defence. Gordon Greenwood's *Australia: A Social and Political History* (1955)[2] similarly focused largely on domestic politics against a background of local depression and the deteriorating international situation.

The first detailed analysis of Australian inter-war foreign policy came to light in 1970 with E.M. Andrews' monograph *Isolationism and Appeasement in Australia: Reactions to the European Crises, 1935–1939*.[3] Andrews argued that the 'Australian Government had wholeheartedly adopted appeasement for its own reasons', thus negating the notion that Australia merely followed London's lead.[4] Andrews' second monograph, *The Writing on the Wall* (1987),[5] switched the focus from Europe to Asia, examining British Commonwealth reactions to the Manchurian crisis with particular focus on Australia, Canada and Britain. Andrews contended that the Commonwealth was incapable of maintaining a uniform foreign policy because the Dominions lacked common interests and the British Foreign Office ignored Dominion views when formulating Britain's foreign policy. Despite the Balfour Declaration and Statute of Westminster, he argued, Australian governments never appreciated fully their lack of influence in London. Several other historians of Australian foreign policy later reached sharper conclusions.

W.J. Hudson and M.P. Sharp (1988), seeking to determine the point at which Australia became an independent nation in a legal sense, maintained that 'Australia and New Zealand never, in fact, sought independence' but 'were dragged along in the wake of others' in the 1920s.[6] Because of the convoluted manner in which the Dominions were granted independence—not 'in one revolutionary step' but 'in a process stretching over more than a decade of singularly tedious talk'[7]—Australia was able to maintain the fiction of not being independent and throughout the inter-war period acted 'as though independence had not occurred'.[8] P.G. Edwards (1983)[9] noted the role played by Australian and international heads of state in the formulation of foreign policy. He suggested that Canada, South Africa and Ireland developed differently to Australia because

> All three had Prime Ministers who remained in office for lengthy periods while their respective Departments of External Affairs were in their infancy: and in all three, despite political differences over Imperial relations, there was a substantial degree of consensus on the desirability of Dominion autonomy in foreign affairs.[10]

The first serious modern works of Australian military history to discuss Australian inter-war defence policy, albeit briefly for the most part, were the early volumes of the Australian War Memorial's official history *Australia in the War of 1939–1945* by Paul Hasluck (1952), Gavin Long (1952), Douglas Gillison (1954) and Lionel Wigmore (1957).[11] However, only Paul Hasluck, a trained historian and professional politician, dealt with inter-war defence policy in any detail. In his two volumes on the home front Hasluck conceded that Australian preparations for war had been insufficient, observing that Australian politicians 'had never had occasion to meditate on the precarious existence of a small nation in a world of power'.[12]

In 1976 John McCarthy became the first historian to make a concerted examination of the relationship between Imperial defence and Australian defence policy.[13] His major work, *Australia and Imperial Defence 1918–39*, asserted that 'Imperial defence arrangements were of little real value to Australia between the wars'.[14] McCarthy maintained that 'As long as Australia remained inside the framework of Imperial defence a viable alternative to sea power and the British diplomatic position could not really be formulated'.[15] McCarthy also viewed Australian governments as passive throughout the inter-war period, asserting that the 'Australian government was prepared to accept too readily and uncritically the United Kingdom's advice and policy'.[16] Although McCarthy interpreted Imperial defence as the Singapore strategy[17] and overlooked local defence—a vital component of Imperial defence that required self-sufficiency 'in terms of materiel at all levels except for the heaviest equipment'[18]—*Australia and Imperial Defence 1918–39* remains a landmark book.

The flowering of Australian defence and military history in the 1970s and 1980s is reflected further in the work of pre-eminent writers such a Jeffrey Grey and David Horner. In his portrait of Defence Secretary Sir Frederick Shedden, *Defence Supremo*, Horner (2000) presents a detailed study of the inter-war period and the role of the public service in the formulation of defence policy.[19] Grey's trail-blazing *A Military History of Australia* (1990)[20] pays less attention to the political and civilian side of defence policy but is an excellent short introduction to the 'depressing [interwar] period' when 'little or nothing was done to increase the government's ability to carry out its military responsibilities'.[21] Grey notes that the 'literature on the inter-war period is uneven' with 'some subjects, especially the Singapore strategy ... well-covered while others have been barely touched'.[22]

The want of a reliable, integrated treatment of Australian foreign and defence policies between the wars leaves David Day's 1988 monograph *The Great Betrayal*[23] to fill the gap. *The Great Betrayal* expands on Day's (1986) allegation in *Menzies and Churchill at War* that British wartime Prime Minister Winston Churchill 'was determined to sustain his policy of total victory at the expense of the Empire that he was entrusted to protect'.[24] According to Day, Britain intentionally deceived Australia and New Zealand about British defence capability in Southeast Asia because 'Australia and New Zealand would have found it untenable to give continued allegiance to an Empire that was plainly not ruling the waves'.[25] Seizing on the Australian War Cabinet's 23 January 1942 statement that 'the evacuation of Singapore would be regarded here and elsewhere as an inexcusable betrayal' and that Australia had 'acted and carried out our part of the bargain',[26] Day argues that there had been an 'abandonment of Australia'.[27] He ascribed this abandonment to the British Government 'following their national interests', evidenced by their failure to send a fleet to Singapore or hold Malaya.[28]

Day's betrayal thesis found influential public support in the form of Labor Prime Minister Paul Keating, who gave the betrayal argument a major push when he adopted Day's view that Great Britain had betrayed Australia at the start of the Pacific War. Keating and Day enjoyed a symbiotic relationship: Keating drew heavily on Day's research and frequently praised him as a historian. Day, in turn, benefitted immensely from Keating's trumpeting of the betrayal thesis. In his foreword to Day's 1992 sequel to *The Great Betrayal*, entitled *Reluctant Nation*,[29] Keating wrote: 'Australians have tended to shy away from the chance to grasp what David Day calls a "possible independent destiny".'[30] As leader of the Australian Labor Party (ALP)—'the bearer of the radical nationalist tradition'—Keating believed it was his prime ministerial duty to guide Australia to its 'independent destiny', injecting a radical nationalist interpretation of Australian history into mainstream political discourse.[31]

Responding during a parliamentary debate in February 1992 about the 1950s, Keating charged that during the Second World War Britain had 'decided not to defend the Malayan peninsula, not to worry about Singapore and not to give us our troops back to keep ourselves free from Japanese domination'.[32] He further contended that as the political heir to the United Australia Party (UAP) the Liberal Opposition was 'not aggressively proud of our [Australian] culture'.[33] Suggesting that the Anzac legend 'fabricated' after Gallipoli was a conservative creation which prevented Australia from becoming a 'social paradise',[34] Keating argued that for Australia to achieve its full potential it needed to acknowledge that Britain had betrayed Australia. He contended that working-class Australians—Labor's 'True Believers'—had struggled continually against the Anglophile bourgeoisie for Australian independence,[35] and that the fall of Singapore was yet another example of Britain sacrificing the 'True Believers' for the Empire.[36] As such it was the fall of Singapore that was the true turning point in modern Australian history. Australia's nationhood began not at Gallipoli but at Kokoda in Papua New Guinea where Australians turned back the Japanese.

In spite of Day's predecessor to *The Great Betrayal—Menzies and Churchill at War*—receiving a number of scathing academic reviews,[37] his subsequent books on defence and foreign policy have largely escaped scholarly review in Australia.[38] The paucity of

The Australian, 28 February 1992

serious comment on *The Great Betrayal* has allowed its argument to be repeated with impunity, with Day's betrayal thesis expounded in a column in *The Australian*[39] and in popular histories of war including a television series.[40] Nonetheless some criticism exists. In an early review for the *Sydney Morning Herald* Peter Hastings observed that *The Great Betrayal* contained 'a great deal of over-simplification and exaggerated interpretation' and that '[t]o all of [these allegations of betrayal] there are numerous answers short of "great betrayal" which implies a policy of deliberate and sinister deceit'.[41] British reviewer Robert Blake, while acknowledging 'this carefully researched and highly revealing book', noted that 'The facts revealed in this book do not really justify its title';[42] Ronald Quinault lamented that 'the contention that Churchill was indifferent about Australia has not been challenged';[43] and John McCarthy, reviewing Day's argument in 1994 in the wake of Keating's pronouncements noted that the assumption that Great Britain's assurances 'lacked integrity and were not meant to be honoured'[44] remained integral to the thesis. *The Great Betrayal* was reissued in 2002 in paperback and in 2003 published with *Reluctant Nation* in a combined volume as *The Politics of War*.[45]

At least half a dozen major books have focused on the construction of the Singapore naval base and Britain's 'Singapore strategy'.[46] Not until recently, however, have the Singapore strategy and Churchill's behaviour in 1940–42 occasioned detailed re-examination, and then only to confirm uncritically Australian certitudes about British perfidy. In *Churchill and Australia*, for example, Graham Freudenberg (2008) examines the British–Australian relationship from the Boer War (1899–1902) through to the 1950s. An admirer of Churchill from his wartime childhood, Freudenberg writes:

> … for my generation, nothing can remotely outweigh the intense conviction that, except for Winston Churchill, the doctrines and practices of Hitler's Germany would have prevailed in Europe and far beyond … and that the British Empire, including Australia, would have been enrolled as an accomplice in Hitler's crimes.[47]

And yet *Churchill and Australia* reads as a strange tribute to Freudenberg's boyhood hero:

> Australia seemed to bring out the worst in Winston Churchill. Often enough to form a discernible pattern, Australia was on the wrong side of the very qualities … that made Winston Churchill … "the saviour of his country, the largest human being of his time". His total self-belief and his urge for action had their stubborn, reckless, and spiteful aspect. Australia often seemed to bring out that side.[48]

Freudenberg's evidence lies in Churchill's Mediterranean and Pacific policies during his period as Chancellor of the Exchequer in 1924–29. However, his interpretation of Australian inter-war defence policy is simplistic and limited by his lack of understanding of the nuances of Imperial defence. Churchill, it is said, weakened Australia's defences by his cuts to British spending and adoption of the Ten Year Rule for defence planning. But the striking fact, as we shall see, is that Australia objected to neither of these decisions.

Freudenberg's criticism[49] of Churchill for treating Australia differently from Dominions that accepted the privileges and responsibilities offered by the Balfour Declaration and the Statute of Westminster is unfounded. Far from being an unwilling participant, Australia readily associated itself with British foreign and defence policy and Churchill's pronouncement in November 1940 to 'Beat Hitler First' was one with which Australia concurred. Local defence was an Australian responsibility and one that British civil servants and military advisers had regularly requested Australia to strengthen. Australia rejected repeated offers of greater autonomy by the British Commonwealth and it was Australia's failure to accept its local defence obligation, not Churchill's strategic outlook, that allowed Australia's northern territories to fall to the Japanese with minimal losses. To put it brutally, Australia refused to grow up. It was Australia, not Churchill, 'who had no conception of the British Dominions as separate entities'.[50] If Australia did not wish to be treated as a colony, as Freudenberg insists Churchill regarded her, then Australia should have stopped acting like one.

Gooch (2003) has made the point more diplomatically, asserting that 'a broad strategic logic governed the wartime politics of Churchill's government'.[51] When the strategic situation faced by Britain changed dramatically with the Fall of France and Italian entry into the war, 'Britain's relationship with Australia ceased to operate according to the norms of peacetime diplomacy'.[52] Australians found subsequent British decisions 'often unpalatable and on occasion unacceptable', but they were 'incontrovertible' and 'the accompanying strategic calculus which both shaped and justified [Churchill's policy] imposed upon Australia a subaltern status which she could not escape'.[53] As John Robertson (1981) observed in *Australia at War 1939–1945* (arguably the best single-volume history of Australia in the Second World War):

> Australia's armed forces in February and March [1942] were unbalanced. Her navy was powerless to stop a Japanese landing. Her air force lacked planes to match the Japanese. On the other hand her relatively large army was better able to withstand a major attack; but it could not be moved quickly over long distances. The implications of these issues need more detailed examination.[54]

Nonetheless, in spite of the detailed and convincing arguments of respected historians like John Robertson, Carl Bridge, Jeffrey Grey, David Horner and Peter Stanley, a number of narrowly nationalist historians continue to reinforce a series of myths about Australia in the Second World War. That Australia was 'armed and ready' as Day and others attest is clearly inconsistent with Australia's failure to invest in local defence or develop a coordinated strategic defence policy. Rather, Australia persisted with her status as a colonial subject of the British Commonwealth and assumed that Great Britain would come to her defence.

CHAPTER 3

AUSTRALIA, THE EMPIRE AND IMPERIAL DEFENCE

> We should realize that for many generations to come it will be necessary for Australia to work in harmony with the British Empire, because only by that means can our safety be assured.[1]
>
> Henry Gregory, Nationalist MP for Swan, Western Australia, 1 August 1923

To work 'in harmony with the British Empire', as the Hon Henry Gregory MP suggested in 1923, necessitated an understanding of Imperial defence. However, between the wars Australians and their governments failed to understand that Imperial defence involved mutual responsibilities for the United Kingdom, the Dominions and the colonies. Too commonly the Singapore strategy was read as constituting, rather than contributing to, Imperial defence, so absolving Australia of its responsibilities for local defence. This chapter asks how this Australian misunderstanding arose and why Australia came to see the Singapore strategy as a sort of one-stop shop for its national defence needs.

THE ORIGINS OF IMPERIAL DEFENCE

The limits of British responsibility for Australia's defence had been accepted by Australian politicians and citizens as early as 1863 when the British Secretary of State for the Colonies, the Duke of Newcastle, informed the Australian colonies that 'the Imperial government had only a limited obligation to contribute to their defence, save in exceptional circumstances'.[2] British assistance could still be expected in the event of a war, but the Australian colonies were strongly encouraged to strengthen their own defences. Indeed, 'It was generally conceded that in a war against two major powers no effective defence of the Pacific could be maintained if one of the adversaries was based upon its shores'.[3] The Royal Navy simply could not protect Australia from a Pacific power while fighting a European war. This was to become evident following the Great War of 1914–19 in Europe.

The 1870s saw the development of an Imperial defence 'ideology'[4] that was 'nicely ambiguous' and left potential threats undefined.[5] Implicit in the concept of Imperial defence, however, 'was the primacy of naval defence'.[6] At the end of 1908 First Lord of the Admiralty Reginald McKenna and the Sea Lords 'insisted that unless six ships were authorized they would not remain in the office'.[7] The Royal Navy asked for a further two new capital vessels in January 1909, exacerbating a struggle within government to reconcile its political ideology to spend less on armaments and more on social services with maintaining numerical superiority over the German High Seas Fleet. The Asquith Liberal Government believed dreadnoughts 'represented staggering sums of money wasted on floating mountains of steel'.[8] The 1909 Imperial Conference, called in part to address the 'Naval crisis', declared that each part of the Empire should 'take its share in the general defence of the Empire'.[9] The Dominions agreed to standardise their armed services in terms of training, administrative practice, ammunition and equipment.[10] More importantly, the Admiralty proposed a Pacific fleet composed of East Indian, Chinese and Australian squadrons. The Australian squadron was to be manned by Australians and under Australian control,[11] with start-up personnel and equipment provided by the Admiralty.[12] Australian Prime Minister Alfred Deakin readily accepted this proposal and Australia subsequently went about the business of establishing its own navy.[13]

The Royal Navy's Admiral Sir Reginald Henderson proposed a navy of 52 vessels with 16 bases around Australia,[14] which was subsequently deemed too expensive. Deakin's Labor successor Andrew Fisher also believed that such a navy 'could not in any way serve as Australia's share in the defence of the Empire'.[15] The advice of British commander-in-chief Lord Kitchener to establish compulsory military training, however, was readily accepted. Kitchener's report also contained the very telling warning that a world war 'might require the concentration of the British naval forces in a theatre at a considerable distance from the Commonwealth'.[16] Australia must therefore be able to defend itself until the Royal Navy could arrive.

Imperial defence was again a major topic at the Imperial Conference of 1911. It was agreed that naval superiority remained the 'central plank of the general principles of Imperial defence',[17] but that naval superiority could never be absolute. John Mordike (2002) observed:

> With the outbreak of hostilities, the Royal Navy would not necessarily be able to deal simultaneously with the fleets of two first-class naval Powers in different quarters of the globe, as well as to provide for all other naval requirements. One major power would have to be dealt with first, because, if Britain's naval assets were spread, the navy risked being defeated in detail. Clearly defence priorities had to be considered.[18]

While it was unlikely in 1911 that Britain would need to assert naval superiority over the Atlantic and Pacific simultaneously because of the Anglo-Japanese Alliance, the Colonial Defence Committee warned that if the Alliance ceased '"local command of the Pacific might for a brief period rest with Japan"' until Royal Navy vessels arrived from Europe.[19] Neville Meaney (1976) argues conclusively that early Commonwealth governments were aware of the limitations of Imperial defence and therefore developed 'consistent, cohesive and comprehensive defence and external policies', albeit within an Imperial framework.[20] Such policies were developed almost exclusively by prime ministers and defence ministers who were 'narrowly self-interested and generally indifferent to the wider issues of peace and war'.[21]

Although there was some progress towards an Imperial defence policy before the Great War, it was not until after the Great War that it was fully developed.[22] The first concrete step towards an Imperial defence policy was the Dominion tour from early 1919 of the recently appointed First Sea Lord, Admiral Viscount John Rushworth Jellicoe. Jellicoe had been commander of the Grand Fleet at the 1916 Battle of Jutland and the tour was designed to support the Dominions in their development of naval policy. Historian Ian McGibbon (1981) noted that Jellicoe's departure so soon after the cessation of war hostilities

> owed little to any British desire to take Imperial defence urgently in hand; rather the genesis of his mission lay in wartime consultations, consequent upon the British invitation in 1917 to the Dominion leaders to participate in the formulation of Imperial war policy.[23]

The Dominions believed that their performance in the Great War demonstrated they deserved to be treated as equals. The Admiralty explicitly told Jellicoe not to broach the topic of Imperial naval defence but to suggest how the individual Dominion navies could be improved.[24]

Jellicoe began his tour uneventfully in Canada before proceeding via several Pacific colonies to Australia. Sydney planned so many festivities in his honour that he 'begged for a minimum of banquets and dances in order that he might devote himself to his mission'.[25] William Watt, Acting Prime Minister for Hughes—who was in Versailles attending the Peace Conference—asked Jellicoe to formulate an Imperial, rather than Australian, naval strategy, which the British government had explicitly prohibited.[26] Jellicoe readily acceded to Watt's request, in doing so disregarding his orders.

Jellicoe went from Australia to New Zealand with the idea of a Pacific fleet apparently forming in his mind.[27] He found a receptive audience when he commented that

> unless the people of the United Kingdom and the Dominions were prepared to put their hands in their pockets immediately it would be impossible to retain that British sea supremacy which was vital to the existence of the Empire.[28]

Jellicoe's interim report to the Admiralty, released in October 1919, proposed stationing at Singapore a Pacific fleet of at least eight battleships, eight battle cruisers, forty destroyers, and 36 submarines.[29] This fleet would preserve the two-power standard against Japan and Russia in the Pacific. Jellicoe reasoned his fleet would cost £19 million a year to maintain with the United Kingdom providing 75% of the fleet's budget, Australia 20% and New Zealand 5%. This translated into A£3.8 million a year for Australia, increasing to A£6 million in 1927.[30] But as *The Times* observed, Jellicoe's Report emphasised

> the desirability of Australia's becoming self-contained in regard to the manufacture of guns, mountings, explosives, and other munitions, and also aircraft.[31]

However, Australia had no desire to become self-sufficient and the 1919 Admiralty debate focused largely on how much was to be pared from the Admiralty budget.[32]

THE CHANAK CRISIS AND EVOLVING IMPERIAL RELATIONSHIPS

The reluctance of the Admiralty to engage the Dominions explicitly in the development of an Imperial defence policy reflected its view of the Dominions as less than equal partners. Whatever the nature of Imperial rhetoric the British Cabinet had no desire to consult the Dominions.[33] The issue of consultation bedevilled Anglo-Australian relations throughout the inter-war period and contributed to

Australia's misconceptions about Imperial defence. There was nothing new in Britain's attitude. In 1929 Hughes observed that

> Up to 1918 the Australian Government was never consulted about any plan; … usually it was told that a thing had been done or was on the point of being done.[34]

The Colonial Office sent the Dominions regular summaries from 1917, but these were often out of date when they arrived[35] and a response was neither sought nor expected. The Dominions had hoped that their signing of the Treaty of Versailles in 1919 as independent signatories would herald a new era in their international standing. Australia—like other Dominions—proved to be naïve in respect to her demand for equal status, and it followed that Australia became a signatory to the Treaty only because the British Government advised the King that she should.[36] Australian politicians were very slow to realise that their views were of minimal interest to Whitehall.

Once Dominion representatives at Versailles returned home, the Foreign Office swiftly resumed total control of Imperial foreign policy.[37] Nevertheless, as Galbraith (1948) noted, when the Dominion premiers went to London for the 1921 Imperial Conference, they did so 'not to be informed of British foreign policy, but to participate in its determination'.[38] They were rewarded with a declaration that there would be a common Imperial foreign policy and that the Dominions would help craft it.[39] However, there was no real attempt at Dominion consultation after the conference, and no Dominion agitated for a change to what was in effect the same system that existed prior to 1914.[40]

The status quo continued until 1922 when an international crisis revealed the limitations of an Imperial policy formulated exclusively by London. The Chanak crisis was the first test of the supposed common Imperial foreign policy.[41] In August 1922 Turkish nationalists under Mustafa Kemal launched a counterattack against the Greek forces occupying Anatolia and by early September the only non-Turkish force in Anatolia was a small British garrison occupying Chanak to protect the straits.[42] In spite of the Near East crisis brewing over several months, official contact between the Dominions and London remained minimal. Consequently Britain's request on 16 September for a military contribution took the Dominions by surprise.[43] It was additionally the first time the Dominions had been asked to provide military assistance to Britain in advance of their offering it.[44] Only Australia and New Zealand offered contingents, which in the end proved unnecessary. Australian Prime Minister 'Billy' Hughes, however, like his Dominion counterparts,[45] was unhappy with London and complained bitterly about the manner in which Australia had been treated. What concerned him most was that he had learned of the crisis from the press rather than official communiques.[46]

To Hughes the entire problem was one of consultation. He reasoned that if the Dominions had been kept well informed about British policy then they would have been more inclined to lend support.[47] However, his view was somewhat optimistic and naïve insofar as the Chanak crisis was concerned as 'Time and circumstance militated against the opportunities for consultation'.[48] At the end of the day the Dominions could endorse or reject but not influence British decisions. Hughes' suggestion of sending uncoded messages was rejected out of hand by London.[49] British Prime Minister David Lloyd George could not understand Hughes' complaints since Hughes had recently declined to appoint a minister to London.[50] Hughes' complaints did, however, result in Australia being better informed about the Lausanne Conference (November 1922 – February 1923), which resolved the status of the straits. Lengthy telegrams followed Hughes around Australia but, barely beating the press, were of questionable value.[51]

The Chanak crisis prompted Canada and Ireland to assert their independence and was a watershed in the development of Dominion status. Canada refused to approve the Treaty of Lausanne and unilaterally made a treaty with the United States in 1923.[52] Ireland appointed its own diplomatic representative to Washington and registered the Anglo-Irish agreement with the League of Nations, even though it was an inter-Imperial agreement. Australia, however, continued to believe the Empire was unchanged and unchanging and that it was entitled to a British foreign policy that reflected

Dominion, or at least Australian, interests. Prime Minister Stanley Bruce, who displaced Hughes as Nationalist leader to head a coalition government from February 1923, even resisted using 'Commonwealth'.[53] A change in terminology might have forced a change in Australian policy and Australia's outlook but presumed a new understanding of Imperial relationships. Bruce did send a liaison officer to London in an attempt to improve communications.[54] Former engineer Richard Casey kept Bruce well informed of what was going on in Whitehall from 1924–29; however, he was only a conduit to Melbourne and Canberra[55] and, although Casey met many senior British policy makers, there is no indication that his advice or insight was ever sought or that his representation of Australian interests was reflected in Imperial policy. Imperial policy was essentially British policy and always had been.

Canada and South Africa were more realistic in their understanding of evolving Imperial relationships. Canada had more than fifty years' experience with self-rule and a close relationship with the United States. South Africa's European population contained a significant non-British segment which dominated its politics and had extensive experience in international relations outside the Imperial context. Moreover South Africa did not consider itself simply as 'British'. It is hardly surprising, therefore, that 'rather than seeking to modify Imperial policies, as Australia attempted', Canada and South Africa began to withdraw from the Imperial framework.[56] Neither country had invested in, or was shaped by, the worldview of the British Empire to the extent of Australia[57] and both were less reliant on British trade. Additionally, neither Canada nor South Africa had potential threats in their region. Australia's geographic isolation offered no such comfort.

Throughout the inter-war period Australians saw world events almost exclusively through British media filters.[58] They were proud to be subjects of the world's largest empire and thought that Australia was the Empire's most important possession. Because Australians of all classes 'viewed the world through an Imperial imagination',[59] they failed to appreciate the changes affecting the Empire and their importance to Australian foreign and defence policy. By contrast, those changes met 'the imperative need of South African and Irish leaders' and were supported by the Canadian Prime Minister.[60]

Australia could ignore the changing nature of the Empire because 'of the conceptual fog that surrounded their [the Dominions'] status'.[61] The fog was thickest at Imperial conferences where the quest for unanimity produced vague and emasculated final statements silent on key issues.[62] This was captured in a Melbourne *Herald* cartoon which portrayed relieved Dominion prime ministers at the 1923 Imperial conference announcing that discussions 'have proceeded amicably, without leading to any cut and dried decision'.[63] The conferences were nonetheless one of the few occasions where Dominion leaders could meet their Dominion and British counterparts.

Hughes could not understand why the other Dominions wanted to follow independent policies. His international outlook was based on the

> unequivocal identification of Australia as a 'British nation', fully entitled to call upon the other states of the Britannic world especially Britain, to help defend the British place in the southern sun.[64]

Australian politicians lacked the experience to appreciate the advantages of evolving Imperial relationships and most worryingly did not realise that Britain traditionally did not resist demands from the Dominions for greater autonomy.[65] Australia also failed to realise that these inconsistencies could only be resolved by the Dominions' acceptance of full independence, and that Australia would always be the junior partner in any alliance where she was not fully independent.

Canada, Ireland and South Africa, however, neither accepted nor aspired to Imperial unity[66] and at the 1926 Imperial Conference South Africa demanded a formalisation of Dominion status.[67] Australia disapproved of any formalisation of links because it would reveal publicly that the Commonwealth was not a military alliance but a loose grouping of former colonies that shared a common monarch and heritage but little else. Australia also feared that the move would ensure that British policy makers pay it even less attention.[68] Australian disapproval, however, proved to be inconsequential since the British Government was 'notably sympathetic to Dominion aspirations'.[69]

THE BALFOUR DECLARATION AND WESTMINSTER STATUTE

In November 1926 the Balfour Declaration decreed the Dominions to be 'Autonomous Communities' 'in no way subordinate to one another in any aspect of their domestic or external affairs'.[70] Hudson and Sharp (1988) describe the Declaration as 'a masterpiece in that almost anything could be read into it'.[71] Hughes viewed the Balfour Declaration as a political stunt to appease Canadian and South African nationalists of non-British stock, later describing it as 'verbose' and 'pretentious'. In a reference to the domestic politics of two Dominions, Hughes contended 'that its *raison d'etre* was to crown Mr. Mackenzie King [Prime Minister of Canada] with a laurel wreath' and to allow South Africa's General Hertzog to save face.[72] He astutely observed that the main flaw in the Declaration was that the Dominions were not equal to Britain militarily, economically or politically[73] but were lesser and therefore in important senses dependent. That the Dominions remained linked to the British empire was a point taken up by John Darwin (1980) who suggested that the purpose behind the Declaration was to frustrate 'the separatist tendencies at work in Canada, South Africa, and Ireland'.[74]

The British Government soon realised the shortcoming of the Balfour Declaration and at the 1930 Imperial Conference offered the Statute of Westminster, which freed the Dominions from any external control and ended the fiction of equality.[75] The Statute gave the Dominions total independence in foreign policy and in doing so ended the myth that the Dominions could influence British foreign policy. Australia could have an Australian foreign policy or Britain's, but it could not exert much influence on the latter.

Leading the Australian Labor Party to victory against Stanley's Nationalist Coalition in 1929, Prime Minister James Scullin disapproved of British 'attempts to fashion a common foreign policy for the Empire', but his government chose not to enact the

Statute.[76] Scullin's failure to realise the opportunity offered by the Statute[77] demonstrates that the Australian Labor Party (ALP) was not overly nationalistic in its worldview. Scullin's views were not unique; the *Round Table* organisation dedicated to close imperial ties also opposed the Statute.[78] They feared that 'advancing status could do nothing to safeguard Australia from attack or infiltration' and was merely a cosmetic change.[79] The Opposition also opposed the Statute. Nationalists leader John Latham described Australia as 'content to accept Great Britain's decisions in the sphere of foreign policy' because a 'divergence of foreign policy which might involve different action is considered "purely academic"'.[80]

Australia's refusal to accept the independence offered by the Statute did not translate into closer Anglo-Australian ties. The status quo of earlier years prevailed and 'neither consultation nor even an adequate flow of information' occurred between London and Canberra.[81] It is questionable if more information would have improved the situation. Expediency was more important to the Foreign Office than Dominion consultation and Australia's refusal to enact the Statute of Westminster implied Australia's acceptance of British foreign policy.[82] That Churchill should make the same assumption in 1940–41 is consistent with this position.[83]

Theoretically, British defence policy considered the views of the Dominions and the Dominions helped shape it. The Committee of Imperial Defence (CID), however, responsible for crafting British defence policy including the Empire defence strategy, had 'very sketchy terms of reference' and little contact with the Dominions.[84] The CID lacked a defence policy-making structure and was supported by a small secretariat with few Dominion representatives. Dominion high commissioners were often invited to participate in its meetings but their military knowledge was minimal.[85] The Australian idea of a peacetime Imperial staff under combined British and Dominion control subsequently never got off the ground.[86] The CID was never intended to create defence by committee; rather it was to placate the Dominions and keep them informed of British strategy. It was inconceivable that Britain would put British troops under Dominion command

Dropping his bundles!

At the time of the Statute of Westminster, George Finey of the Sydney *Labor Daily* (1 November 1930) viewed John Bull as staggering under his Imperial responsibilities.

when the British contribution would be larger than all Dominion contingents combined.

Both the Empire and Australian notions of the Empire and Imperial relations had a deep effect on understandings of Imperial defence within Australia. Australia's economic and military reliance on Great Britain appeared to be highly advantageous to Australian politicians. Britain's apparent security guarantee allowed Australia to spend minimal amounts on defence and ensured the protection of the sea lanes upon which Australia's exports depended. With its small population and large coastline Australia was unattractive as a potential ally and, when formulating defence policy, the United States as Australia's only potential ally in the Pacific gave Australia minimal consideration.[87] Even after Curtin's 'Look to America' declaration in December 1941 'Australia never achieved anything more than the status of a significant but minor ally'.[88] Australia was incapable of protecting itself without a major internal policy shift but as a British dependency was well protected. Furthermore, most Australians felt a strong emotional tie to the United Kingdom and would have demanded Australia support Britain in a major war.[89]

THE SINGAPORE STRATEGY

The Singapore strategy arose out of an Imperial need for a strong naval presence in the Indian and Pacific oceans and, in part, accommodated Australia's obsession with a perceived threat by Japan. Considerable satisfaction was thus expressed in Australia at the announcement on 20 June at the Imperial Conference in London of the British Cabinet's decision of 6 June 1921 to develop a naval base at Singapore.[90] The original plan was ambitious, envisaging

> a massive facility with a floating dock, two sealed inner basins, at least ten docks, and large enough wharfage, maintenance and repair, supply, and above all petrol storage capacity to handle the main fleet itself: at least a dozen capital ships and a full complement of escorts.[91]

The Dominions were called upon to provide financial or material contributions for the construction of the base, which commenced some eighteen months later. New Zealand rushed to announce a contribution of £100,000.[92] Australia's Prime Minister Stanley Bruce, however, was less enthusiastic and confessed:

> I have not yet got clearly into my mind, from the strategical point of view, the effect of having a base at Singapore in relation to the defence of the Pacific generally.[93]

Progress towards the base was largely stalled till the Imperial Conference of October 1923 when the contentious issue of Imperial preferences dominated proceedings. The final resolution of the Conference noted 'the deep interest of the Commonwealth of Australia, the Dominion of New Zealand, and India, in the provision of a naval base at Singapore'.[94] Bruce's concerns had apparently been allayed.

The British General Election in December 1923 swept Ramsay MacDonald into 10 Downing Street as Britain's first Labour Prime Minister. A dedicated pacifist and internationalist, MacDonald objected to most military spending.[95] His Labour Party had 'always taken the view that no adequate reason has been shown for the very large expenditure' required for the Singapore base.[96] His government nevertheless promised to 'examine the case for the scheme before announcing their decision'.[97]

MacDonald's Government explored the Singapore naval base for just over a month before Charles Ammon, Parliamentary Secretary for the Admiralty, announced that 'the government has decided not to proceed further with the Singapore scheme'.[98] Leo Amery, former First Lord of the Admiralty, charged that 'by dropping this project of Singapore, the government are practically renouncing all co-operation with the Empire in future'.[99] MacDonald disagreed stating, 'I think I may claim that we have a large measure of sympathy in the Dominions',[100] a statement he based on bland Canadian and Irish statements.

Australia and New Zealand, the two Dominions most concerned about the Singapore direction, were adamantly opposed to MacDonald's decision. Bruce announced that 'The British

Government's decision regarding the Singapore naval base had caused the deepest regret among the vast majority of Australians' and that it 'manifested a distinct lack of Empire vision which is dangerous'.[101] But the Australian Opposition, the deeply pacifist ALP, congratulated 'the British Government on its decision not to build a naval Base at Singapore and hopes that other nations will follow the splendid lead towards disarmament'.[102]

Spared from contributing to the Singapore base, Bruce initiated the first five-year programme of defence measures in his 1924–25 Budget. 'The restoration of the Royal Australian Navy was the main feature of the programme.'[103] The Royal Australian Navy (RAN) ordered two cruisers, two submarines and a seaplane tender, a 'pointed reference', Hasluck writes, 'to the fact that Great Britain had suspended work on the Singapore naval base'.[104] It also exposed Australia's either/or approach to Singapore and local defence.

Stanley Baldwin's Conservative Government, elected in October 1924, swiftly resumed construction of the Singapore base. But it was a different base from that originally envisaged. The base would now have one floating dock and one graving dock, but no sealed basins and less than half the wharfage of the original proposal.[105] The new Chancellor of the Exchequer Winston Churchill criticised the government's decision to develop Singapore quickly, exclaiming: 'Why should there be war with Japan? I do not believe there is the slightest chance of it in our lifetime'.[106] Australia made no objection to the changes in spite of them potentially restricting the level of British assistance that could be offered through the diminished facility.

In reality Singapore's commercial harbour would have been used for naval purposes in the event of a war. Additionally, Australia's northern port city Darwin had been developed as a supporting naval base with wharfage and fuel storage facilities.[107] Construction of the Singapore base proceeded slowly. Baldwin's opening speech to the 1926 Imperial Conference concluded: 'There could be no more valuable contribution' than a financial grant to Imperial defence.[108] Bruce's reply—'It is very gravely doubtful whether we can now do anything further'[109]—underscored Australia's reluctance to contribute to the core of its own defence strategy. It was clear that the future of the base was still far from assured.

The election of another MacDonald Labour Government in May 1929 seemed destined to threaten the existence of the Singapore naval base. However, it became apparent that not all contingencies had been entertained when Labour backbencher Joseph Kenworthy questioned in parliament

> Whether there is any break clause in the contracts for the construction of the naval base and dockyard at Singapore in order that the contracts can be altered or modified in certain eventualities?[110]

The confronting response and realisation that Baldwin's Conservative government had failed to build a 'specific "break" clause in the main contract'[111] transformed the Singapore debate. That the government could be sued by the developer Jackson Limited for breach of contract should the tender be cancelled was a worthy consideration. And so it came to pass that the lack of an opt-out or partial performance clause entrenched Conservative policy beyond a Labour victory.

A major component of the base was delivered in March 1938 when the King George VI Graving Dock—the largest dry dock in the world—was opened. By early 1941 the base was completed and defended by artillery, searchlights and the newly built Tengah Airfield.

LIABILITY OR ASSET? HISTORIANS ASSESS THE SINGAPORE STRATEGY

As an inter-war subject the Singapore strategy has been relatively well covered by the military historians,[112] although the literature continues to be predominantly British-centred. Between 1979 and 1981 no less than four major books appeared on related subjects with a further two appearing in 1999[113] and 2005.

The first four of these books told a story of British self-deception (William David McIntyre's (1979) *The Rise and Fall of the Singapore Naval Base, 1919–1942*), of duplicity (Paul Haggie's (1981) *Britannia at Bay: The Defence of the British Empire against Japan 1931–1941*), of timidity (Ian Hamill's (1981) *The Strategic Illusion: the Singapore Strategy and the Defence of Australia and New Zealand, 1919–1942*) and of utter incompetence (James Neidpath's (1981) *The Singapore Naval Base and the Defence of Britain's Eastern Empire, 1919–1941*). Neidpath's approach was first supported by Malcolm Murfett *et al.* in 1999 (in their book *Between Two Oceans*, expanded and reissued in 2004) and Brian Farrell in 2005 (*The Defence and Fall of Singapore 1940–1942*), who further entrenched the idea of British betrayal of the Australasian Dominions.

McIntyre, the first historian to use newly declassified British, Australian and New Zealand documents, asserted that the Singapore strategy, 'born out of economy and nurtured on parsimony',[114] was flawed from its inception because Britain failed to appreciate its weakened naval power. Haggie's *Britannia at Bay*, based entirely on British archives, claimed that Britain was reluctant to confess to the Pacific Dominions 'the full extent of the Empire's weakness in the Far East' lest the Dominions reduced their Imperial commitments in favour of home defence.[115] Hamill saw the construction of the naval base in the main as an attempt to placate Australia and New Zealand,[116] and Neidpath argued that it would have been impossible for the Main Fleet to reach Singapore before the base had been captured.[117]

Neidpath's view was supported by Murfett who additionally noted that Singapore lacked sufficient resources to support a battle fleet of 20 capital ships. Murfett concluded that the British operational strategy was 'reactive rather than proactive' with 'contingency planning for a war with the Imperial Japanese Navy ... fitful at best'.[118] While Murfett believed that Britain had acted 'disingenuously' toward Australia, Farrell went even further, arguing that 'The defence of Singapore rested on a promise never meant to be kept',[119] a charge he found confirmed by a forensic examination of the disastrous Malayan campaign that ended with the fall both of Singapore island and city and the capture of the naval base.

Notwithstanding the populist acceptance of such accounts of British betrayal, there exist central weaknesses in these characterisations of Britain's Singapore strategy. In the first instance, the authors tell us little about Australian thinking. In *Between Two*

Oceans, for example, Murfett (2005) promises to demonstrate British disingenuousness and Australian 'strategic myopia'[120] but makes no further reference to these matters. And, even if one were to accept Farrell's assertion that 'Singapore was doomed',[121] he offers no insight into why Australia placed so much faith in the Singapore strategy and why it mistook that strategy for the only defence policy Australia needed. Indeed, this is a common weakness in the literature of the Singapore naval base and defence strategy. Historians eagerly discuss the tortured history of the British conception, construction and functioning of the naval base, offering varied accounts of alleged flaws in the Singapore defence strategy, but have little to say about Australia's acceptance and conception of the strategy. Why the Australian Government and military failed to realise and plan for the possibility that the British fleet might not reach Singapore before it was damaged or occupied is unclear.

With the exception of Ross (1995), who claims that Australia had always doubted the Singapore strategy and therefore armed and readied itself for war,[122] most Australian historians agree that Australia supported the Singapore strategy, although they have been unable to agree why. McCarthy (1976) suggests that the Australian Government lacked the desire or the ability to question the Singapore strategy.[123] Similarly, Horner (1982) believes that Australia had doubts about the Singapore strategy because of the numerous times it was informed of the strategy's flaws, but that the Australian Government and Opposition lacked the will to act on those doubts.[124] And David Day argues that Australian politicians—especially conservative ones—supported the Singapore strategy because of British trickery—a view echoed by Freudenberg (2008) who, contending that Australian politicians were 'fobbed off with false assurances',[125] describes the Singapore base as 'Australia's security blanket'.[126]

Australian expectations of the Singapore strategy must be seen in the context of Imperial defence planning for the Pacific after the Great War and the place of a Singapore naval base in that planning. These expectations were of course greatly influenced by Australia's experience of the Great War and attachment to the Empire. Jellicoe's proposal in 1919 for a base at Singapore was preserved by the Admiralty but modified to allow for the despatch to Singapore in the event of a Pacific War of the Home Fleet rather than a Pacific fleet. The Singapore strategy that eventuated was a poor substitute for Jellicoe's Pacific fleet. As the historian Christopher Bell notes, the strategy did not mean that the fleet simply steamed to Singapore in the event of war—a point that has escaped most historians. Such historians have tended to focus on the fleet's failure to arrive at Singapore without considering what it would have done once there. Murfett reveals that in the event of a Pacific War the Royal Navy would 'take offensive actions against the Imperial Japanese Navy', while in the event of a wider conflict 'its task would be to assume defensive duties to protect and deter the Japanese from moving South'.[127]

Far from failing to appreciate its weakened naval power as McIntyre suggests, Britain developed the Singapore strategy, at least in part, in recognition of her weakened state, as a substitute for a Pacific fleet, and in acceptance that the Royal Navy could no longer maintain or station a primary fleet in Singapore. Britain had substantial interests to protect in Southeast Asia and the Pacific and intended to defend them as best she could. The naval base was therefore more than an attempt to placate the Pacific Dominions, as Hamill suggests. Nor can the argument about British duplicity be sustained. Far from concealing her uncertainty as to what forces could be sent to the East as Haggie maintains, Britain repeatedly made clear the conditionality of her commitments. The period before naval relief could be accorded in the event that Singapore was under attack was repeatedly and incrementally increased from six weeks in 1921 to six months at the outbreak of war. Australia was never prepared for even six weeks of Japanese naval supremacy.

David Day's accusation of British and Australian conservative perfidy enumerates many acts of betrayal: the Lyons and Menzies governments' backing of Britain; the UAP commitment of Australian forces to the European war from 1939; Britain's failure to defend Australia from threatened invasion by preventing the fall of Singapore; and Britain's giving of assurances 'when none was warranted' and which were not met in 1941 and 1942.[128] The story of British assurances is complex. In May 1935, Chamberlain admitted to Lyons and Menzies that 'Singapore had become something of a liability which had to be converted into an asset'.[129] Further, Britain could not fight Japan and Germany simultaneously.[130] In 1937 the Chiefs of Staff noted:

> We cannot accurately forecast the delay which might occur before we could despatch a fleet to the Far East, since it must depend on the naval and political situation at the time.[131]

In April 1939 the Admiralty telegraphed the Australian Government via the British High Commissioner in Canberra that 'the strength of fleet actually sent out in such circumstances [war with Japan] must depend on numerous unpredictable circumstances including the situation in Europe'.[132] Shortly after this telegram the Committee of Imperial Defence observed:

> It is not possible to state definitely how soon after Japanese intervention a Fleet could be despatched to the Far East. Neither is it possible to enumerate precisely the size of the fleet that we could afford to send.[133]

Murfett is thus quite correct to characterise British operational strategy as reactive and naval defence planning as 'fitful at best',[134] contingencies being so manifold. But Australia was not kept in the dark. British statements of support for Australia in Southeast Asia and the Pacific, far from being ironclad assurances, were perforce highly conditional, issued when Europe was still at peace and France an ally. Day judges the conditionality of such pre-war British assurances as irrelevant because in his view 'Ever since the First World War, it had been acknowledged that the Pacific Ocean would probably be the arena for the next world conflict'.[135] British policy makers should therefore have focused on the Pacific but 'Churchill wanted an all-out war with Germany until it was utterly defeated' and this prevented Britain from strengthening Singapore.[136] Indeed, Day maintains that peace was still possible until France was invaded in 1940.[137]

The idea that an agreement could have been reached with the Nazi regime resulting in a long-term European peace is fanciful if not ludicrous. This is the same regime that systematically violated every treaty it entered and enslaved and exterminated its own citizens. Any attempt at a negotiated peace would have been seen in Berlin as further evidence of the weakness of the democracies and would have delivered Japan entirely the wrong message.

The fall of France in June 1940 and entry of Italy into war utterly transformed the conflict between the Allies and Axis Powers and spelt disaster for British strategy in Asia. Britain now stood alone against Nazi Germany and fascist Italy. Despite Britain's desperate plight, Winston Churchill, who had only become Prime Minister in May, stated categorically that if 'Japan set about invading Australia or New Zealand on a large scale', then 'we [Britain] should then cut our losses in the Mediterranean and proceed to your aid sacrificing every interest except only [the] defence position of this island on which all depends'.[138] As none of the stipulated conditions for Britain to send a fleet to the Pacific were met, such a drastic decision was unnecessary and, consequently, there was no betrayal of warranties to Australia or New Zealand.

Nor was Singapore left defenceless. A British army contingent was in Malaya and the British Government sent two capital ships to Singapore late in 1941: HMS *Prince of Wales* and HMS *Repulse*. The warships sailed from Singapore to intercept the Japanese invasion fleet and failed narrowly in their attempt. Dismissed by Day as 'the most minimal contribution',[139] this is surely the most compelling argument against a British betrayal. What else Britain could have done, given the global strategic situation it faced late in 1941, Day leaves unclear. But he asserts without evidence that 'It was only by chance that they [the *Prince of Wales* and *Repulse*] were at Singapore on the outbreak of war', because Churchill planned to have them retreat to the Indian Ocean.[140] Day's accusation is without credence. The *Prince of Wales* was one of the most modern warships in the Royal Navy—its movements were not left to chance. Ultimately the ships lacked air cover and were sunk two days after the commencement of hostilities. Had Churchill wished it their retreat to Ceylon could easily have been ordered or planned to occur once the Pacific War began.

Finally, we can dismiss Brian Farrell's argument that 'The defence of Singapore rested on a promise never meant to be kept'.[141] Even if one accepts that the Malayan campaign revealed incompetent leadership and underperforming troops, incompetence does not necessarily demonstrate a lack of faith. A serious attempt *was* made to defend Singapore: an army was lost and two capital ships sorely needed in the North Atlantic were dispatched to Singapore to intercept the Japanese invasion fleet. Australia accepted the Singapore strategy, sending reinforcements for its 8th Division AIF—which had been badly mauled in Johore—that ultimately arrived just weeks before the surrender.

The Singapore base alone was never meant to ensure Australian security. Had Australian politicians realised that the Singapore strategy was but a component of Imperial defence, they might have adopted different defence policies. Imperial defence expected Australia 'to become self-sufficient in terms of materiel at all levels except for the heaviest equipment' so that it could defend itself against enemy raids.[142] Australia never achieved that level of self-sufficiency. It had been warned that naval relief for Singapore might take as long as six months but was unprepared for even six weeks of Japanese naval supremacy.

PRINCIPLES OF IMPERIAL DEFENCE REVISITED

The construction of the Singapore naval base, then, did not resolve Australia's security or defence needs or absolve Australia of its responsibility to develop and implement a local defence strategy. The principles of Imperial defence had been laid out at the 1923 Imperial Conference—the first to deal with the changed strategic situation brought about by the Washington Naval Conference. Imperial defence was based on the premise that each Dominion was responsible for its own local defence; that the maintenance of Imperial communications was crucial; that sufficient naval bases existed throughout the Empire; and that Dominion air forces had interchangeable aircraft.[143] These principles were to ensure that it would be possible to mount a successful defence of British possessions and interests with British, Dominion and colonial forces.[144] Australia, however, failed to develop its own air force or the other forces necessary to provide for a strong local defence.

Australian inter-war governments believed their defence policy either should be centred on the Royal Navy or totally independent and focused solely on local defence. Advocates of the Royal Navy solution were encouraged in their belief because the notion of an exclusively local defence was grounded in isolationism and pacifism and so unrealistic that it failed to attract significant electoral support. The ALP, which advocated the latter policy, formed only one inter-war government. Both the Singapore strategy and local defence were, however, components of Imperial defence and not options from which the Australian Government might selectively choose. Local defence was mandatory in order that Australia protect itself against enemy raids—the most likely form of attack.

Archdale Parkhill, Minister for Defence in the Lyons UAP Government from 1934–37, argued that the Government supported Imperial defence because 'The strength of the British Commonwealth is the strength of one Dominion' and, therefore, 'A manifestation of solidarity is of itself a deterrent to aggression'.[145] He continued:

> No Dominion is capable of providing absolutely for its security by its own efforts alone ... The loss of trade with even one Dominion would react to the disadvantage of the whole. Security is, therefore, important for economic reasons alone ... Mutual help does not therefore, consist solely of aid to the partner in need of succour.[146]

In short, Parkhill summed up Imperial defence as 'United we stand; divided we fall',[147] though in reality it meant that Australia would fall without Great Britain.

The main advantage of Imperial defence undoubtedly was the savings it meant for the Dominions. The United Kingdom spent far more on defence than they: in 1937, 5.6% of Britain's national income was allocated for defence, whereas Australia allocated only 1%.[148] Had Australia and New Zealand spent the same percentage as the United Kingdom it would have provided more than a third of the Royal Navy's annual budget. As the historian G.C. Peden (1984) observed:

> It would be fair to say that the difference in levels between British and Dominion defence expenditure is a sufficient explanation of the strain placed on Britain by responsibility for Imperial defence.[149]

This strain became apparent when Britain stood alone in 1940–41.

AUSTRALIA'S SERVICES FAIL TO UNITE

The failure of Australian governments to understand the nuances of Imperial defence is at least partly attributable to the Australian military's inability to arrive at a common understanding of Imperial defence and to agree among themselves as to the sort of defence policy Australia should adopt. The culture of the RAN partly explains why that service had complete confidence in the Singapore strategy. The Naval Board was overwhelmingly British in character, many RAN Officers having trained in the Royal Navy.[150] RAN support also reflected its strategic outlook: 'If sea power fails, there is no alternative measure within her [Australia's] power, that will secure Australia'.[151] The Navy assumed that Japanese naval supremacy would lead to an invasion that could not be stopped or to a blockade which would starve Australia into submission. Since it was impossible for Australia to match Japan in naval terms, 'Australia's defence must therefore, of necessity, be dovetailed into Empire Defence'.[152] It was a logical argument, but it was flawed in that it largely overlooked the importance of local defence to Imperial defence—notwithstanding the naval component. The RAN argued that if Australia and its allies lost control of the sea—viewed as highly unlikely and unimaginable—a successful defence of the continent would be impossible.

The Australian Army saw the issues differently. It rejected the assumption that the Imperial Japanese Navy would invariably be halted and, although unsure whether or not a Japanese invasion was probable, believed that an invasion could be defeated.[153] The Army began to voice doubts about the viability of the Singapore strategy as early as 1923, when the base was still on the drawing board.[154] Such doubts were encouraged by the base's troubled development, but were never aired with a coherent alternative strategy.

Army critics of the Singapore strategy never addressed key issues such as Australia's lack of an adequate transport infrastructure to move troops or want of adequate munitions production to arm them, both of which would have been crucial if Australia were to defend itself. Indeed, the Army's primary contingency plan—Plan 401—considered only the possibility of another Great War and focused on expeditionary warfare in Europe or the Middle East.[155] It was completely silent on the issue of local defence.

The Army did not comprehend that Australia's failure to prepare a strong local defence was a cardinal violation of Imperial defence.[156] It further failed to appreciate that the Singapore strategy needed to be complemented, not supplanted, by local defence as laid out in the 1923 Imperial Conference resolutions. Australia was expected to maintain sufficient defence forces and fortifications to counter enemy raids on the Australian mainland. If the Army had been less adversarial and cast its case as supporting the Singapore strategy and strengthening Imperial defence it might have achieved better results. Army criticisms of the Singapore strategy appear to have been primarily a product of inter-service rivalry rather than evincing a clear-eyed concern for the larger picture of Australia's defence.

The view of the Royal Australian Air Force (RAAF) of an appropriate defence for Australia was even more confused and self-centred than the Army's. The RAAF questioned the Singapore strategy while it threatened RAAF independence, but ceased its opposition to the Singapore strategy once its budget was increased and independence assured in 1935.[157] This change reflected its fears that an increase in Army funding would translate into a reduction in the RAAF's budget.

The RAAF should have benefited the most from Australia's adherence to Imperial defence, for the development of Dominion air forces was a core principle. The RAAF was also ideally suited for local defence and patrolling Australia's extensive coastline.[158] As

Air Marshal Trenchard wrote in a 1925 report for the Australian Government:

> It is apparent that the most efficient method of defending Australia as a whole has not yet been fully investigated. If defence in water-tight compartments of sea and land could be replaced by a coordinated scheme of the three services, wherein the Air Force could amplify and partially replace some of the functions of the Navy and Army, it should be possible to obtain a more efficient defence of Australia itself.[159]

British proposals to strengthen the RAAF were ignored or emasculated,[160] leading the RAAF to deal with inferior aircraft and limited personnel. Imperial defence and the Singapore strategy were subsequently secondary issues for a RAAF chronically under-resourced and focused on survival.

IMPERIAL LESSONS AND A 'POCKET HANKEY'

Faced with conflicting views from the services on the Singapore strategy, the Australian Government was further hindered by a supine Public Service which failed to present alternative strategies or even clearly examine Imperial defence. The most knowledgeable public servant was Edmund Piesse, an expert on Japan who joined the intelligence corps in 1909. Piesse advised governments on the Anglo-Japanese Alliance and accompanied Defence Minister Pearce to the Washington Naval Conference of 1921–22.[161] However, he resigned from the Public Service in 1923 and, as will be shown later, was thereafter unsuccessful at influencing policy.

The public servants responsible for defence policy after Piesse's resignation were largely non-entities, as defence had not been considered an important policy area. Frederick Shedden, Secretary of the Defence Committee from 1929 and Secretary of the Department of Defence from 1937, was the next important public servant to focus on defence policy. Sometimes labelled the 'Pocket Hankey', because the power he wielded within government was similar to that of the all-powerful British Cabinet Secretary Sir Maurice Hankey,[162]

Shedden used his position within the Public Service to tightly control the information provided to politicians and thereby hinder the advancement of ideological foes.[163] Shedden's power was further facilitated by the lack of university educated public servants.[164]

In spite of a number of senior public servants and military officials attending Britain's Imperial Defence College, Australia's elites continued to interpret Imperial defence differently from London. Established in 1927, the College attempted to provide Dominion staff officers and public servants with a comprehensive understanding of Imperial defence and contemporary military thinking.[165] College Commandant Admiral Herbert Richmond was a strong supporter of the Singapore strategy,[166] but believed that the Dominions needed to embrace a wide Imperial outlook for Imperial defence to be meaningful.[167] Richmond was highly critical of Australian policy and noted, correctly, that Australia could not prevent Japan from taking the 'stepping stones' to Australia and also New Guinea, which fell within the local defence component of Imperial defence.[168] He advocated a strong Australian navy as part of local defence[169] and argued that Australia should contribute to the defence of Singapore and Malaya for the Singapore strategy to be viable.[170] Australia refused.

Shedden attended the College in 1931. His notes reveal that students studied numerous scenarios involving all parts of the Empire, including possible British responses to a simulated successful Japanese attack down the Malay peninsula against Singapore.[171] However, despite an instructor's comments about the potential size of a Japanese invasion force and the ramifications of such a scenario for Australia, Shedden appears to have been unimpressed.[172] Further, despite the College encouraging the notion that the Royal Navy was but a key component of Australia's defence, Shedden's research led him to believe that the Singapore Naval Base ensured Australia's defence.[173]

Australian attendees should have learned from these exercises that Australia was on the periphery of the Empire, and that strong local defence was therefore extremely important. While Shedden ensured that Richmond's views on Singapore were presented to key members of the Australian Government,[174] he does not seem to have pointed out that Richmond was unimpressed with the Australian defence strategy for its territories. The most important Australian civilian to attend the Imperial Defence College, Shedden seems only to have sought to have his preconceived views on Imperial defence confirmed there. Too few members of Australia's elites attended the College. This prevented an informed debate within Australia's armed services and the Public Service.

The paucity of Australian attendees at the Imperial Defence College contributed to political confusion about Imperial defence, for it gave the views of those who did attend, such as Shedden, an undeserved stature. Australian politicians failed to acknowledge that British power was greatly reduced and did not seriously debate defence policy. The ALP Opposition was particularly confused. According to its official historian, Ross McMullin, the most damaging political development of the inter-war period was the 'ALP's intellectual bankruptcy',[175] which allowed the ALP to avoid the challenges posed by the rise of fascism and hide behind pacifism and unarmed neutralism.

The ALP was split into pacifist—and socialist—leaning wings which combined to produce a party that offered unrealistic foreign and defence policies. Many in the ALP's left wing believed Britain would protect Australia because it was in Britain's financial interests to do so.[176] According to these MPs war was the fault of warring capitalists and British capitalists would demand Australia be protected.[177] The pacifists on the other hand argued that if Australia remained insular and isolationist the nation would be safe.

The UAP was only slightly more realistic in its outlook. Facing a weak and divided opposition, however, UAP policy looked much better. The electoral strategy of the conservatives—first as the Nationalists and then as the UAP—was to portray themselves as the party of Imperial defence without ever explaining it, save to reveal the ALP as isolationist.[178] Their navy-centred policies reveal a failure to understand the nuances of Imperial defence and a readiness to equate the Home Fleet steaming to Singapore with Imperial defence. Such an assumption relieved Australia of the need for in-depth local defence. This miscalculation was grounded in the unfounded assumption that the Royal Navy could protect Australia at any time and under any circumstances.

THE HUNGRY CANNON: "Hurry up, Cook; I don't care what fodder you put into my mouth, so long as there's plenty of it."

Will Donald *Australian Worker,* 16 October 1935

The Bulletin

Registered at the General Post Office, Sydney, N.S.W., Australia, for Transmission by Post as a Newspaper.

CO-OPERATION IS THE ONLY SAFE DEFENCE POLICY!

JOHN BULL

Australia may need his help some day

AS IN 1914, THE BRITISH NAVY IS STILL AUSTRALIA'S FIRST LINE OF DEFENCE

Lyons's Defence Policy, which is based on EMPIRE CO-OPERATION, means that, if Australia were threatened with attack, the whole might of Britain would be on our side. Our shores would remain inviolate. Curtin's policy of ISOLATION means that Australia would be alone and friendless in a world where one lonely and friendless nation after another has been mercilessly attacked and beaten to the ground. Lyons's policy is Security. Curtin's policy is tantamount to National Suicide. That is the choice before you on October 23.

The Bulletin, (Sydney), 20 October 1937

The absence of substantial political debate ensured that Australia failed to appreciate the intricacies of Imperial defence. Even if one accepts that with the Singapore strategy as its main component Imperial defence was a logical strategy for Australia—given its small size and relative isolation—the nation should have reacted more swiftly and more firmly when it learned of emerging weaknesses in the Royal Navy. The Shanghai crisis of 1932 had revealed that the Royal Navy's Chinese squadron was totally outgunned and outclassed by the Imperial Japanese Navy.[179] At the same time, Admiral Kelly described the Singapore naval base as 'moribund', yet Australia's defence budget remained minimal and did not supply money or troops for Singapore.[180] In May 1935, Lyons and Menzies were told by Chamberlain that 'Singapore had become something of a liability which had to be converted into an asset'.[181] They were also told that Britain could not fight Japan and Germany simultaneously.[182] This should have prompted Australian politicians, public servants and military officers to re-evaluate Australia's local defence requirements. That re-evaluation was never made. Why those revelations were never made is the focus of the remainder of this book.

CHAPTER 4

AUSTRALIAN RESPONSES TO INTER-WAR CRISES

We shall be wise if we do not anticipate trouble[1]
Prime Minister James Scullin, 9 January 1931

The inadequacy of Australia's political and military response to international crises in the inter-war period revealed a failure both on the part of the elites and the Australian public to realise the dangers posed by the rise of fascism and Japanese militarism. That Australia did not relate to increasing hostilities in Europe and Asia—the Italian invasion of Abyssinia, Hitler's remilitarisation of the Rhineland, the Spanish Civil War, the Czechoslovakian crisis, the Sino-Japanese War—or appreciate that the challenges presented by American isolationism owed much to the continent's geographical isolation and to an isolationist opposition. As a result of these failures, Australia would be caught off guard on its homefront and in the Pacific.

THE WASHINGTON NAVAL CONFERENCE

Japan's victory in the Russo-Japanese War of 1904–05 worried both the Australian elites and the public.[2] The Anglo-Japanese Alliance of 1902 had not stilled Australian fears of the 'Yellow

Peril'—a term coined in the 1870s to describe the Asian threat[3]—and novels about Asian invasions of Australia proliferated up to the First World War. Australia's blasé attitude toward its northern neighbours and its almost exclusive focus on domestic matters was the product of the Washington Naval Conference of 1921–22. On 11 July 1921, American President Warren G. Harding invited the world's naval powers to Washington to discuss naval disarmament through his Secretary of State Charles Evans Hughes.[4] Australian Prime Minister 'Billy' Hughes, who forcefully argued for the renewal of the Anglo-Japanese Alliance at the Imperial Conference in London, believed he could persuade the United States to join the Anglo-Japanese Alliance and thus ensure its renewal.[5] Government advisor Edmund Piesse, however, advised Hughes that 'Japan [was] an unworthy ally', a view which the United States shared.[6] In any event, the Washington Conference did not begin until November and Australia was not invited.[7]

Australia instead was represented at Washington by the British delegation, which prevented an automatic British majority.[8] It was also standing State Department policy not to treat the Dominions as fully independent states.[9] 'The United States of America [having] slammed the door in our face', Hughes returned to Australia convinced that America was out to destroy the British Empire.[10] Such attitudes would plague Australian–American relations for years to come. At the end of September 1921 the State Department agreed to a British Empire Delegation led by Lord Balfour. Because Hughes had attended Versailles as an equal to the American and British leaders, he remained obdurate that he could not attend Washington as a delegate subordinate to the British representative. So George Foster Pearce, Minister of Defence, was dispatched swiftly to Washington as the Australian member of the British Empire Delegation charged with preserving the Anglo-Japanese Alliance while reducing budgetary outlays for defence.[11]

Pearce signed six of the Washington treaties for Australia as an independent signatory.[12] The most important of these was the Four Power Treaty which limited the size of Pacific fleets and established a 5:5:3 ratio for capital ships with Japan entitled to three capital ships for every five allowed each of the American and British navies. This ended the two-power standard which had been the cornerstone of British naval policy. Another treaty limited fortifications, but the Singapore naval base could proceed as planned and the possibility of a defensive alliance with the United States remained.

The treaties gave Australia almost everything it desired—White Australia was protected and no financial commitments were made.[13] Pearce would later claim that he had saved Australia millions of pounds at Washington.[14] The Four Power Treaty meant Australia's biggest and most expensive warship HMAS *Australia* was soon scrapped. As Hughes noted, however, 'There is no force behind the Treaties', and there was no new alliance to replace the Anglo-Japanese Alliance which the Conference effectively terminated.[15] Consequently, Hughes concluded his observations on the treaties with the words: 'We are as dependent as ever on the Navy of the Empire'.[16] The Washington Conference concluded in early 1922.

Despite Hughes' incisive observation, Australia was slow to appreciate the significance of the Washington Treaty, especially the increased stress placed on the Royal Navy by the abandonment of the two-power standard and the subsequent risk this posed to Australia.[17] Australia's obsessive fear of Japan was replaced almost overnight by an even more dangerous ignorance, though 'a popular suspicion of Japan' remained.[18] As historian Jacqui Murray has observed, 'When the [Australian] media did provide information about Japan it was sporadic, lacked context … and invariably reinforced cultural stereotypes'.[19] In 1925 the Committee of Imperial Defence applied to Japan the Ten Year Rule, which meant no war was expected within the next ten years.[20]

Australia's lack of interest and concern about Japan was understandable given the faith in internationalism and disarmament that dominated international affairs in the immediate postwar period. With Japan not engaged in a military build-up no public support existed for massive military spending. Australia continued to be dominated by the spirit of the Ten Year Rule long after London rescinded the rule in 1932 following the Shanghai crisis.[21]

ABANDONED—A FUTURIST STUDY.

Jimmy Bancks comments on naval disarmament: *The Bulletin* (Sydney), 3 November 1921

EUROPEAN CRISES, ISOLATIONISM AND APPEASEMENT

The focus on Europe in the inter-war years reflected the importance of Imperial defence to the majority of Australians and Australian politicians. Most international news came from British sources and was European-centred,[22] with no full-time Australian correspondents based in Asia until shortly before the start of the Pacific War.[23] Public ignorance of the intricacies of European geopolitics allowed Australian politicians to avoid the difficult moral and strategic questions posed by appeasement and its repeated failures. In any case, appeasement enjoyed widespread Australian support—not because appeasement was British policy, but because of an abhorrence of war and the economies it allowed. Prime Minister Lyons was desperate to avoid another war and the ALP's strident pacifism and neutralism allowed his government to remain exceedingly cautious while appearing bold and attentive.[24]

David Bird has gone so far as to credit Joseph Lyons with playing a crucial role in British appeasement, arguing that 'It was Lyons from 1933 [not Chamberlain in 1938], who first implied and demonstrated that conciliation and rearmament were compatible'.[25] Lyons was 'an optimist' seeking 'to impose a new pattern on external policy—cunctation and then appeasement'.[26] While Bird's thesis is the most detailed analysis of Australian foreign policy in the 1930s, his argument is overstated. Lyons certainly believed in appeasement as did Chamberlain, but it is unclear that Lyons was responsible for Chamberlain's appeasement policies or even if Chamberlain would have embarked on a different policy had he not met Lyons.

That Chamberlain used Dominion opinion to bolster his 'already determined positions'[27] is undeniable and unsurprising. One of the first historians to use the records of the Dominion Office, David Carlton, noted that

> No British government was prepared in any matter affecting its vital interest to defer in the least to the views of a Dominion government.[28]

Bird provides no evidence to the contrary; at most Lyons encouraged Chamberlain to follow a policy of appeasement to which the British

Prime Minister was already committed. Nor does Bird ever demonstrate effectively how Australia could have appeased Japan, notwithstanding his claim that 'The theory of Australian eastern appeasement had arguably been sound and defensible'.[29] Although Bird asserts that Lyons' foreign policy was focused on the 'Asia-Pacific region, specifically at Japan',[30] he does not fully appreciate that every European crisis made it more difficult for the Royal Navy to steam East of Suez. However, there is no indication that Australia realised that a European war increased the risk of a Pacific war. British politicians and defence officials, on the other hand, were greatly worried that a European War would stretch their resources far too thinly.[31]

The first major European crisis of the 1930s was the Italian invasion of Abyssinia in 1935. As Carl Bridge observes, the crisis is little researched even though it 'marks an early stage in the development of Australia's and, in particular, Lyons' own appeasement policy'.[32] Lyons, who had recently met Mussolini and departed Italy with a sympathetic view of Italy and Mussolini, nevertheless supported sanctions. Indeed, Lyons' support of sanctions against Italy sits uneasily with Bird's contention that Lyons continued to maintain a sympathetic view of Mussolini's Italy.[33] Admittedly, the Government did not encourage debate and cabinet discussions on the topic were brief.[34] A crisis in the Mediterranean could be particularly damaging to the Australian economy, as Italy was Australia's fourth or fifth largest customer[35] while Suez

> was also the Imperial artery along which 95 percent of Australia's wool clip [the country's primary export and 90 per cent of Australia's refrigerated cargoes [meat, dairy products and fruit] were shipped to the British market.[36]

This is all the more remarkable since Lyons confided to the American consul, Jay Pierrepont Moffat, that he 'could never forget that Australia might someday find herself in the plight of Abyssinia', dependent on someone else to protect it from an invader.[37] The Government favoured imposing sanctions on Italy because, as Lyons eloquently stated, 'The Mediterranean has become almost as much an Australian sea as the Tasman' and 'To stand for isolation and non co-operation with Britain would be national suicide'.[38] It is hard to balance such statements with Bird's assertions that Lyons was sympathetic to Mussolini and favoured appeasing Italy. Lyons' placed HMAS *Australia* in Alexandria and HMAS *Sydney* in Portsmouth 'at the disposal of the Admiralty' in September.[39]

'If it were not for the oil-fields of Abyssinia' claimed the ALP's acting leader Francis Forde 'there would not be these manoeuvrings for war'.[40] Forde then declared that the policy of the ALP was 'Non-participation'.[41] This would become the ALP's standard response to any international crisis in the inter-war period. John Curtin, who would become Labor leader within weeks, announced that Australia must persuade Mussolini's Italy 'to return to a sense of its obligations', though just how this would be achieved was unclear.[42] Other Labor MPs blamed the Abyssinian crisis on Standard Oil, the League of Nations (for failing to outlaw nationalism), and even the United Kingdom and France.[43]

The Government swiftly seized the opportunity to attack the Opposition's leadership qualifications, though mainly in the Senate. George Foster Pearce, a former Labor minister, denounced the ALP as having 'blown its brains out' while 'endeavouring to bring together a mass of words to cover up its nakedness'.[44] It is difficult to disagree with Pearce's interpretation, if not his exact words.

The imposition of League of Nations sanctions was opposed by the ALP with the somewhat tortuous logic that this would prevent war.[45] Jack Beasley (ALP, West Sydney, NSW) claimed 'If Australia opposes sanctions then there cannot be war'.[46] This position was espoused by a party that had preached internationalism and had once worried that the League of Nations would fail.[47] The ALP's isolationism was strong—the party was willing to see the League fail its first major European test which, coming four years after its failure to resolve the Manchurian crisis, would ensure the League of Nations was forever impotent. Once installed as the ALP's leader, John Curtin admitted: 'I have not come into the leadership to alter the Labor Movement'.[48] The ALP's isolationism thus remained policy. Curtin soon compared the imposition of sanctions to Austria's 1914 demands on Serbia and questioned the need for an urgent Australian response.[49]

There was a very good reason for Australian politicians to counsel restraint in the Abyssinian crisis. The Royal Navy opposed a conflict with Italy because it feared it would be unable to send a fleet to Singapore if engaged in the Mediterranean.[50] There is, however, no indication that Australian politicians realised how important this crisis in the Mediterranean was in relation to the Singapore strategy—Australia's primary defence strategy. Yet the British Government had warned that the Italian cruiser *Quarto* 'might endeavour to emulate the activities of Emden' and thus disrupt Australian trade considerably.[51] To counter possible raiding by the *Quarto*, HMAS *Canberra* and HMS *Sussex* and *Stuart* were dispatched to Darwin while the remainder of the Australian squadron remained in Fremantle and 'elements of the British Far Eastern Fleet moved from Hong Kong to Singapore'.[52]

The imposition of sanctions probably had the support of most Australians.[53] Public support, however, should not be mistaken for comprehension or the existence of deep-seated views. Historian E.M. Andrews convincingly argues that an outcry similar to that which erupted in Britain following the revelation of the Hoare-Laval Pact, a proposal by the British Foreign Secretary Sir Samuel Hoare and the French Foreign Minister Pierre Laval to give Italy part of Ethiopia, is impossible to imagine in Australia.[54] Indeed, the Australian press did not believe Hoare should have resigned as Foreign Secretary. Australia's representative in London and to the League of Nations seems to have supported what became the Hoare-Laval Pact.[55]

Once sanctions were imposed, the ALP repeatedly demanded their immediate removal and urged a swift resumption of trade with the fascist state.[56] Indeed, many of the ALP's arguments in favour of resuming trade make the ALP appear to be the party of business. The Melbourne Chamber of Commerce, however, supported sanctions and curtailing trade—even though nearly half of Italy's wool came from Australia—arguing: 'This country is not sacrificing trade because it wants to lose trade, but for the sake of principle'.[57] Racism not economics is a better explanation for the ALP's views, which could be shocking: 'Abyssinians are on the lowest rung of civilization' and did not have a 'place on the map of the civilized

Labor Daily (Sydney), 19 November 1935

"The situation is very delicate. Nothing must be said or done that will," etc., etc.—Prime Minister Lyons on the Abyssinian crisis.

"Hush! He's a very sensitive dog. Don't speak above a whisper or he'll think you're sooling him on!"

Will Donald, *Australian Worker*, 13 September 1935

world' were all too common sentiments within the ALP.[58] The *Advocate*, Melbourne's Catholic newspaper, claimed that the issue 'is how Italy's needs are to be satisfied and how Ethiopia is to be civilised',[59] though the *Advocate* 'alone among the Catholic papers, actually defended the sovereignty of Abyssinia'.[60]

Although Australian Catholics were overwhelmingly found in the ALP, Pauline Kneipp argues that 'Catholics were as confused by and divided over the issue [Abyssinia] as most other groups in Australia'.[61] The attempt by Brisbane Archbishop James Duhig to equate the British colonisation of Australia with Italy's actions in Abyssinia and general sympathy for Mussolini 'were probably not shared by the majority of Australian Catholics',[62] most of whom were of Irish descent and questioned Australia's 'dependence on Britain'.[63] Catholic newspapers may have criticised British and Australian policy but 'they offered no alterative policy. They were thoroughly isolationist'.[64] The heavily Catholic ALP reflected this isolationism and 'The troubled years of the 1930s did nothing to disturb the remarkably stable alliance between Catholics and the ALP'.[65]

The ALP was equally isolationist concerning European crises when all the parties were European. In March 1936 Hitler remilitarised the Rhineland violating the Treaty of Versailles which Australia had signed. This was the first concrete indication that Germany had expansionist ambitions and, coming so soon after Italian expansion, should have greatly alarmed the Lyons Government and ALP Opposition for there were now two potential European foes for the Royal Navy to consider before they could dispatch a fleet to Singapore. However, the remilitarisation of the Rhineland had little impact on Australian politicians or the population.[66] The ALP largely ignored the issue, though it strongly objected to the Government's decision to accelerate its three-year defence plan.[67]

The Spanish Civil War, which broke out three months after the remilitarisation of the Rhineland, also failed to arouse significant interest within the ALP in spite of the Spanish cause being the 'supreme issue for many idealistic radicals' around the world.[68] Lyons' announcement on 11 September 1936 that the policy of the Commonwealth Government 'is one of strict neutrality' was wholeheartedly endorsed by the ALP and most Australians.[69] The ALP's silence on Spain reflected the party's deep divisions. Its sizeable Catholic constituency tended to favour Franco's Nationalists while the Left favoured the Republic.[70] Curtin himself claimed that the Spanish Civil War did not warrant panic.[71] The fear of another ALP split ensured that its front bench said nothing. The ALP's strict neutrality also reflected a fear that intervention would lead to a European-wide war which might lead to conscription.[72] It was left to the hard Left to argue for the Spanish Republic.

The Lyons Government realised that the 1938 Czechoslovakian crisis might lead to a war but still hoped appeasement would produce a comprehensive peace. Lyons personally approved of and supported Chamberlain's last ditch efforts at Munich to avert war.[73] David Bird contends that Australia's involvement and influence during the Munich crisis 'was far stronger than has been acknowledged by any commentator'.[74] Lyons urged Chamberlain not to underwrite Czechoslovakian independence and argued that the Czechs' desires were unrealistic.[75] Bird argues that because of Bruce's placement as High Commissioner in London and his status as a former Prime Minister, Lyons 'was thus able to remain well-informed throughout September, as well informed as the most senior (British) cabinet ministers themselves'.[76]

Lyons was not alone in his views. The Attorney General Robert Menzies also advocated pressuring the Benes Government to back down,[77] a view supported by all major Australian newspapers.[78] The Opposition was even more outspoken in its desire for a peaceful settlement. John Curtin announced on 28 September that Hitler's demands 'do not justify resort to force in Europe; nor do they warrant war in Europe'.[79] Most Australians probably agreed with Curtin's views and appear to have been completely ignorant of Czechoslovakia.[80] All the major Australian newspapers supported appeasing Hitler with Czechoslovakia, but the same arguments Australia used to oppose returning New Guinea to Germany were equally valid for the Czechs.[81] Curtin believed the Czech crisis was only a war scare and claimed that 'After the present period of tension, things will then calm down'.[82]

Lyons prepared the country for war with a radio address on 20 September 1938. He claimed that he wanted peace and had worked hard for it, and if war came it would be solely because of Germany.[83] He remained hopeful, however, that a war could be avoided. Lyons sent a personal message to the American President Franklin D. Roosevelt, and suggested to Chamberlain that Mussolini's intercession be sought. However, it is unclear if he gave Chamberlain the idea of using Mussolini or merely 'reinforced Chamberlain's intention'.[84] War was averted, but the Czech crisis finally forced the Australian Government, if not the Opposition, to realise what dangers were lurking in Europe. Hughes acknowledged that Australia was presently safe from air raids but asked 'Will it be the same tomorrow'? and warned that Australia could soon find itself in a similar strategic position to Britain, under constant threat of attack.[85] Thereafter Australia began to strengthen its defences, but as will be shown in later chapters, it was too little too late and started from a very low level of preparedness. The Militia was expanded, though training remained voluntary, and the Army's budget almost doubled.[86]

Richard Casey could claim that the 'Scales fell from our [the Lyons Government's] eyes' when the German Army entered Prague in March 1939, but the ALP could not claim anything of the sort.[87] The ALP was far from convinced that Munich was a warning. Curtin announced that 'The danger which threatened has been averted' and objected vehemently to increased defence spending.[88] The ALP did not offer constructive criticism; the Opposition criticised merely to score political points, members reaffirming their faith in pacifist isolationism or their belief in Marxist theories on the economic causes of war, which were increasingly impractical.[89] Hughes succinctly replied to the ALP's isolationism by pointing out that the ALP 'will not face the fact that there are today nations which stand for force'.[90] The ALP's failure to appreciate the seriousness of the threats facing Australia or to suggest realistic alternative policies—even though the Opposition's duty arguably is to provide an alternative government—renders hollow David Day's notion of the ALP as somehow Australia's saviour or better qualified party to defend Australia.

THE SINO-JAPANESE WARS

The ALP and most Australians had also failed to appreciate the seriousness of a crisis much closer to home and involving Japanese aggression, which Australia had feared to varying degrees since the Russo-Japanese War. The Sino-Japanese conflicts are particularly revealing because both the ALP and the UAP were in government during those conflicts.

The Scullin Government was already in crisis when Japan invaded Manchuria in September 1931. Parliament did not even debate the crisis and Scullin's one statement on it was incredibly naïve: he did not believe there was a war and declared that 'We shall be wise if we do not anticipate trouble'.[91] It was wishful thinking at its worst, indicative of political immaturity rather than ignorance. The Dominions Office provided Australia with extremely detailed reports of the ongoing crisis.[92] Edmund Piesse had warned as early as 1922 that if Japan acquired Chinese resources 'the world would be endangered'.[93] The press supported Japan out of fear of the Soviet Union.[94]

The election of the newly-formed United Australia Party (UAP) under Joseph Lyons in December 1931 did not lead to a substantial change in governmental policy towards Asia. Lyons was willing to concede that it was a war and his government adopted a policy of strict neutrality.[95] Only the Australian Army strongly questioned neutrality, because they saw the conflict as a way to dispose of obsolete rifles at a profit.[96] The dominant political view was that Japan had 'bitten off as much as they can chew in Manchuria for the next 30 years' and thus spared Australia.[97] This view became increasingly popular as Japan became deeply entangled in China.

The Sino-Japanese War should have caused serious alarm in Australian political and military circles. The Shanghai crisis of 1932 revealed that the Royal Navy had far too few ships in the Pacific and most of them were obsolete or lightly armoured.[98] Yet the crisis had no effect on Australian policy and was quickly forgotten. The publication of works such as *White China* by John Sleeman (1933), a journalist and former New South Wales Treasury publicity agent, had minimal effect on Australian policy, though Sleeman argued forcefully that Japan would threaten Australia if China was not helped.[99] Sleeman's descriptions of Japan's modern tactics and weapons were ignored. Australian military officials attributed Japan's success to the inferior quality of the Chinese military. The RAAF did not consider the Sino-Japanese War a 'serious war', although it received detailed reports from an advisor to Chiang Kai Shek.[100]

The renewal of Sino-Japanese hostilities in July 1937 should have alarmed Australia. The Japanese landings along the Chinese coast in November 1937 demonstrated that the Imperial Japanese Navy was capable of complicated amphibious operations in heavy seas. Historian Jacqui Murray notes that 'Japanese brutality at Nanking did not excite the intense condemnation' we would expect today.[101] Furthermore, Japan had prepared for these operations in utmost secrecy.[102] The Australian Government finally realised how important Japanese amphibious operations were when more took place in 1939.[103] Yet even then, the Commonwealth's response was to express great regret about the situation and to worry that it had disrupted Anglo-Japanese talks.[104] All Australian services, including the Army, had received detailed intelligence reports from the British embassy in Tokyo on the Japanese military and its modernisation and expansion.[105] The Army did not grasp the increased threat Australia faced if Japan could conduct such combined operations.

There was a widely held belief in Australia that Japan was too preoccupied with China to contemplate or undertake southern operations.[106] Lyons himself confided to the American Consul that he hoped 'that her [Japan's] energies would be absorbed there [China] for a generation'.[107] One UAP parliamentarian, Albert Lane (UAP, Barton, NSW) even argued that 'Probably, Japan's influence will be to the benefit of China'.[108] The ALP took comfort in the view of Maurice Blackburn (ALP, Bourke, Victoria) that 'I do not think Japan desires outlying possessions'.[109] The pacifist community in Australia assumed that a Japanese success in China was a *fait accompli* and strongly argued for a rapprochement with Japan to prevent Australia being drawn into an American–Japanese war.[110]

A few especially prescient commentators such as Dr Rupert Hornabrook, a leading anaesthetist who tried to awaken Australia from her slumber, and Norman Angell, a British internationalist and frequent commentator on International affairs, realised that Japan's advances into China endangered Australia. They appreciated that if Japan succeeded in China it could then turn to the South and suspected that Japan might do so to extract itself from China. Furthermore, such commentators knew that Singapore's value was decreasing with every Japanese success. Japan's influence was increasing in Siam, and it was advancing dangerously close to Indo-China and thus Malaya and Singapore.[111] Furthermore, even if a British fleet arrived at Singapore, these commentators realised that the Royal Navy and therefore Australia would face a very difficult situation should Japan have established firm control over the South China Sea.[112] Such interpretations of the significance of the Sino-Japanese conflict were rare and far from influential.

Australia's most important response to the Sino-Japanese War was in the diplomatic sphere: the Australian Eastern Mission. In March 1934 the Deputy Prime Minister and Minister for External Affairs Sir John Latham went on a goodwill tour of Asia. It was the first mission of a diplomatic kind Australia had sent to any foreign country'.[113] David Bird argues that 'it constituted a step toward a regional foreign policy'.[114] Latham spent nearly two weeks in Japan and China and returned fully supportive of Japan.[115] Japan may have been 'isolated and looking for friends', but as Ian Nish observed 'the practical results of the mission were small'.[116] It was unlikely that the mission could achieve major results as Japan viewed Australia as 'a secondary power'.[117]

Australia's status as a secondary power was one that Lyons could never overcome. Australia could not appease Japan—only the United States and the United Kingdom could do that. Australia could not influence American policy and British policy makers, nor could it risk offending the American government. Australia's limited ability to influence British policy was demonstrated at the Imperial Conference the year following the Far Eastern Mission at which Lyons' first plea for appeasement 'was immediately brushed aside without any detailed scrutiny'.[118]

Latham viewed the Chinese as inept and noted that Japan had accepted the White Australia Policy and was a good customer for

Australian goods, especially wool.[119] Trade was one of the main considerations in Australian–Japanese relations throughout the inter-war period but Australian insecurity meant that Australian politicians feared becoming dependent on Japanese markets.[120] Australian politicians such as Latham did not appreciate the threat posed by Japanese aggression. Indeed, as late as 1938 John Curtin was more worried about Western Australia's economy in the event of an embargo on trade with Japan than he was about the defence of China.[121]

THE UNITED STATES AND AUSTRALIA: AN AMBIVALENT RELATIONSHIP

The Australian Government was equally ignorant of its potential Pacific ally, the United States. This was clearly demonstrated at the 1937 Imperial Conference when Lyons proposed a Pacific Pact, an agreement among all Pacific Powers to aid any member that was attacked and to resolve disagreements between themselves peacefully. One historian has recently labelled the Pacific Pact a 'Great Initiative'.[122] David Day attributes its failure solely to the British[123] and argues that

> there was little attempt to replace or even supplement, Britain with America as the guarantor of Australian security in the Pacific.[124]

But Day appears not to have consulted the American archives and assumes all that was necessary for Australia to secure American aid was to ask for it. Both his conclusion and his assumption are simplistic and incorrect.

Ian Nish correctly described the Pact as an 'amorphous proposal'.[125] The idea sprang from Lyons' 'idealism and his abhorrence of war'.[126] Hart further argues that Lyons had been trying to arouse support for the idea for over a year.[127] He had discussed the Pact with President Roosevelt when he visited the United States in 1935, and Bird claims that Roosevelt had 'left the door ajar' for a Pacific Pact.[128]

Ruth Megaw, however, demonstrates that Roosevelt did not even raise the proposal with the State Department.[129] Considering the isolationist feeling in the United States, especially within the Senate whose approval would have been necessary for the United States to join such a Pact, the prospects of American agreement were minimal. Japan had responded slightly more favourably to the Pact idea, but even their response was only lukewarm. According to Ian Nish their response 'killed the initiative'.[130]

The British view that Lyons was merely 'flying a kite' with an eye to the upcoming elections is difficult to dismiss.[131] Only the Soviet Union responded favourably to the concept, saying that the Pact 'would answer the needs and interests of all countries in the Pacific'.[132] Australian communists dutifully supported the Pact.[133] Indeed, they even suggested Curtin resurrect the idea in 1939.[134] The United States, whose participation was crucial, was uninterested and passed the Neutrality Acts shortly after the Pact was proposed.[135] Indeed, America's ambassador to the Court of St James interpreted the Pact as a ruse by Australia to gain American protection.[136] The ambassador warned the Foreign Office that such protection was impossible. Lyons himself acknowledged that he understood America's refusal to participate in a Pact while Japan was attacking China.[137] Writing shortly after its proposal, Edmund Piesse offered the most damning critique of a Pacific Pact and one to which historians who laud the idea have yet to respond: 'What justification does recent history give us for thinking that a Pact would be observed?'[138] None, given Japan's expressed disregard for the Nine Power Pact and the Kellogg Briand Pact. A break in Anglo-Australian relations without an American guarantee would have only left Australia more exposed.

As evidence of Australia's failure to endear itself to the American Government, David Day cites its refusal to grant Pan American World Airways (Pan Am) landing rights at Sydney.[139] While a direct air link would have facilitated communications between the two nations, one must object that it would not have produced a sense of fealty between the two nations in either direction. Nor would it have automatically led to defence links for Pan Am serving many countries.

Indeed, Pan Am's attempts to establish an air link are an excellent example of Australian misconceptions about the United States. Pan

Am, the world's largest and most advanced airline in the 1930s, was controlled by Juan Terry Trippe. UAP governments repeatedly and incorrectly assumed Trippe spoke for the American Government and that Pan Am was the *de facto* American flag carrier. President Roosevelt, however, described Trippe as 'the most fascinating Yale gangster I ever met',[140] and a Trippe supporter said that 'His most disturbing characteristic was his deviousness. If the front door was open he would go in by the side window'.[141] Australia refused to even consider granting Pan Am landing rights unless the United States allowed an Imperial carrier to land in Honolulu so there could be an Imperial air route around the world linking Sydney to Vancouver.[142] Pearl Harbor was the only suitable location for a flying boat base, but the US Navy would not allow foreign carriers to land there. The Lyons Government assumed the State Department would force the US Navy to relent after Pan Am was denied landing rights in Sydney.[143] But the State Department was largely uninterested in Pan Am's South Pacific expansion.

Trippe was not about to let State Department indifference or Canberra's resistance get in the way. If Pan Am could not serve Australia directly it would go in through the 'side window': New Zealand. Pan Am's representative, Harold Gatty, convinced New Zealand that if Pan Am served New Zealand first it would 'establish the supremacy of New Zealand overnight'. Landing rights were promptly granted, but the New Zealand–Pan Am agreement required the United States to give a New Zealand or Imperial carrier landing rights at Pearl Harbor when requested.[144]

The State Department, however, promptly informed Prime Minister Forbes that

> The agreement between the New Zealand Government and Pan-American Airways, does not impose any legal or moral obligation of any character whatever upon the Government of the United States.[145]

Just in case New Zealand had any doubts, Gatty was ordered to 'Declare his lack of authority to obligate the United States'.[146] On 11

March 1937 New Zealand granted Pan Am unconditional landing rights. This did not lead to an improvement in New Zealand relations and certainly not a United States–New Zealand alliance.

The Pacific Pact and Pan Am show that Australia simply did not understand American policies. This ignorance is unsurprising. Australia's image of America came from lurid tales in the press of lynchings, crime and sexual debauchery, and Hollywood movies often featured all three. There was no Australian representative in Washington until 1940, and the position of Australia's trade commissioner in New York was little more than that of a 'glorified commercial traveller'.[147] The Department of External Affairs received copious reports from the British Embassy in Washington on the United States, but these provided only a description of political events with little insight.[148] Australian politicians and public servants lacked the resources to make insightful analysis of the American political system.

This ignorance and superficiality was reciprocated in the United States. The average American gave Australia little thought and knew very little about it.[149] Those Americans who were aware of Australia had a 'dim and unfavourable view' of Australia, especially of its business methods and social customs.[150] The United States Government had no sense of paternal or financial obligation towards Australia. In terms of trade, Australia was insignificant.[151] Australia did not even bother appointing a trade commissioner to the United States in the period 1931–38.[152] Australia would struggle for years to overcome America's lack of interest, but Australian misconceptions of the United States greatly hindered its attempts at better relations.

Australian politicians seem to have viewed the United States as 'an errant Dominion', which precluded a deep and sound relationship between the two Pacific nations.[153] Richard Casey did concede that they 'might be a useful people'.[154] The American State Department appreciated this misunderstanding but viewed it as an Australian problem. Cyril Wynne of the State Department wrote to Moffat: 'It would naturally be a shock to find that the eagle was not willing to have his feathers plucked to make a downy quilt for the lion's whelps'.[155] Australia was repeatedly shocked that America's outlook differed from Britain's.

The United States had no desire to aid or protect Australia. Lyons was correct when he observed that 'America was indifferent to Australia'.[156] Attorney General Robert Menzies visited the United States in 1935 and criticised virtually every aspect of American life: New York's subways, the Congress, the Secretary of State and even Pullman railcars. He believed that Americans were obsessed with money and concluded his damning description thus:

> We err if we regard the Americans as our blood cousins. The majority of them are not Anglo Saxons; their language is by no means identical; their ideas are cruder; their standards are lower; they engage in a nauseating mixture of sentiment (Mother's Day) and dollar chasing not palatable to the English mind; they have no consciousness of responsibility for the well being or security of the world; no sense of an Imperial destiny except in so far as it sounds in terms of collaring the world's trade and washing the hands of responsibility.[157]

Menzies was not alone in his dislike of the United States. The *Bulletin* proudly proclaimed in 1922 that 'Australia is experiencing a general reaction against the craze for things American' including magazines, books, chewing gum and 'the nigger dance, the ugliest product of U.S. civilisation'.[158] The *Bulletin* was quick to assert that it was not anti-American *per se* and would welcome it 'if some of the finer features of Americanism came across the Pacific' but lamented that the 'virtues and graces of America mostly remain on the far side of the Pacific'.[159]

Predictions of a decline in 'Americano-Mania' were overly optimistic. A mere four years after the *Bulletin's* prediction 90% of the movies shown in Australian movie theatres were American.[160] Hughes warned in 1929 that 'The influence of American films upon Empire and outlook is very considerable, and constitutes a direct menace to Empire unity'.[161] Many Australian intellectuals were equally critical, believing American culture was 'degenerate and socially dangerous' and would destroy Australia's nascent popular culture.[162] 'Inky' Stephensen was the most prolific and vehement critic of American culture. He was not alone. As the historian Jill Julius Matthews notes, Sydney film critic Beatrice Tidesley, Sydney academic and attorney Richard Windeyer, Judge and social reformer Albert Bathurst Piddington, and writer and critic Nettie Palmer were all concerned with the debasing influence of American culture on Australia.[163]

Most Australians, perhaps, disliked the United States because of its late entry into the Great War, its refusal to join the League of Nations and its commitment to Philippine independence,[164] but they flocked in vast numbers to cinemas to see the latest films from Hollywood.[165] Phillip and Roger Bell judged Australian working-class audiences as 'sympathetic to the imported popular and populist entertainments'.[166] Yet America was also seen as 'an icon of excess, anti-puritanism, and the celebration of masculinist populism'.[167] The Bells note that 'such contradictory images of America were to continue in the popular media and become increasingly complex'.[168] Even Japanese expansionism 'did not undermine the fear of contamination by vulgar Americanism that many Australians so keenly felt'.[169] Opposition to certain aspects of American culture and fear of cultural contamination did not translate into 'effective resistance to the spread of American culture'.[170] Indeed, as the Bells observe, 'Resistance at the popular cultural and consumer levels to overt or acquisitive American values had little effect'.[171] Australian audiences could, however, distinguish 'the entertaining dream from the reality of their own work'.[172]

The alarm of cultural critics was not shared by those concerned with the national defence, yet Australia's misunderstanding of the United States had dire consequences for Australia's defence planning. Australian strategic thinkers viewed an alliance with the United States as one in which the United States Navy would supplant the Royal Navy at Singapore.[173] This was a self-centred outlook that did not consider the global implications of American policy. American strategic planners viewed a future war with Japan as essentially a two-nation affair. They believed such a war would be fought across the vast expanses of the Central Pacific, nowhere near Australia.[174] An Admiralty suggestion that the United States

THE WINNER.

"During the War and since the Peace the late European Allies have got into debt to the U.S.A. to the extent of more than £2,000,000,000; and the question has now arisen whether they can support the burden."

VON HUN: "Yes, mein friendts, der Yankee vos quite right—he von der var."

The Bulletin (Sydney), 3 November 1921

THE NEW DEVILFISH (*Octopus dollaris*).

The Bulletin (Sydney), 10 November 1921

send a strong naval force to Singapore or Manila was contrary to American naval philosophy.[175] American planners had long ago accepted the inevitability of the fall of the Philippines and the futility of rushing a fleet to Manila or Singapore.[176] The Royal Australian Navy Attaché in Washington, Henry Burrell, informed Australia of America's policy.[177] Australian defence planners, continuing to ignore American policy in spite of Burrell's reports, expected the American fleet to come to Singapore or balance any Japanese threat.[178]

IN SEARCH OF BETTER RELATIONS WITH UNCLE SAM

Australian governments did attempt to improve relations with the United States, making several independent attempts to interest the United States in the Pacific. Prime ministers Bruce and Lyons each visited the United States during their terms of office, and Lyons stayed at the White House as a guest of President Franklin Roosevelt. But American commitments were still not forthcoming and Australia's understanding of the United States remained flawed. In the words of the United States Attorney General, Homer Stille Cummings, Australia was 'a hell of a way off'.[179]

Lyons visited the United States in 1935 following a trip to the United Kingdom and Italy. Crossing the Atlantic, Lyons expressed his desire 'to correct the oversight which makes Australia the only Dominion of the Big Four not represented in Washington by its own diplomatic mission'.[180] Australia's decision not to enact the Statute of Westminster was the reason Australia was not represented in Washington. Lyons arrived in New York on the 6 July 1935 where his wife Enid noted that everyone 'had a question to ask, and about one in five wanted an answer'.[181]

The American media was enchanted by this 'short, well-built man with curly gray hair, ruddy complexion, and a jovial manner'.[182] He made the cover of *Time* magazine and urged better American–Australian relations in a nationwide radio address stressing that 'America and Australia had a common factor in the Pacific'.[183] Lyons travelled to Washington from New York. He felt an immediate affinity with President Roosevelt who arrived joking that Lyons 'should have been with me just now. I was receiving a deputy from some of your co-religionists'.[184] Roosevelt, with typical disregard for the State Department and protocol, informed Lyons that 'if the Commonwealth of Australia appointed a Commissioner to Washington he would be accorded recognition similar to that granted to Ministers of other countries'.[185] This would allow Australia to avoid inaugurating its own foreign service. Secretary of State Cordell Hull, however, was indignant when he heard of the proposed commissioner arrangement. 'No commissioner could be treated as if he had diplomatic rank', Hull roared.[186] Such a commissioner would be placed 'at the end of the line where he would necessarily always remain'.[187] Australian–American relations thus remained cool. Richard Casey, who was appointed Australia's first minister to Washington in February 1940, was tireless in his attempts to improve Australian–American relations. His instructions, in the words of Casey biographer Carl Bridge, were:

> To create a sympathetic awareness of Australia in isolationist America. And, much more important, he was to make sure that British and American preoccupation with the war in Europe did not lead them to forget to provide properly for the defence of British Pacific territories, foremost among which, of course, was Australia.[188]

Casey had visited the United States shortly after the Great War, but his knowledge of the United States was limited. He failed to appreciate that the Governor of Iowa really was 'in charge of a state whose "real life" was based on corn and hogs',[189] and frequently criticised the 'softening influences' in American life while having silk socks sent via diplomatic pouch from London.[190] On arrival Menzies instructed him to employ public relations expert Earl Newsom, who was instrumental in Casey making contact with America's leading broadcasters, journalists and media proprietors.[191] Casey's impeccable sense of fashion and his 'daylight air raids'—he flew himself to some engagements—ensured his speeches were well covered.[192] He gave 70 major speeches—a combination of requests for aid, information about Australia, and warnings about the danger posed by Nazi Germany and Japan—including three that were broadcast 'coast to coast'.[193]

Casey urged Americans to realise that if Japan 'thrust its tentacles down to the democratic countries of the South-Western Pacific' America would be menaced.[194] Even though Casey often referred to himself in his speeches as British and described Australia as a British country,[195] he made it clear that Australia was at war 'voluntarily', that it was Australia's war, and that Australia

> went to war because we realized that if every one of us did not stand by Britain and throw ourselves across the track of this Nazi juggernaut—the writing was on the wall for democracy and for our way of life.[196]

Casey's speeches were recommended by the Foreign Office as an 'ideal format' for diplomats.[197] He soon formed good relationships with President Roosevelt, Secretary of State Hull and Undersecretary of State Sumner Wells. However, Casey arrived in the midst of the 1940 presidential campaign and President Roosevelt, seeking an unprecedented third term, had to be especially cautious in international relations. American isolationism was not easily overcome and President Roosevelt bluntly told Casey:

> Australia's distance from the United States meant that he could not guarantee any American military aid should Australia be invaded.[198]

Casey nevertheless sought an American guarantee in the event of a Japanese attack on the Dutch East Indies—which was not forthcoming. The United States policy was that: 'The loss of raw materials now drawn from Malaya and Netherlands East Indies would not be fatal'.[199] Casey's suggestion that a statement from the State Department to the effect that 'The United States of America is not prepared to entertain any attempt at intervention in the Dutch East Indies, ... would be most beneficial and welcome', was rebuffed.[200] The United States remained extremely isolationist and there was nothing Australia could do to change that. Declining an invitation to the Anglo-Australian–New Zealand staff conference at Singapore in November 1940,[201] it showed that it was just not interested in being the guarantor of Australia or any other country. There were no alternative allies. Australia was not going to be a major player and Australia had to act accordingly.

The European and Chinese crises of the 1930s were a warning of the dangers threatening Australia. Yet Australia's elites failed to heed these warnings and inaction remained the preferred course. Australia's failure to appreciate the significance of world events was not the product of perfidy. This failure was a product of Australia's inability to appreciate its peripheral status in world events, and its false assumption that Australia was a key factor in American plans for a Pacific war. Astute Australian political leadership was rare, a problem exacerbated by the Opposition's failure to offer realistic alternatives to government policies and a general failure of intra- and inter-elite communication. This weak and ineffective political leadership will be explored in the next chapter.

CHAPTER 5

CRITICS OF COMPLACENCY AND THEIR RECEPTION

> We are, as a people, little interested in theoretical problems of strategy.[1]
>
> *Argus* editorial, 17 February 1940

Previous chapters have discussed the failure of the Australian Government to appreciate the increasing dangers posed to Australia by European and Pacific crises in the inter-war period, or to acknowledge its responsibilities under Imperial defence to develop a strong local defence capacity. This chapter examines the efforts of individuals who through their writings and speeches attempted to influence public policy in Australia and alert Australian leaders and the general public to the threats posed internationally and locally by the rise of fascism, Nazism and Japanese militarism.

HUGHES' DEFENCE OF AUSTRALIA

The most prominent person to attempt to alert the Australian Government and public to the dangers Australia faced was 'Billy' Hughes. Hughes was Labor Prime Minister from 1915–22 and later served in the Lyons Cabinet as Minister for Health and Repatriation

(1934–35, 1936–37), Minister for External Affairs (1937–39), Minister for Industry (1938–40) and Attorney General (1939–41). Hughes was always wary of Japan and had questioned the efficacy of disarmament and the League of Nations as early as 1922. Japan's 1931 invasion of Manchuria confirmed Hughes' fears,[2] and he attempted in speeches and articles to alert the Australian public to the dangers lurking in the international arena.

Hughes often led the Australian delegation to the League of Nations Opening Session in Geneva and had become increasingly alarmed by international developments.[3] In April 1933, following his return from Geneva, he warned the Constitutional Club that 'Australia must not regard her position as secure because of her isolation from the rest of the world'.[4] He attempted to reach a much wider audience in August where he declared in a column for the *Sydney Morning Herald* that Australia was 'not in a position to defend herself' and that 'the British Navy is no longer mistress of the sea'.[5] The former Prime Minister astutely observed that the world situation had changed dramatically since the Great War, that the Army was undermanned and that the RAN lacked sufficient vessels to protect the Australian continent, let alone its vital trade routes. He concluded that 'these facts should surely spur the most apathetic Australian to action'.[6]

Hughes' warnings did prompt some Australians to action, but only briefly. Several letters of support were published by the *Sydney Morning Herald*.[7] A series of articles and editorials on British and Australian defence strength appeared over the next week. However, they were all superficial and ignored the significance of Royal Navy deficiencies for Australian defence policy.[8]

In September 1933 Hughes created the Defence of Australia League 'to further his crusade' for stronger defence and enhance his standing.[9] Hughes gave a series of speeches to large crowds claiming 'The British Navy is no longer what it was'[10] and that 'Every nation has not only the right to defend herself against attack but civilization imposes that duty upon it'.[11] He warned:

> Weakness invites attack. Ineffective defences such as we possess are worse than none at all because they create an

> illusion of security … Once an enemy got within gun shot range of Sydney it would be all over in Australia. In half-an-hour they would destroy our bridge, wreck the Bunnerong power-house, plunge the city in darkness, stop our trains and trams and factories, shatter the Newcastle steel works and so make major repairs impossible, and we would be on our knees rendered impotent.[12]

The League pledged 'to do anything possible to ensure the adequate defence of the Commonwealth'.[13] Public interest in Hughes' pronouncements was short-lived. By October a *Sydney Morning Herald* article dismissed Hughes' arguments as 'an attempt to stampede us into hysteria'.[14] No response from Hughes was published and there is no indication in his papers that he bothered to reply. The uproar prompted by his charges had already died down.[15]

Hughes' elevation to the UAP Cabinet in October 1934 did not convert him. He developed his critique of defence policy into a book entitled *Australia and War To-Day: The Price of Peace*,[16] which opened with the bold proposition: 'War is not an illusion; it is a grim fact that must be faced'.[17] Hughes was loathed by the ALP because he had 'ratted' on the party and was distrusted by the UAP because of his role in bringing down the Bruce Government. He claimed to be motivated by the conviction that

> The present position of Australia is without precedent in her history, and is such as should arouse her people to a full realization of the necessity for putting the defences of their country on an effective footing.[18]

His biographer Laurence Fitzhardinge noted that the book cast him in 'The role of prophet without honour'.[19]

Hughes' book warned that disarmament had failed and the League of Nations was impotent.[20] Of greater concern was its revelation that the Royal Navy, the cornerstone of Imperial defence and the Singapore strategy, was weaker than it had been either in 1914 or 1918 and would be unable to defend Australia if Europe were at war. Hughes pointed out that 'Britain is under no more obligation to defend Australia than is Australia to defend Britain',[21] which must have shocked most of his readers. Therefore, Hughes reasoned, 'Australia must at least take whatever steps are possible to ensure her own safety from aggression'.[22]

Hughes proposed a much larger Army, RAAF and RAN. He acknowledged that it would be expensive but pleaded: 'Surely we can find the money to protect ourselves from a still more disastrous war coming to our very doors'.[23] Hughes did not offer suggestions as to where the money could be found but opposed deficit spending. His book, which argued for what might be termed 'forward defence', was also a pointed critique of the ALP's policy of fighting only within Australian territory. Hughes' proposals would have met Australia's local defence requirements and thereby ensured that Australia met its Imperial defence obligations.

Australia and War To-Day was praised in *The Australian Rhodes Review*[24] by Lewis Wilcher, Dean of Trinity College, University of Melbourne and future lecturer in British History, who noted:

> It is useless saying another major war will mean the destruction of our civilisation; the only way to avert it is for the right-minded nations so to equip themselves that any attack on them would be more disastrous to the aggressor than to themselves. This is not fire-eating, but mere common sense.[25]

A former First Lord of the Admiralty and critic of appeasement, Leo Amery congratulated Hughes on the book,[26] but his own Cabinet colleagues were appalled by it—especially by Hughes' vehement critique of the League of Nations. Hughes persisted with his unpopular stance.

Prior to the publication of Hughes' book the Lyons Government had decided to support the League of Nations in the Abyssinian dispute. Hughes took little part in the Cabinet discussions on sanctions and was 'contemptuous of their [his cabinet colleagues'] ostrich-like unreality'.[27] He supported imposing sanctions because in his view 'they offered the only, and perhaps the last, chance to make the League effective and stop the dictators'.[28] Hughes surely hoped that his decision to support sanctions would allow him to stay in the Cabinet. He told Lyons that he had written *Australia and War To-Day* before the Government decided to impose sanctions. Lyons, however, demanded and received Hughes' resignation.

Hughes was soon invited back into the Cabinet but would not tackle defence issues again until 1937 when as Minister for External Affairs he launched a scathing attack on the ALP's defence policy. He still argued that 'There is nothing Australia can do to prevent war' and 'Nothing it can do to prevent war coming to Australia if it does break out'.[29] He now contradicted his argument in *Australia and War To-Day*, asserting that 'Britain and "Collective Security" could do something to prevent war'.[30]

Hughes still argued that Australian local defences needed to be improved and played a crucial role in strengthening Australia's local defence—but not because of his writings. In 1938 Lyons asked Hughes—owing to his enthusiasm and concern about Australia's defence—to lead the campaign to expand the Citizen Military Forces (CMF) to 35,000 men. Lyons acknowledged that if Hughes failed 'We face disaster'.[31] Hughes preferred compulsory service, but he campaigned vigorously for volunteers.[32]

THE GOVERNMENT'S 'ALBATROSS': EDMUND PIESSE

Hughes' attempts to arouse his government colleagues largely failed in spite of ready access to the Government and levers of power. Many of his observations were prescient, but his past did not engender confidence. Former public servant and lawyer Edmund Piesse, however, had neither prescience nor confidence but possessed a detailed knowledge of Japan and friends in Army Headquarters. Piesse had joined the Australian Intelligence Corps in 1909. He was the first Director of Military Intelligence in 1916 before becoming head of the Pacific Branch and Foreign Affairs section of the Prime Minister's Department in 1919. Piesse was not anti-Japanese; he had objected to Hughes' conduct at the Versailles Conference and accepted Japan receiving former German colonies in the Pacific as League of Nations mandates.[33] In 1920 he drafted a report which suggested easing

Australian immigration restrictions on Asian immigration.[34] Hughes responded to this report by denying Piesse important information and ignoring his advice. The Bruce Government's failure to implement different policies or improve Piesse's access to information caused him to resign in 1923.

While practising law, Piesse remained deeply interested in Australian–Japanese relations and Australian defence policy. In 1926, writing for the journal *Foreign Affairs*, he alleged that Bruce's anti-Japanese attitude reflected undue RAN influence on the Government. Piesse maintained that 'Japanese population growth is not a danger to Australia'.[35] As an active member of the *Round Table*, he contributed articles which criticised Australia's foreign policy.[36] The Sino-Japanese War, however, changed Piesse's attitude towards Japan and convinced him that Japan was a real and imminent threat.

In 1935 Piesse published *Japan and the Defence of Australia*,[37] his most detailed analysis of Australian defence policy and Japanese intentions, under the pseudonym Albatross to minimise government ire.[38] According to Piesse's biographer it was aimed at 'Professors who believe in collective security in the Pacific' and 'Admirals who believe in Imperial defence for Australia'.[39] It was also aimed at Australian politicians. *Japan and the Defence of Australia* was commended by the *Argus*, the only major newspaper to review it, claiming that 'It will dispel many of the obscurities and perhaps some of the prejudices—whether infantile or senile—by which speakers and writers on this subject are too often beset'.[40]

In an attempt to influence the political elite, Piesse sent a copy of his book to every federal Member of Parliament and Senator, but Neville Meaney concludes that Piesse had very little effect on any of them.[41] In a thank-you note Attorney General Robert Menzies stated: 'I have already read much of it with interest and am glad to have it'. However, his views on defence did not change and when Prime Minister his policies did not reflect an acceptance of Piesse's views.[42] General John Lavarack, Chief of the Australian General Staff, forwarded a condensed version of the work to his officers. Lavarack also arranged for Colonel Henry Dennis Wynter, an Army

Applying Sanctions at home.

LITTLE BILLY: "Oh, spare me, Mother! I didn't mean to do it!"

Will Donald *Australian Worker*, 13 November 1935

staff officer, to comment on a draft of Piesse's work. Wynter's role is discussed later in this chapter.

Japan and the Defence of Australia commenced with the claim that 'War is a natural way of achieving the purposes of a nation' and warned that Japan was interested in expanding to the South.[43] Like Hughes, Piesse pointed out that the Royal Navy was weaker than it had been in 1914 and that 'Japan takes [the] offensive when [the] rest of [the] world [is] engaged'.[44] Therefore, Piesse argued, 'The only safe doctrine is to rely solely and finally on local defence'.[45] By 'local defence' Piesse meant the Army and RAAF, but did not provide specific figures or consider how such a defence programme would be funded.[46]

Piesse had the misfortune to release his book shortly after Hughes and lacked Hughes' reputation and flair for publicity. Only 500 copies were printed and Piesse worried that he would not even recoup his printing costs.[47] He later acknowledged his inability to influence defence policy or inspire debate. In a 1939 book review he conceded that in spite of his and others' efforts, 'Australia has become too well accustomed to feeble generalities and hazy half-truths from government speakers on defence'.[48] The commercial failure of *Japan and the Defence of Australia* did not stop Piesse from attempting to raise the alarm. He wrote more articles as 'Albatross' for the *Sydney Morning Herald*, which again stressed the need for a stronger Army and RAAF,[49] and a series of anonymous articles for the *Age* in March 1936.[50] The *Age* series began with the indictment that 'Australia to-day is bordering upon a state of impotence with regard to its available organisation for defence'.[51] Piesse recommended the Army form Australia's primary defence. The response was minimal to these articles and others like them. The *Age* lamented the lack of public interest a month after Piesse's articles appeared, observing that the 'Public did not realise the danger' Australia faced.[52]

CONCERNED OFFICERS, OR POLITICAL PROPAGANDISTS?

Colonel Henry D. Wynter, a serving army officer who had commented on Piesse's work, assumed, somewhat incredibly, that he could leak secret reports to the press and collude with the Opposition with impunity in an attempt to change government policy. This was an improper way to attempt to influence the political elite but the only one available to an army with few sociometric ties to the political elite. Wynter was a Great War veteran who had attended the British Staff College at Camberley in 1921–22 and the Imperial Defence College in 1930.[53] He was described by an early biographer as an 'intellectual beacon in Australia's military society, made arid in his time by public apathy and want of ministerial inspiration'.[54] He also had a reputation 'for looking at old problems in new ways' and was a close friend of General Lavarack.[55] Minister of Defence Parkhill suspected that Wynter had commented on Piesse's *Japan and the Defence of Australia*, but that the Colonel did not appreciate the dangers inherent in politics.[56]

Wynter first seriously questioned Australia's reliance on the Singapore strategy in the April 1927 issue of the British *Army Quarterly*, which had a specialised and limited readership of serving Army officers. He was one of the few published Australian officers; as Warren Perry observed, 'The Australian Government of the inter-war period did literally nothing to encourage "pen and ink" soldiers'.[57] Wynter believed that it was unrealistic to 'rely on just one service to defend a nation', implying that Australia's reliance on the Singapore strategy was a dangerous mistake.[58] He went on to state that the Royal Navy was unlikely to arrive in sufficient strength to protect Australia even if the Singapore base were completed. In any event, Wynter argued, it was on land where decisive results were to be achieved.[59]

Wynter did not, however, believe this meant that Australian troops should defend the Malayan peninsula; he favoured defending Australia only on Australian soil. However, his argument for an Army-centred outlook smacked of heresy to an island nation which had always relied on the Royal Navy and was well versed in the accomplishments of Sir Francis Drake and Admiral Horatio Nelson.[60] Further, he failed to consider the advantages of 'forward defence' and trade protection, and never addressed the issue of cost for his army-based strategy or its efficacy. He also failed to appreciate that a stronger Army could be developed as Australia's local defence.

Wynter, however, continued to advocate for a defence based on the Army. In 1935, during lectures to fellow officers at the Royal

United Services Institutions in Melbourne and Sydney, he stated that 'A fortified base such as Singapore cannot be regarded as a defence, for example, of the trade routes through the Indian Ocean or of Australia except in conjunction with a fleet based upon it'.[61] (He did not discuss ways in which the Army or the RAAF would protect Australian trade routes either.) Wynter doubted a British fleet would be available when needed because an Asian enemy would probably make demands 'when Great Britain is involved or threatened to become involved in a war in Europe'.[62] He argued that 'A greater degree of self-reliance in Australian defence is essential'.[63] Wynter concluded that 'The principal means available to us for attaining greater local security are land and air forces', otherwise Australia was 'doomed to failure at every point'.[64]

Wynter's views eventually came to the attention of the Lyons Government, which forwarded his views to London for comment by the Chiefs of Staff (COS). The COS was highly critical of them, arguing correctly that 'The defeat of Great Britain in Europe would mean the breakup of the British Empire'.[65] It also noted that Japan was not likely to attempt operations against Australia without absolute command of the Pacific, which required the defeat of the Royal Navy and not simply the preoccupation of the Royal Navy with European or Mediterranean matters. The COS also observed:

> It seems scarcely conceivable that Australia, in time of peace, could build up an armament industry capable of supplying the requirements of the military forces on the scale advocated by the writer.[66]

Wynter's lectures came dangerously close to political 'propaganda by Service Officers on the political aspect of Defence policy'.[67] In April 1936 the Sydney *Daily Telegraph*, where Wynter's son was a reporter, ran an article by 'Our Military Writer' which was similar to Wynter's lecture and smacked of Army politicking.[68] The article claimed that Australia 'must be self-reliant',[69] but did not explain how that could be accomplished. The article's argument for self-reliance was based on a misunderstanding of Imperial defence, alleging that

> It has long been the fashionable view, particularly in Whitehall, that Imperial defence is one and indivisible and that the only sound course is a general contribution to an Imperial scheme.[70]

Whitehall was frequently urging Australia to strengthen its local defences, because local defence was a key component of Imperial defence.

The publication of the article indicated that Wynter had almost certainly broken Army regulations. Australian military regulation 309(2) warned:

> Officers and soldiers will be held responsible for all breaches of Defence Act 73.4 (relating to the communication of information) and should bear in mind its provisions when communicating with their friends.[71]

Defence Minister Archdale Parkhill demanded the Military Board investigate the article and discover its source. Major General Lavarack would later describe the Military Board's handling of the article as an attempt at 'white-wash'.[72] The Board therefore reported that they had 'considerable difficulty in criticizing the article' because many in the Army agreed with the article's general theme, and they had 'no knowledge regarding the identity of "Our Military Writer"'.[73] Parkhill did not believe the Board, noting 'I do not agree'.[74]

Wynter's lectures and views might have remained forgotten had they not somehow found their way to the Opposition leader, John Curtin.[75] On 5 November 1936 Curtin rose in the House and gave a speech which 'except for the introductory remarks, odd interpolations, answers to interjections and a general conclusion' was Wynter's Royal United Services Institute lecture.[76] Curtin stated, as had Wynter, that 'A greater degree of self-reliance in Australia's self-defence is essential'.[77] He continued: 'The principal means available to us for attaining greater local security are land and air forces'.[78] Minister of Defence Parkhill's fury at hearing Curtin repeat 'secret' Army lectures in Parliament was predictable and understandable.

This time the Military Board, rather than try to white-wash Wynter, acknowledged that Curtin's speech had drawn on Wynter's views and most probably came from his lectures. This admission allowed the Board to safely claim that 'no actual leakage of Departmental information from a Departmental document has taken place'.[79] It did, however, go on to assert:

> Colonel Wynter, therefore, appears to have acted quite innocently both in the delivery of the lecture and in the presentation of copies to various persons.[80]

This might have been technically true, but Wynter had clearly engaged in 'political propaganda'.

Wynter was forced on the defensive but began by arguing that he knew nothing about the newspaper article in April—a secondary issue. It is unclear why Wynter embarked on this strategy and his explanation was unimpressive. Wynter claimed he 'had no idea such an article would be published' though conceded that 'It appears not improbable that my son was the author'.[81] Wynter admitted that he and his son often discussed defence but claimed disingenuously that

> These discussions, like all others of the kind were of a purely academic nature and not involving the passing of any "information" as distinct from "opinion".[82]

Wynter naïvely believed that his explanation would be 'generously accepted'.[83] It was not. Parkhill labelled Wynter's explanation 'absolutely absurd' and noted that

> Colonel Wynter's action and attitude in this matter is most unsatisfactory, and he has been guilty of a serious breach of trust in not informing of his superior officer of his son's connection with a serious matter.[84]

Parkhill therefore ordered that 'Colonel Wynter should no longer be employed at Army Headquarters'.[85] The Military Board transferred

Wynter to Queensland four days later with orders that 'he take up duty as early as possible'.[86]

The Military Board had finally appreciated the dangers of engaging in political propaganda. But Wynter apparently did not appreciate the seriousness of his acts and requested a court martial on the grounds that he had been denied 'natural justice' by the Defence Minister.[87] The request was denied. The Government maintained, correctly, that 'nothing has been introduced to controvert the original and plain facts'.[88] To ensure Army officers refrained from political activity, the Government deferred making Lavarack a Companion of the Order of the Bath.[89]

Wynter had exhibited a 'lamentable lack of discretion and vision', which ensured that his vision was ignored.[90] The Army could not attempt to influence government policy by leaking its views to the Opposition or the press. Embracing this tactic ensured that the Army came to be seen by the Government as marching arm-in-arm with the Opposition. This in turn helped ensure that the Government viewed the Army and its suggestions with suspicion, thus further hindering communications between the Army and UAP elites.

Horace Robertson was also concerned with Australian defence policy, but he wisely avoided politics. Robertson had attended the Staff College, Camberley (1923–24) and would soon become the director of military art. His 1934 article 'Defence of Australia' was also published in the British *Army Quarterly*, and as a pamphlet.[91] Robertson argued that 'Australia must be prepared to defend itself'.[92] 'How far', he wondered, 'can she [Australia] rely on these bulwarks of Imperial defence [the Royal Navy and the Singapore naval base] under all conditions'?[93] Robertson, like Wynter, believed Singapore was useless without a fleet, and therefore he argued that 'Australia's local defence should be organised around the Army, the other services conforming to the needs of the Army'.[94] Robertson's criticisms were valid, though he failed to argue for stronger local defence *per se*. His essay was awarded the Gold Medal for the best essay by a member of the Australian Military Forces.[95] However, the Government was unimpressed because the article lacked detail.

Thomas Blamey, a former high-ranking Army officer and Victorian Police Commissioner, made few criticisms of government policy. Blamey's weekly radio broadcasts in 1938 and 1939 tended to support reliance on the Singapore strategy without considering Imperial defence requirements for local defence. 'The advance toward peace', Blamey claimed in February 1939, 'goes step by step with the British Empire's capacity to insist on her policy being carried out'.[96] However, Australia was not carrying out the Empire's policy because it was neglecting its local defences.

The concern for Australian defence and the world situation expressed by Hughes, Piesse and Wynter is hardly surprising. All of them had expert knowledge and were intimately familiar with the details and strategic foundations of Australian defence. Hughes was a member of the political elite, while Piesse and Wynter realised the importance of communicating with the other elites; however, all were unsuccessful in getting their ideas across. Hughes' membership of the political elite could not overcome the lingering suspicion and resentment among his political colleagues related to his defection to the UAP and role in bringing down the Bruce Government. Wynter's attempt only angered the political elite and further divided the UAP and Army elites, while Piesse's book was but one of many. However, it was not only those with an expertise in defence who attempted to raise the alarm.

MEDIA REPORTING AND COMMENTARY

One did not have to be a politician, serving officer or public servant to appreciate the dangers Australia faced in respect to its defence capability and attempt to alert the Government and public. The media also attempted, albeit haphazardly, to raise the alarm. Newspapers, books, journals and radio broadcasts about Australian defence are a valuable indication of public interest. Historians have noted that Australian newspapers covered international events sporadically and inaccurately.[97] Defence was also covered sporadically in newspapers, and articles about defence were usually written by those who had written books on the subject and drew heavily on those books. Admittedly, this increased the audience for authors such as Hughes and Piesse, but it does not seem to have produced a more informed or robust debate.

Until the move to Canberra 'defence departments were covered by federal roundsmen' who shared their stories with the press of the Federal Parliamentary Press Gallery.[98] The roundsmen system meant few reporters had much knowledge about defence policy. The move to Canberra made coverage of departments even more difficult as it 'removed the strong departmental rounds base which had been an important component of political reporting in Melbourne'.[99] The Press Gallery also became smaller, 'at most, six or seven', although the number increased during parliamentary sittings.[100] Furthermore, some ministries remained in Melbourne, which separated parliamentary reporters 'from the departmental work which had given coherence to their job'.[101] The move to Canberra also meant reporters from every major newspaper in Australia had to cable their stories to their editors.

Occasionally articles did appear about Australian defence that had not been written by experts.[102] As early as 1924 the *Argus* reported in a story about parliamentary debates that 'Australia had fallen behind in the necessary provision in defence'.[103] But defence was a minor issue in the Australian papers until the 1930s when a series of features appeared, albeit sporadically. In August 1935 the *Argus* ran a series of articles extolling the benefit of Imperial defence and a naval-centred defence strategy, which it believed were one and the same. The faith of the *Argus* in the Singapore strategy was grounded in the belief that 'The principle of sea power as the basis of Imperial defence will not alter until it becomes possible and cheap to transport cargo in bulk by air'.[104] By 1937 even the *Argus* was questioning the wisdom of 'placing all her eggs in one basket'.[105] Articles also appeared on British and Japanese defence spending. These should have concerned or alarmed the Australian Government, but they appear to have had little effect on politicians.[106] The public remained apathetic, and this lack of public interest insured that defence remained only sporadically covered.

Public apathy continued in spite of more detailed articles in various magazines and journals on Australia's defence, though like the newspapers these were sporadic and found in publications with a limited, albeit occasionally influential, readership. As this survey suggests, in spite of reaching a key group of the Australian population, these articles seem to have had no effect on policy making. The *Australian Quarterly* was the first serious journal to raise the issue of Australian defence. A contributor using the pseudonym 'Observer' warned in June 1935 against considering defence as solely a naval responsibility. 'Observer' warned that Singapore in Japanese hands would greatly facilitate an invasion of Australia.[107] He also urged Australia to 'build up land and coastal defences capable of defeating a 60,000 strong invasion force'.[108] Recommendations were made as to the exact composition of Australia's defences which would be centred on the Army and RAAF. This article was found in the Shedden papers, but there is no indication that Shedden, Secretary of the Department of Defence, or anyone in the Public Service paid much attention.

Not all the articles or papers about Australian defence policy were couched as warnings. Economist J.G. Crawford believed economic appeasement of Japan was the only viable option for Australia to follow. Crawford argued in 'Australia as a Pacific Power' that the RAN was too weak to protect Australia and that Singapore was too far away to assure Australian safety.[109] He believed the British Empire had mistreated Japan, and Japan deserved economic and naval concessions. Yet Crawford also absurdly claimed that aggressors should not be appeased and by 1938 Japan was clearly an aggressor.

The recently-created *Australian Rhodes Review,* which consisted of articles by Australian Rhodes Scholars—an important if small Australian group—considered Australian defence only once in a major article, and then only in the last quarter of 1939 when it was too late to effect a major change in governmental policy. 'We must face the fact', warned Neil MacNeil, a Great War veteran and Headmaster of Wesley College, 'that the Empire is no longer supreme'.[110] He added that Australia could not expect a declaration of war and that therefore stronger defences were needed.[111]

Newspaper and journal articles were, by their very nature, brief. More detailed warnings and prescriptions were found in several books written between the wars. Some of them, such as Hughes' and Piesse's, were serious attempts at investigating Australia's defences based on first-hand knowledge of Australian policy. However, one did not need to be a high-ranking politician or public servant to write a book urging Australia to strengthen its local defences.

E. George Marks, a journalist for the Sydney *Sun* and spokesman for the Navy League, wrote two books on the danger Japan posed to Australia.[112] As early as 1924, in *Watch the Pacific!: Defenceless Australia*, he argued that 'Japan aims at the hegemony of Asia'[113] and that the 'League of Nations [was] too impotent to deter the policy of Japanese expansion in the Pacific'.[114] He also claimed that Japanese mandated islands were a threat to Australia and charged that 'Japan having a mandate is a betrayal to the Anzacs'.[115] Today, Marks's arguments seem prescient, but when he wrote his first book Japan was still peaceful, the League of Nations had yet to fail and Marks did not make a convincing argument that Japan was aggressive or that the League was impotent.

Marks's second work, *Pacific Peril, or, Menace of Japan's Mandated Islands*, was better researched and, coming two years after the outbreak of the Sino-Japanese War, was more realistic.[116] The Singapore strategy—reliance on the Royal Navy as Australia's primary defence—was still the preferred strategy. Yet he also warned that

> Australia must first look to the protection of her own people; she can do so by keeping the troops within her own confines during any struggle in the Far East between Asiatic peoples.[117]

Marks also took aim at the ALP and pointedly wrote that 'if the ALP is really opposed to preventing cheap labour it must be willing to defend White-Australia'.[118]

J.M. Fowler, a former Labor MP, writing two years after Marks's first book, was not impressed with the Singapore strategy.[119] In *Australia's Perils: Real and Imaginary*, Fowler claimed that few Australians realised 'what a near thing it was that Prussian officers are not to-day swaggering about our streets as our lords and masters'.[120] But now, Fowler claimed, the 'International danger zone has spread to the Pacific'.[121] Singapore was 'too far away from the vital parts of Australia to take any material share in their defence'.[122] While it is tempting to see Fowler as ahead of his time, his work was heavily influenced by racial stereotype. He argued that Japan was only a threat because 'There was a considerable introduction of Caucasian or white blood and many Japanese have features which are quite European'.[123] The United States, which Fowler regarded as a potential enemy, was an 'undigested welter of nationalities'.[124] Australia therefore should develop close relations with Japan, the 'mistress of the Pacific'.[125]

W.C. Wentworth, a conservative New South Wales politician, believed that Japan, the 'mistress of the Pacific', would turn South by 1942 if not earlier.[126] Wentworth described his *Demand for Defence: Being a Plan to Keep Australia White and Free* as a 'Call for action and hope, not to despair' though he clearly despaired of Australia's defence policy.[127] Wentworth wanted Australians to realise that there were 'the soundest strategic reasons why' the Royal Navy could not 'be spared for Britain for operation in the Pacific'.[128] Wentworth also warned that 'Owing to the size of the Japanese fleet it is probable that multiple Japanese operations will be undertaken thus ensuring Singapore is virtually useless to us here'.[129] Wentworth therefore argued for a massive increase in the defence budget across all services. He called for higher taxes, restricted civil rights and minimal non-defence associated public works. Wentworth concluded *Demand for Defence* with the sharp comment 'We should not be frightened of offending Japan' and that Australia therefore must do everything possible to help China.[130]

Demand for Defence was not favourably reviewed. Gerald Packer, a Duntroon graduate who worked on intelligence and planning for the Army, condemned it:

> Mr. Wentworth has not made a comprehensive study of modern war and the solutions he propounds are but imperfectly related to the naval, military and air facts of the position.[131]

Packer did, however, concede that 'Military criticism in Australia is very nearly non-existent and, in recent years, professional opinion has been silenced by Ministerial command'.[132]

In addition to the print media, there was a new means of mass communication: radio. Billy Hughes had informed the House in 1927 that 'No step has been taken that is more calculated to bring about not only progress and happiness among mankind, but also the peace of the world' than radio.[133] Lesley Johnson observed that 'No country, it was said, had embraced radio so eagerly' as Australia,[134] but the new medium played a limited role in the public debate about defence and foreign policy. In 1929 'Most Australians were still relatively unsophisticated in their listening habits'.[135] Even the creation of the Australian Broadcasting Commission (ABC) in 1932 did not increase the role of radio in public debate as 'Most stations, both national and commercial, closed down between sessions [and] Weekend programmes were usually minimal or non-existent'.[136] Furthermore, governmental control often severely restricted the ABC's international and political coverage.

Even if stations had broadcast more frequently, it is unlikely radio would have been more effective at influencing debate. Australian radio in the inter-war period was not a major source of news. The ABC's inability to break news stories was in marked contrast to the United Kingdom, where the BBC was fast becoming a major source of news, and to the United States where four networks sought to be first with news. C.J. Lloyd notes that 'There was strong opposition within the ABC to the broadcasting of hard news items which were collected directly by the ABC news staff'.[137] Australian newspapers with their excellent wire services also 'wished to preserve the prerogative of being first with the news',[138] and as most commercial stations were owned by newspaper companies, they therefore had no incentive to provide the ABC, a competitor, with news.[139]

The ABC was limited to two morning news bulletins between 10 am and 11 am and one evening bulletin after 7.50 pm.[140] The ABC was further limited in that Australian Associated Press (AAP), which had the rights to Reuters and Associated Press, provided the ABC with only '200 cabled words per day'.[141] Consequently, as Alan Thomas notes:

> Most ABC news bulletins degenerated into an announcer reading articles from a newspaper. There was no policy

> on what constituted news, the selection being merely the personal preference of the announcer on duty.[142]

The ABC did not even have a full-time journalist in the parliamentary press gallery until Warren Denning was appointed in 1938.[143] Denning was given the near-impossible task of supplying 'a summary of every important story that broke at Canberra, irrespective of the day or time'.[144]

The ABC did occasionally dramatise real events. In 1935, it presented 'a play-with elaborate sound effects of war and crowds cheering as an actor spoke the words of the Emperor Haile Selassie' in a recreation of the Italian invasion of Abyssinia, but dramatic recreations of news events were rare.[145]

Coverage of political events was also limited. The ABC Act allowed only coverage of election 'speeches'.[146] Limited coverage of news and politics suited both the Government and Opposition, neither of which wanted their policies scrutinised or debated. During the Czechoslovakian crisis the Lyons Government considered banning anything 'unduly disturbing to the peace of mind of the listeners'.[147] Radio's effect on public debate was also limited by ministerial command. The Government claimed that the 1936 *International Convention on the Use of Broadcasting in the Cause of Peace* prohibited broadcasts that were 'likely to harm good international understanding'.[148] The ABC could thus 'broadcast only in the interests of peace'.[149] The National Joint Committee for Spanish Relief was thus told not to mention the word 'German' in its broadcast on the Spanish Civil War.[150] The weekly League of Nations Radio Club was relegated to the ABC's 'mid-morning Women's Session'.[151] By 1936 the ABC considered some of the League of Nations programmes uninformative.[152]

The ABC was not entirely devoid of constructive analysis of foreign affairs. E.A. Mann, a former Nationalist MP and Melbourne businessman broadcasting as 'The Watchman', was—according to K.S. Inglis—'the nearest thing Australian radio had in the 1930s to an oracle'.[153] But he had little competition. He was not seen as an oracle by ABC management, which pressured Mann to tone down his views and led to his resignation from the national broadcaster.[154] Mann was fierce in his opposition to appeasement, denouncing the Pact of Rome as one of the 'gravest challenges to liberty which history has yet produced'.[155] He described Munich as 'only just the beginning' and pointed out that Australia's rearmament paled in comparison to Britain's.[156] Ken Inglis noted that

> When his loud voice differed from the government's as it did on Chamberlain's appeasement of Hitler, the Commission would instruct him not to do it again; but on he would go.[157]

There is, however, no evidence that Mann's commentaries accomplished anything more than irritating the Government. Alan Thomas contends that 'Despite pretensions to independence, it is clear that the ABC's approach was to avoid a fuss wherever possible'.[158] Thomas concludes that 'Government pressure on the ABC was fairly successful', making the ABC 'a politically compliant institution during its formative years'.[159]

Commercial radio also carried commentaries on Australian defence policy. Edmund Piesse was the most prolific commercial commentator, giving talks on commercial stations that drew extensively from his book. He noted on 29 November 1936 that

> East of Aden scarcely a British cruiser remained. On the China Station there were a few small vessels, and a cruiser and some destroyers in Australian waters, together far too weak to oppose other naval forces in Pacific waters if a clash had come with them at the same time as the threat from Italy.[160]

Although Piesse's radio broadcasts reached a larger audience than his book, there is no evidence that they had any noticeable effect on government policy or led either to a public outcry or re-examination of defence policy.

***

This chapter has shown that questions were raised about the viability of the Singapore strategy and Australia's local defence. Serving officers, politicians, public servants and private citizens attempted to arouse public concern. Their suggestions ranged from the prescient and realistic, such as Hughes', to the utterly fantastic, such as Fowler's. Few of these warnings, however, appear to have reached a large audience or to have had a noticeable effect on public thinking or government policy. Critics found little support among the Labor Opposition because Labor remained profoundly isolationist, and had no support from the services, which had their own preferred solutions. Furthermore, it should be noted that none of these warnings adequately explored the cost of increased defence, and few of them seemed to realise the importance of trade or Australia's need for an alliance with a strong power. Yet the critics further demonstrate that Australia was not simply duped by Britain. The facts were available if anyone cared to look or listen, but few politicians took them seriously, even when presented by one of their own colleagues. Why such attempts failed to alert Australians to the perilous state of national defence is explored in the next chapter.

CHAPTER 6

WHY THE WARNINGS WERE IGNORED

> Military criticism in Australia is very nearly non-existent[1]
>
> Gerald Packer, 'Demand for Defence'

The many warnings about Australia's vulnerability failed to alarm key groups within Australia's elites and to excite wider public interest. The Government's flawed interpretation of Imperial defence therefore went largely unquestioned. Although the Singapore strategy was an appropriate component of Australian defence, it alone could never have offered Australia total security and was never intended to. Britain repeatedly informed Australia of the Singapore strategy's limitations, but the lack of close scrutiny ensured that its intricacies were not appreciated. The warnings were too infrequent and too varied to force a change in official policy without Opposition pressure. And most of the warnings came too late to compel any effective change in governmental policy. The inadequacies of Australian defence policy were further aggravated by a divided military. The Army and the RAAF were incapable of agreeing on the exact nature of the threat Australia faced, while the RAN believed the Government's policy was correct. The various services never appreciated that local defence and the Singapore strategy were both necessary and complementary elements of Australian defence. The public preoccupation with domestic issues such as unemployment and the economy spared the Government from public scrutiny of defence matters.

NO VIABLE ALTERNATIVE

Historian Carl Bridge correctly claims that the traditional historiography of Australian inter-war defence policy attributes the failure of the Australian Government to fully understand the Singapore strategy to a naïve faith in the United Kingdom and in British defence preparedness, especially the Royal Navy. But David Day's notion that

> Security against an invasion of Australia relied as it had always done on Britain's promise to reciprocate Australian co-operation in a European conflict with the timely dispatch of a fleet to the Far East[2]

might be widely held but is an overly simplistic view of British defence policy and promises.

Either way, such beliefs should not have translated into weak local defences and had not done so before the Great War when Australia had universal military training and developed its own Navy.

Late in 1940 an American diplomat observed that among Australians, including members and supporters of the ALP, 'there is no doubt of an intense loyalty to Britain'.[3] Even Curtin clothed his inchoate defence policies with Imperial rhetoric and claims of Imperial loyalty. Campaigning in the 1937 election, he announced, 'When we defend Australia, we defend not only these seven million British subjects, but also three million square miles of British territory, and one thousand million of British investments'.[4] Historian James Curran observes that whenever Prime Minister Curtin 'was called upon to rouse national feeling or express ideas of cultural identity, he gave voice to a British race identity'.[5]

Historian Stuart Macintyre has recently written that the ALP 'in no way constrained the conservative government'.[6] The ALP did in fact restrict government policy. Although the Labor party was weak throughout most of the inter-war period and sought to avoid debates that might create division, the Government was all too aware of the ALP's reserves of strength on notoriously touchy issues, such as military training and conscription. The Opposition set the parameters of the debate.[7]

The ALP's position on international affairs throughout the inter-war period may be summed up by quoting its future leader James Scullin, who asserted in 1923 that Australia's policy should be: 'Politically, militarily, and diplomatically we shall mind our own business'.[8] Apparently Australia therefore did not need to worry about being attacked. In November 1936 Frank Brennan (ALP, Batman, Victoria) reiterated this viewpoint stating: 'This country has never been threatened with attack'.[9] Labor's policy was one of isolationism, pure and simple.

Additionally, the Government saw no need to embark on bold policies when confronted by such a weak Opposition. The UAP was essentially a residual party composed of those uncomfortable in the two major parties[10] and lacked even a federal platform. Lyons' Cabinets were not inclined to embark on new defence policies and saw no reason to question the established policies of their conservative predecessors.

New policies were politically risky because the ALP was almost always, as John Latham (NAT, Kooyong, Victoria) commented, 'perfectly prepared to give the fullest credit for pacific intentions to Japan, but never to the government of Australia'.[11] Therefore Labor would resolutely oppose government proposals for a defence build-up, and the Government was not eager for a debate. The ALP, charged Donald Cameron (UAP, Lilley, Queensland), was even unwilling to send 'a ship or an aeroplane or a man to the assistance of the sister Dominion [New Zealand]' without first holding a plebiscite.[12] The *Argus* described Curtin's defence policy of not sending troops overseas or forming alliances thus: 'Mr. Curtin is not constructive. He suggests a policy, but rejects the only possible means by which it can be carried out'.[13] *Time* magazine described Curtin as 'a born oppositionist'[14] while his biographer noted that a journalist labelled him 'Jaded Jack'.[15] If Australia were to rely entirely on its own resources it needed a large body of trained professional soldiers,

Mr. Curtin's defence policy provides for the taking of a referendum before Australia commits herself to fighting oversea.

The Argus (Melbourne), 21 September 1937

airmen and sailors, and that would probably require compulsory training and a much larger defence budget. The ALP's weaknesses served to constrain debate and ensured defence policy was neither seriously examined nor searchingly debated.

The ALP believed defence and foreign policy were secondary issues in comparison with better wages, hours and working conditions.[16] The ALP even suggested that Australia should leave the League of Nations, and The Melbourne Trades Hall Council and ALP Victorian branch even formed an antiwar committee. Thomas Sheehan (ALP, Cook, NSW) claimed that the Government,

> by associating Australia with the collective security proposals of the League, has cut right across the path of peace which the Australian people should follow. It is a policy that will eventually embroil the Australian people in war.[17]

Such outright isolationism was unlikely to win Labor elections. The belief that Australia by opting out could prevent or at least avoid war led the ALP to advocate overly simplistic policies. Statements that the ALP 'is opposed to war' were unhelpful, for most Australian politicians were opposed to war and such statements were unlikely to impress would-be voters because opposition to war was not going to prevent war.[18] A 'Policy of War Resistance' did, however, have its advantages to the Government as it was exceedingly vague and easily dismissed and did not examine government defence policy in any detail.[19] Additionally, it was easier politically for the ALP to advocate outright isolationism than to debate Australia's defence needs.

Langite Eddie Ward (East Sydney, NSW, ALP) claimed that 'a naval vessel is not an arm of defence but one of offence' and therefore Australia did not even need a navy.[20] The Government had already pointed out that 'As Australia is an island continent, foreign aggression against the Commonwealth must come from overseas'.[21]

The ALP opposed increases in the defence budget. It claimed Lyons' 1935 budget, which increased defence spending markedly, 'Does not give anything to anybody'.[22] John Curtin could not understand why the Government had decided to spend the defence budget in one year instead of the three originally planned in spite of the ongoing Sino-Japanese War and the Abyssinian crisis.[23] In 1937 John Curtin was forced to concede that 'We [an ALP Government] will maintain the Australian Navy', though his concession was vague.[24] In 1938 Curtin opposed a loan to strengthen Australian defences in spite of increasing tensions in Europe.[25] The ALP's opposition to increases in the defence budget renders hollow the notion that it was the party that would have better protected Australia.

In view of the ALP's opposition to increases in the defence budget and the strengthening of Australia's defences, the logical alternative policy was to form alliances with stronger nations. The ALP, however, was adamantly opposed to alliances for fear that they would involve Australia in a 'foreign' war. Curtin stated his party's position following the 1937 Imperial Conference:

> The Labor party declares against participation in partial pacts and treaties which would commit the country to support, or oppose, as the case may be, groups of powers.[26]

The ALP's outright isolationism explained to a considerable degree why the Party was so electorally unsuccessful, and this ensured that the UAP's policies were not seriously debated. Some members of the ALP acknowledged that the Party's isolationism hurt it in the 1937 election.[27] Yet the ALP's defence and foreign policy remained pacifist and isolationist. John Curtin was not 'a prophet' and, as biographer John Edwards stated, throughout the inter-war period Curtin did not believe Fascist Italy or Nazi Germany posed threats which 'required an Australian response'.[28] Consequently, any UAP response was criticised by the Opposition, and this encouraged Government caution. Curtin objected to the Government's decision to bring forward defence estimates in response to the German annexation of Austria. In a mangled statement, he naïvely claimed

> There is no justification for dealing with defence estimates until it [the government] explains what changes have taken place in the world in respect of foreign relations, which are

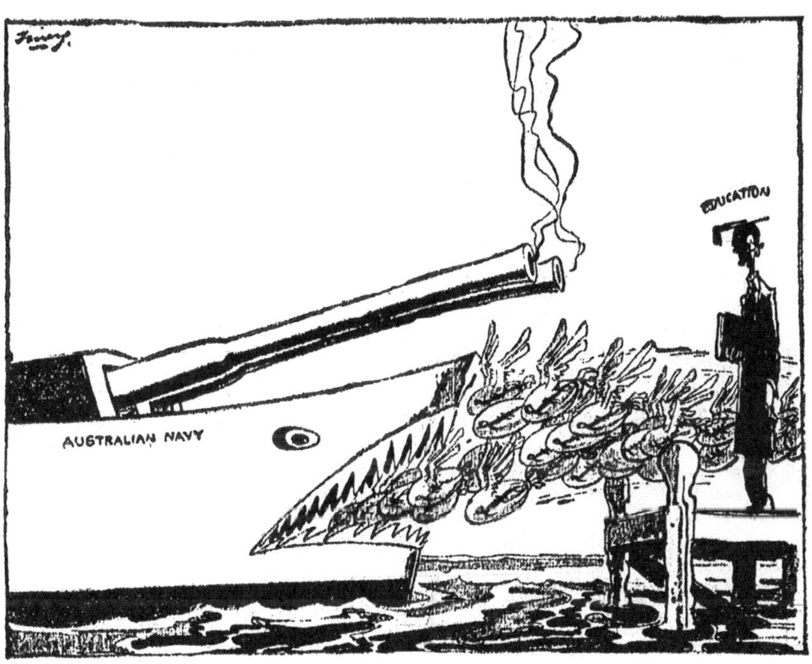

George Finey, *Labor Daily* (Sydney), 15 November 1930

> of such character as to increase the menace against which Australia must make provision to be safeguarded.[29]

He then went on to say: 'I venture to say that from the viewpoint of Europe, the position is less inflammable than it was two or three months ago'.[30] Just five months later German troops occupied the rest of Czechoslovakia.

A FAILURE OF IMAGINATION

The extra-parliamentary critics of defence policy discussed earlier also failed to change governmental policy because the Government had been committed firmly to the Singapore strategy since the base was first proposed in the early 1920s. It was a pragmatic and economical policy and the ALP's opposition to it remained vague.[31] As a result the Singapore strategy remained almost entirely unexamined until the mid-1930s, by which time 'The Lyons Government was locked into' it.[32] Yet, as discussed in chapter 3, the Singapore strategy was merely a component of Imperial defence, and Australian defence was not Whitehall's only concern. As historian Ian Hamill has written, 'So long as the British fleet was liable to enter the Pacific, the enemy would not dare to take the risks involved in mounting an invasion'.[33] Therefore, Australia need not fear invasion unless Britain faced defeat in Europe.

No criticism of the ALP's strategy addressed this key factor. In ALP terms, Australia merely needed a friendly fleet somewhere in the world to be relatively safe. Clearly the ALP's opposition was not grounded in sound strategic analysis or an understanding of Imperial defence. It did not argue for stronger local defence to supplement the Singapore strategy. The choice therefore became one of taking part in Imperial defence or not; hence the UAP could thus defend its policy with generalities and sweeping statements that were never closely examined. The Opposition's objections to the Singapore strategy did not acknowledge that another strategy would have cost more, not less. Indeed, improving Australian defence to the degree required to ensure Australian territorial integrity in the face of overwhelming Japanese naval supremacy would have cost considerably more than was then allocated to defence.

Throughout most of the inter-war period there was no reason to question the ability of the Royal Navy to reach Singapore. Government faith in the Royal Navy sending a fleet to Singapore before Australia was forced to rely on its local defence allowed the Australian Government to keep defence expenditure at lower levels than was advisable.[34] Once the two-power strategy had been abandoned in 1923 there was, however, no good reason to assume that the Royal Navy would always be able to come to Singapore.

British promises to send a fleet to the Pacific were always conditional, and the amount of time needed for the Fleet to arrive in Singapore was continually adjusted upwards. In 1937 the Royal Navy increased the period before relief from 48 days to 70 in response to European crises, but this was at a time when the Sino-Japanese War was beginning in earnest. Two years later, it was increased to 90 days, and with the outbreak of war in Europe it was doubled to 180 days.[35] Thus Australia could expect to be alone for the first six months of any Pacific war with only its local defences for protection.

The significance of the period before relief would be available was continually reiterated to Australian governments. As early as 1934 Sir Maurice Hankey warned Australia

> His Majesty's Government in the United Kingdom cannot yet provide in time of peace all the Air Forces needed for the naval bases and coaling stations in the Far East.[36]

He also requested that Australia undertake 'strengthening one or other of the strong points on the Eastern Route'.[37] In 1935 the War Office warned that 'The capture of Singapore will, however, probably prove to be so decisive that a fleet action may never take place'.[38] The War Office further warned that Singapore had less than enough food to last a fortnight.

At the 1937 Imperial Conference British promises were exceedingly vague. Whitehall warned that 'The intervention of Italy against us [UK] would at once impose conflicting demands on our fleet' and that 'The strength of the fleet that we could send to the Far East must be governed by consideration of our home requirements'.[39]

Furthermore, the Admiralty warned that it 'must retain in Home Waters a fleet sufficient to neutralise the German Fleet'.[40] The only encouraging note at the 1937 Imperial Conference was the rather bland assurance that

> Even if Japan captured Singapore, she could not absolutely rely on preventing operations in the Far East by the British Fleet, despite the great difficulties with which it would be faced in such circumstances.[41]

It was a clear indication that reliance on the Royal Navy alone was not a sufficient guarantee of defence, especially against raids, as they might occur before the Royal Navy was in a position to intercept or deter them.

The possibility of a British fleet steaming to Singapore decreased as a European War became increasingly likely. In May 1939 Leo Amery warned recently appointed Prime Minister Robert Menzies that in the event of a war against Germany and Italy 'there may be a very big military problem for Australia to solve'.[42] The Royal Navy might not be able to leave the Mediterranean for Singapore. In November 1939 Churchill, the First Lord of the Admiralty, told Australian and New Zealand representatives that an unconditional promise to send the fleet to Singapore would 'give to Japan the power to immobilise half our fleet by a mere paper declaration of war'.[43] This logical restriction meant that Australia could not rely on a Royal Navy deterrence and that the Royal Navy might not even steam to Singapore until actual hostilities had commenced. In view of this qualification, Australia needed strong local defences.

In spite of the restrictive nature of British promises and the ever-increasing amount of time required for the Fleet to reach Singapore, the Australian Government remained firmly committed to the Singapore strategy. Government faith in the Singapore strategy was succinctly stated in the *United Australia Party Monthly Bulletin*. 'Foreign aggression against the Commonwealth must come from overseas. British sea power is therefore our first line of defence'.[44] Defence Minister Parkhill pointedly acknowledged that

'No Dominion is capable of providing absolutely for its security by its own efforts alone. Imperial co-operation is therefore the most economical basis'.[45]

Parkhill's statement was undoubtedly true, but it did not absolve Australia from strengthening its local defences. Local defence required a strong air force with the requisite infrastructure. It also required a large and well-trained militia, preferably one based on universal service. Compulsory training, however, was not reinstated until after the war had begun. Local defence also required non-military infrastructure expenditures such as a uniform national rail gauge and well-developed road system. The failure to implement such programmes reflected a lack of Opposition pressure as well as the failure of the Government and services to agree on the nature of the threat Australia needed to focus on repelling.

WHAT THE THREAT MEANT

Demands for a different defence strategy or improvements in Australian defence policy did not arise until the mid-1930s. Those demanding different defence policies did not consider how such changes would be funded, or the time necessary to implement the policies. Nor, with the exception of Hughes, Wynter and Piesse, were those advocating different policies experts in defence. Most of the warnings related to the threat of a Japanese invasion, but few politicians believed invasion was a serious threat so the warnings were easily dismissed.

As Opposition leader, Scullin claimed in July 1934 that raids 'constitute the only danger to Australia in time of war'.[47] Therefore, he argued, Australia did not need to strengthen the RAN. The UAP Government also believed raids were the only threat facing Australia and that it was better 'to provide efficient protection against raids rather than inefficient measures against invasion'.[48] Shedden firmly believed that 'The danger of a Japanese invasion does not exist'.[49] Raids, however, remained a contingency that should have been met by local defence but the variety of possible raids and targets made this a difficult task. Further, Australia's shortcomings in 1942 imply that it would not have been up to the task.

The military was best placed to analyse the threat Australia faced and the veracity of the warnings discussed earlier, but the services were terribly divided. Inter-service rivalry was inevitable, but Australian services between the wars could not even agree on the need for each other. The *Herald* astutely observed in 1934 that the only thing the Army and RAN could agree on was 'their dislike of the air force'.[50] The three services did not practise combined operations or develop strategies which involved the other services.[51] The inability of the services to present a united front allowed the Government to avoid making tough choices regarding defence spending because whatever strategy it adopted was bound to be supported by at least one service and criticised by one other service if not by two.

The RAN enjoyed a preferential status because it was the 'First line of defence'.[52] It always had been, and it would 'remain so as long as oceans link the shores of its members'.[53] As far as the RAN was concerned, a naval defence was the only hope of defending Australia. According to the RAN, if Japan ever enjoyed total naval supremacy it was 'extremely improbable that it would be possible for Australia then to provide for its own defence'.[54] Since Australia had relied on a naval-centred defence since Federation it was an attractive argument and one that supported the RAN's preferred status.

The RAN's preferred status ensured that it had its own administrative agency to oversee its functions: the Navy Board.[55] The Board was essentially British in its character and held complete faith in a naval-centred defence. This meant that the 'service had its own special governing body', a privilege not granted to any other service.[56] The RAN could thus always present a coherent and comprehensive defence strategy, whereas the Army and RAAF were constantly changing their recommendations. This ensured that the Government viewed the latter's proposals more sceptically.

The Government was already inclined to view Army proposals with scepticism following its inability to recognise Treasury limitations. Its scepticism was increased following the Wynter Affair. Furthermore, Frederick Shedden, Secretary of the Department of Defence, was a firm believer in the Singapore strategy and the Royal Navy as Australia's pre-eminent defence.[57] He did not believe that Australia could defend itself and thus its defence was possible only if a major power (Britain) came to its aid. Shedden had much better access to the Government than the Army elite. He also actively disliked the head of the Army and Chief of the General Staff, General John Lavarack.[58] The Army, especially Lavarack, failed to appreciate the logic of the Government's position or that it might be more successful if it argued that local defence against raids was lacking and that this was a contingency that the Singapore strategy did not cover.

Local defence should have allowed all three armed services to co-operate and present a detailed strategy for combined operations. The RAN's fleet was designed to serve as support vessels with Royal Navy task forces.[59] Australia lacked the mine sweepers, mine layers and motor torpedo boats crucial for local defence. A Naval Board report presented in 1921 conceded that the RAN had few vessels capable of local defence, including protecting the harbours. Throughout the inter-war period the ability of the RAN to provide local defence decreased. The report also conceded that shore batteries were 'hardly considered as effective means of defence', but the Government continued to rely on shore batteries and built more of them with its limited defence budget.[60] The RAN's ability to provide local defence was thus minimal throughout the inter-war period.

Local defence, which the Army could have used to link itself with the Singapore strategy, became merely another issue on which the services could disagree. The Army firmly believed that 'in the last resort the principal factor in our local defence will be land forces'.[61] It failed to appreciate the importance of air superiority over a battlefield or the risk posed by naval bombardment. Instead of seeing local defence as an area where the Army could complement the Government's naval-centred defence strategy and meet its Imperial defence requirements, the Army argued that the RAN's preferential status was 'precluding the Commonwealth discharging its responsibility for defence'.[62]

The Army was unimpressive at proposing alternative defence strategies, but it was prolific in its criticisms of the Singapore strategy. As far as Lavarack was concerned, the RAN was 'useless'.[63]

Lavarack embarked on two strategies to aid the Army. He argued repeatedly against over reliance on the Singapore strategy and attempted to strengthen the Army for the war he believed was inevitable.[64] However, the Chief of the General Staff did not propose strengthening the Army to ensure Australia's local defences were sufficient to protect Australia until the Royal Navy arrived. Lavarack lacked tact and made enemies of Shedden and the Minister of Defence which ensured that the Army's views were quickly dismissed.[65] Lavarack's biographer, A.B. Lodge, claims Lavarack maintained a distinctly Australian outlook,[66] but his was just an Army outlook that failed to realise the effect of Australia's geo-strategic position.

As early as 1923, the Army voiced doubts about the then proposed Singapore strategy.[67] It is tempting to see the Army's criticisms as especially prescient, but their criticisms were weak and grounded more in inter-service rivalry over limited finances than strategic acumen. A 1932 Army report stated, 'There is no guarantee that the British fleet will arrive in time', but this served only as a preface to a lengthy request for more funding.[68] In 1933 Lavarack observed that 'You either rule the waves or you do not', but such statements were not going to convince a Government which firmly believed that Britannia still ruled the waves and could not accept that it might not be able to come to Australia's aid.[69] Furthermore, if the Royal Navy had the ability to rule the waves by sending vessels to the Pacific, Australia was still protected. It would have been far more profitable if the Army had argued for greater funding so that it could complement the Singapore strategy and defend Australia until the Royal Navy arrived. When 10 years of Army criticisms of the Singapore strategy failed to produce any noticeable change in defence policy, a change of tactics was clearly indicated but the Army persisted in using the same argument.

As Ross has justly observed, the Army's fundamental problem was that it

> wished to prepare for the Defence against invasion contingency, which was only one of several possible

contingencies and was the least likely to occur and the most costly for which to prepare.[70]

Invasion was the threat most discussed by critics of defence policy because it was the threat most likely to alarm readers. It was, however, impossible politically and economically for Australia to support the military apparatus necessary to prevent an all-out enemy invasion, especially in view of the defence cuts initiated in the 1920s. This ensured that most of the warnings discussed earlier were ignored. The Army's belief that an invasion was possible was contradicted by the other services. By contrast, the RAN believed, with considerable justification, that such an amphibious operation was beyond the shipping capability of the Imperial Japanese Navy. If an invasion were mounted, it was impossible for a country with seven million to repel an invasion from a nation of seventy million.[71] The RAAF believed raids were the most likely sort of threat Australia faced and that stopping them should be the focus of Australian defence policy.[72]

The Army had not always claimed Australia should prepare to face an invasion. The Army's campaign for defence against invasion was driven by emotion and greed. It was unsupported by anyone in Government, and the Army was never able to rebut charges such as that of Senator Johnson (NAT, Lang, NSW) that 'We cannot successfully defend Australia within Australia' because the continent was too large and dependent on overseas trade.[73] The Army's contingency plans for an invasion were unrealistic and did not consider the resources available for Australian defence. According to Shedden, General Chauvel opined after the war that there was never any possibility of an invasion.[74]

The RAAF was more realistic in its approach to defence policy than the Army. It was also much more conciliatory and accepting of its junior status. Although the RAAF had been created as an independent service in 1921, it was forever in fear that it would lose its independence. The Swinburne Committee had supported an independent RAAF primarily because it was cheaper than a separate fleet air arm and an army air corps. The Army believed that the RAAF's role was primarily reconnaissance and therefore it 'should be under Army command'.[75] Once its independence was assured the RAAF ceased to question government defence policy.

There is a tendency to portray the ALP as a friend of the RAAF.[76] However, the RAAF was always wary of the ALP. Statements by Curtin, such as

> The question of Australian defence boils down to how many aerial fighters, bombers, and carriers are adequate to Australia's needs and within her means to sustain. Until that is decided Australia has no effective preparedness

reflected an attempt by Curtin to keep his party together, rather than faith in the RAAF or an appreciation of Australia's strategic needs.[77] Scullin's budget cuts had hit the RAAF especially hard because of its small size. It was allocated A£326,000 in the Scullin budget, a decrease of nearly A£200,000 and only a third of the Army's budget and less than a quarter of the RAN's annual budget.[78] Furthermore, Curtin's statements favouring a RAAF-centred defence did not appreciate Australia's limited aircraft production capacity which made such a defence strategy impossible.[79]

AN INDIFFERENT PUBLIC

The warnings failed to produce noticeable results. The public was preoccupied with domestic matters, the Government discouraged public interest in defence policy and lack of public interest ensured there was little debate concerning the sort of defence best for Australia.

The lack of public interest in the outside world discouraged the Government from debating or changing its defence policy. Contending that the lack of public interest was actually a product of the Singapore strategy, Geoffrey Serle claims that 'reliance and trust in British protection was a sedative which induced somnolence and apathy towards both the trend of world events and geographical realities'.[80] The warnings thus had to arouse a public lulled into complacency by a misunderstanding of British security guarantees.

The preoccupation with domestic issues was further encouraged by the press which rarely covered international events. A preoccupation with domestic affairs was even found in the Returned and Services League (RSL), the one organisation which might have been expected to have a deep and abiding interest in defence. It was, however, mostly concerned with matters such as soldier settlement schemes and preferential employment for returned soldiers.[81]

Warnings failed to make a significant impression on the crucial audiences. The Opposition was unable to use the warnings as the basis of alternative policies because it was unsure if Australia even needed an active defence policy. The Opposition's inability to seize on the warnings allowed the Government to ignore them with impunity and ensured its interpretation of the Singapore strategy was not questioned and its weaknesses discovered and rectified. The military, which was best qualified to comment on Australian defence policy, was consumed by inter-service rivalries and could agree on little. The warnings had also been too late for there to be any realistic hope of even a serious examination of Australian defence policy, especially with an uninterested public. The warnings failed to prompt responses from the governing elites which ensured that the Singapore strategy was not closely examined. As a result Australia did not fulfil its local defence commitments.

CHAPTER 7

DOMESTIC POLITICS AND AUSTRALIAN DEFENCE

A financial burden which they are unable to bear[1]

The Times, 24 May 1923

The weak state of Australia's defences can be attributed to the nature of Australian domestic politics and the ineffectual performance of politicians who played the primary role in the formation of defence policy. At the time there was no bipartisan agreement on the nature of the threats Australia faced and therefore no bipartisan agreement on an appropriate defence strategy for Australia. The memories of the Great War and an overriding desire to avoid another war—whatever the cost—combined with the fiscal restraints necessitated by the Great Depression to ensure that bipartisan consensus was impossible. The parties drew very different lessons from the Great War and were at odds as to the causes and cures for the Great Depression. The conservatives subscribed to a blue water strategy, while the more isolationist ALP's failure to develop a comprehensive defence strategy precluded productive political debate. Debate was further hindered by the small but extremely vocal pacifist movement and supporters of the League of Nations. This chapter argues that the lack of productive debate ensured Australian defence policy was insufficient to defend Australia against raids or invasions, or to protect Australian trade.

THE QUESTION OF AUSTRALIA'S DEFENCE

The issue of Australia's defence produced a variety of arguments. Some politicians, for example Gerald Mahoney (ALP, Denison, Tasmania), believed that 'the difficulty which Japan would have in bringing an army large enough to conquer this country to its shores' was adequate protection.[2] Hence, Australia did not need a defence policy. David Day more recently claimed that 'Australia was simply too far and too big for Japan to conquer' and that this 'should encourage us [Australians] to shake off the lingering insecurities'.[3] Thus Australia should have relied (and should still rely) on its geographical isolation for security. Geographic isolation offered—and for some still offers—a false sense of security. But such an argument ignores the importance of trade.

Admiral Herbert Richmond of the Royal Navy and the Imperial Defence College correctly noted in 1936 that the economic dislocation resulting from even a partial blockade would be considerable, and the lack of consumer goods would soon have a detrimental effect on Australian morale.[4] He astutely observed that it was 'one thing for a fortress like Gibraltar to hold out [but] quite another for a country'.[5] The widespread alarm caused by the bombing of Darwin in February 1942 and by the incursion of miniature submarines in Sydney Harbour in June 1942 give some indication of the effect of Japanese raiders on Australian morale and the Australian population.

Isolationism, however, was attractive especially if one viewed the Great War and the Great Depression as the fault of a particular group—be they warmongers, armament manufacturers, international capitalists or militarists. But even if one accepted that such groups were responsible for wars and economic upheavals, isolationism could not guarantee that Australia would not be drawn into the wars such groups caused.

The alternative to erecting strong defences was to appease the most serious potential enemy, Japan. Although David Bird demonstrates that Australia certainly tried to appease Japan and encourage Great Britain to do so as well, an Australian agreement with Japan was impossible.[6] Japan could have been appeased only by the United States—certainly not by Australia. Since the inauguration of the Commonwealth in 1901, Australia had feared Japanese supremacy of the Pacific. The appeasement of Japan would have meant, at the very least, agreeing to the Japanese occupation of large parts of China and probably large parts of Southeast Asia. Even so, Australian recognition of Japanese sovereignty over China would have been meaningless to the Japanese, and Australia was not in a position to grant Japan any territory in Southeast Asia. Nor was Australia in a position to stop Japan taking any Asian territory it desired. A weak nation cannot appease a strong one. The United States would not have agreed to such a settlement, and neither Britain nor Australia could have risked offending the United States. An Australian attempt to appease Japan would have precluded any alliance with the United States and thus left Australia even more exposed.

INTER-WAR POLITICS—THE PARTIES

The parliamentary parties' composition reflected urban trade union, rural grazing/farming and urban-industrial middle-class interests. The Country Party, consisting largely of farmers and graziers, was formed in 1913 'as a protest against alleged exploitation of regional and rural Australia'.[7] Its focus was mainly on domestic politics, especially the tariff. Following the 1922 election the Country Party held the balance of power in the House and chose to support the Nationalists (though not Billy Hughes) rather than the ALP. The Country Party was therefore 'a vital factor in the maintenance of non-Labor power in the 1920s and remained so for most of the 1930s'.[8] Joan Rydon argues that the Country Party's support for the non-Labor side of politics was 'partly because the Senate electoral system still limited its ability to compete independently'.[9]

Graziers and farmers also predominated in the National and United Australia parties which were not dominated by businessman, let alone a 'ruling industrial elite'. Their working-class numbers were boosted by those who defected from the ALP, some of whom continued in the UAP.[11] The conservative parties were far from a cohesive political organisation. They were, as the historian Joan Rydon has observed, 'a changing mixture of conservative, ex-labor and Country Party men'.[12] The Nationalist party was composed of the old Liberal Party and those ALP MPs and Senators who had crossed the floor with Hughes following the defeat of the 1916 conscription plebiscite. The Nationalists governed until 1929 under the leadership of Billy Hughes (1916–23) and Stanley Melbourne Bruce (1923–29). John Latham succeeded Bruce as leader. However, Joseph Lyons' crossing of the floor in 1931 altered the party structure markedly.

Lyons and his supporters swiftly joined the non-Labor ranks which were reconstituted as the United Australia Party with Lyons as its leader. Because it was formed from the top, the UAP lacked a developed party organisation.[13] Furthermore, like its Nationalist predecessor the UAP was a residual party with a 'grab-bag character' which, as C.J. Lloyd notes, led to 'constant attrition and rebuilding'.[14] It was

> a miscellany of political and populist elements including the Political Independents Group, a small breakaway from James Scullin's ALP Government, the minute Australian Party led by Hughes and a sprawling Citizens' Movement which was adverse to political organisation.[15]

The party was generously described as a 'big-tent party', but it housed so many shades of opinion that its critics called it the 'Disunited Australia Party'.[16] Judith Brett, in her groundbreaking study of Australian non-Labor voters, acknowledges that they 'Did not achieve organisational stability until the formation of the Liberal Party in 1945'.[17] The same sort of person regularly voted for the Nationalist as voted for the UAP but the parties' structures reflected a much more diverse makeup.

In terms of faith, the ALP was heavily Catholic while the conservative parties were predominantly Protestant, albeit spread across seven denominations. This ensured no Protestant sect approached the dominant position enjoyed by the Catholic Church in the ALP where 41% of ALP MPs and over half of ALP Ministers and party officials with a known faith were Roman Catholics. The heavy Catholic presence in the ALP made it extremely difficult for the party to formulate a policy in response to an international dispute that involved a predominantly Catholic country such as Mussolini's Italy. In terms of occupation, the parliamentary ALP was overwhelmingly composed of manual tradesmen and party and trade union officials. The party was split into left and right factions which often clashed bitterly. Kim Beazley Sr described the inter-war ALP as:

> an ideological battleground—Irish Nationalism, I.W.W. [Industrial Workers of the World], Communism, Socialism, pure industrial unionism, industrial groups, all certainly more intent on destroying one another than the alleged enemies.[20]

The lack of war veterans in the Australian Parliament meant no Opposition MP could assume the role of military expert and ask pointed questions or make informed suggestions. Throughout the inter-war period slightly more than a quarter of MPs had military experience (52) but they were disproportionally in conservative ranks. Only ten ALP MPs had military experience, just 12% of the ALP. The first returned soldier to be elected to the House, J.H. Lister, was in the ALP but left the party over conscription and remained in parliament as a Nationalist until 1929.[22] Ideologically the ALP was still dominated by a strong anti-war sentiment and vehement opposition to conscription. Indeed, Senator W.A. Gibbs 'had formed the Returned Soldiers' No Conscription League'.[23] The narrow margin over conscription had been a Pyrrhic victory. The other major ideology influencing the ALP was pre-Bolshevik socialism heavily influenced by the Victorian Socialist Party (VSP) to which both Brennan and Curtin had belonged. Others such as Scullin and Calwell tended to be even more socialistic in their outlook, though they had never joined the VSP.

Conservative MPs were much more likely to have served in the military. Nearly a third of Country Party MPs (9) had military experience, as had 38% of the NAT–UAP MPs (35). They did not usually become career politicians: 'The officers elected for the Nationalist party rarely served long; several were defeated in 1922'.[25] They were, however, unlikely to question government defence policy when the Opposition's policy was utterly unrealistic. A few of the returned men did remain concerned with defence issues. Captain T.W. White, elected in 1919, 'retained an interest in the Army'[26] and E.F. Harrison, a staff officer, remained in the Militia while an MP.[27] The small number of returned men in the House of Representatives ensured that the political elite struggled to comprehend fully Australia's defence requirements or the threats posed by new technology on the battlefield. The Senate also had returned servicemen—particularly on the conservative side in the 1920s—but few would still be in the Senate in the Lyons years.[28] Subject to party discipline, Senators were not likely to question or delay legislation and non-Labor governments enjoyed large majorities throughout the inter-war period. As Coulthard Clark has concluded:

> Those for whom the armed services represented a livelihood, and a career demanding commitment to a military ethos, have been until relatively recent times an insignificant numerical actor in Australian society.[29]

INTER-WAR POLITICS—THE PRIME MINISTERS

William Morris 'Billy' Hughes, the first inter-war Prime Minister, led the Nationalist Government until the December 1922 election gave the 14 Country Party MPs the balance of power. The Country Party under Earle Page refused to support a Hughes Government and obtained 5 of 11 cabinet portfolios in the subsequent Bruce–Page Government. Stanley Melbourne Bruce, who at the Country Party's behest replaced Hughes as Prime Minister, was a veteran of the Great War and had served at Gallipoli and the Western Front.

The conservative parties' hold on power was broken only once between the wars. In 1929 Billy Hughes led several MPs across the floor to vote against a bill returning industrial relations powers to the states. Bruce promptly called an election and the ALP scored an impressive victory winning 46 of the 75 seats including Bruce's own constituency. Then ALP Prime Minister Jim Scullin, a former Ballarat grocer, had to contend with a hostile Senate where his seven senators were outnumbered by 29 conservative senators. This was a rarity in the inter-war period when the winner-takes-all system of Senate elections ensured the Senate was usually overwhelmingly government-controlled. Scullin, however, was elected without the benefit of a Senate election. Thus the upper house was dominated by the Nationalists who delayed or blocked several domestic and budget measures—but not Scullin's defence cuts. Scullin was himself undone less than two years later by internal party strife.

In March 1931 five ALP MPs led by Joseph Lyons (Postmaster General, Minister for Works and Railways and the former acting Treasurer) crossed the floor. Scullin's thin majority had evaporated. He was now dependent on the support of five New South Wales MPs who were loyal to renegade New South Wales Premier J.T. (Jack) Lang.[30] Although only one of the MPs from New South Wales had actually campaigned as a Lang candidate and 'shunned federal Labor's policy during the his recent by election',[31] the four other New South Wales MPs supporting Lang were all excluded from the Federal Parliamentary Labor Party Caucus. A special ALP conference held in Sydney at the end of March, boycotted by the New South Wales branch,[32] expelled the New South Wales (Lang faction) from the ALP.[33] In November the Langites voted with the Opposition to defeat the Scullin Government, earning Langite leader Jack Beasley the sobriquet 'Stabber Jack'.[34]

The Langites would exercise a malign influence on the ALP for years in spite of becoming 'an inner-city rump' following the election.[35] Ross McMullin observes in his history of the ALP that 'Langite "basher gangs" violently disrupted federal Labor meetings', noting that all unions in New South Wales except for the Australian Workers' Union remained loyal to Lang.[36] Even once the Langites were re-admitted in 1936 'on terms which in practice favoured Lang's faction',[37] they remained a disruptive influence on the party. The UAP seized on fears of Lang in the 1937 federal election by urging voters to 'look behind the Curtin' as they 'maximized the spectre of Lang'.[38] In 1938, the *Australian Worker* opined that the ALP 'must take action. It must restore in New South Wales the democratic charter which the Langites have suppressed'.[39] The Langites left the party again in 1940 following the adoption of a 'Hands off Russia' resolution at the ALP's state conference in Easter 1940.[40] McMullin surmises that the problems in New South Wales 'probably prevented Labor from winning the 1940 federal election'.[41]

The Langites were not the only problem the ALP faced in internal politics. The Communists, a much more difficult group to identify than the Langites, were also a malign influence within the ALP. In 1924 Communists were 'driven out of local Labor branches', but some 'refused to identify themselves'.[42] Indeed, 'Labor needed the Communists for they were the best and most reliable fighters',[43] and by 1939 Communists were 'an active presence in every major union'.[44] But they were not committed to the ALP and were fiercely pacifistic and isolationist for much of the inter-war period, the Spanish Civil War being a notable exception. Following the German–Soviet invasion of Poland Australian Communists dutifully accepted Moscow's instructions that the Second World War was an imperialist war, and by the end of 1939 they argued that 'Australians must have nothing to do with the war'.[45]

Lyons' crossing the floor was a seminal event in inter-war politics. He dominated political life until the eve of the European War and unlike his predecessors, as C.J. Lloyd observes, 'had one brilliant and indisputable gift as PM—he could win elections'.[46] The UAP's origins also meant that Lyons' Cabinet 'was fundamentally an administrative body and not a policy-formulator'.[47] The UAP was able to govern without the Country Party in its first term. The UAP and Country Party then formed a coalition government with a comfortable majority following the 1934 election. The 1937 election saw the UAP and Country Party secure another easy victory over the ALP which 'failed to make significant headway in the Representatives'.[48] When Lyons died of a heart attack on Good Friday 1939, he was succeeded by the Country Party's leader and Deputy Prime Minister Earle Page as caretaker Prime Minister until Robert Menzies was elected leader of the UAP and thus Prime Minister three weeks later.

Menzies led Australia into the Second World War and narrowly won the first wartime election in 1940. The UAP's much-reduced majority forced Menzies to rely on two independent MPs. Believing that it would be better for the UAP, which was bitterly divided, and the war effort—the ALP had repeatedly rejected his proposals for a national government—Menzies resigned as Prime Minister and UAP leader at the end of August 1941. He was succeeded by the leader of the Country Party Arthur Fadden who governed for a mere five weeks before his budget was rejected by the independent MPs. In a deteriorating international situation ALP leader John Curtin was then called on to form a minority government.

A POWER BEHIND THE THRONE?

The Nationalist and United Australia Parties,

> unlike the ALP and the Country party, have never had outside organizations—corresponding to trade unions and primary producer bodies—formally affiliated.[49]

There were, however, two organisations dedicated to keeping the ALP out of power: the Consultative Council in New South Wales and the National Union in Victoria, particularly their Finance Committees. Lex Watson, one of the few historians to write on these organisations, laments that 'little is known, even today, about their activities'.[50] Unfortunately we are unlikely to learn much more about them as 'there are no records for the two principal sponsor organisations' and 'all federal records of the UAP were destroyed'.[51] It is likely that the records would reveal little information as 'secrecy was something of an obsession' with the National Union and Consultative Council. They were 'usually composed of important businessmen in each of the capital cities'.[52] These organisations were thus simply filling a gap in conservative politics.

The idea that a section of the commercial elite was instrumental in conservative politics during the inter-war period has its origins in the inter-war period itself. *Smith's Weekly* claimed in February 1926 that 'SEVERE PRESSURE is being exerted by the National Union to induce him [Bruce] to do what he believes to be a political wrong', though the policy was unnamed.[53] In the next issue the National Union was labelled 'The money bags behind the present party in office'.[54] These articles were long on innuendo and short on evidence. John Archibald McCallum, State President of the Federal Labor Party in New South Wales, warned the Australian Institute of Political Science that

> the importers, the wholesale traders, the great retail business men, the manufacturers, the private banks and the insurance companies stand solidly as the economic foundation of the conservative core in the UAP.[55]

McCallum admitted his claim was an 'inference from a very few facts'.[56] As Irving observes, however, 'claims that the Nationalists were "tools" of these "secret societies" were a gross exaggeration'.[57] The National Union and Consultative Council 'played their most active political role when there was a need to unify the Right and remove a Labor government'.[58] Their primary function was to raise money and assist non-Labor parties secure election. There is no indication that the commercial elite—so important in these bodies—desired much more than 'to be left unmolested and untaxed'.[59] C.J. Lloyd in his history of the UAP referred to only one example of the National Union initiating policy, the 'partial restoration of parliamentary salaries' in 1933.[60] Lloyd also believed that the National Union undertook some services for Lyons but 'of a rather trivial kind'.[61]

The few available facts that have come to light since McCallum's observations confirm that the organisations were 'usually composed of businessman in each of the capital cities',[62] but one of the primary weaknesses they faced was that there was 'not the same homogeneity of interest among bankers, importers, merchants, and farmers'.[63] Baiba Irving, who has made the only attempt to discover who was in these organisations,[64] concluded that

> In no cases, on the basis of these lists, is it possible to speak of a committee as being dominated by a particular "business interest".[65]

Furthermore, they 'belonged to a variety of business associations' and 'various clubs'.[66]

Lyons' main communication with such organisations was through the Party.[67] He did occasionally dine with the Consultative Council but as Lyons' biographer Philip Hart observes, 'such meetings were infrequent'[68] and when Lyons dined with some important businessmen in Sydney he

> had to be told which company or organisation each man belonged to [which] indicates his unfamiliarity with them, and his papers do not record any further contact between Lyons and [any] of the sixteen.[69]

Hart believes that the tariff was 'foremost in these private discussions'.[70] Lex Watson further comments that

> Ex-Labor leaders, one might surmise, were also not likely to be particularly appealing to the intensely conservative men in the sponsor groups.[71]

The lack of communication is also partly explained by the fact that 'no major issue is known about on which the two [the National Union and the Nationalist Party] had different ideas'.[72]

In an attempt to provide a sample of the makeup of the National Union and the Consultative Council, a search has been conducted of the *Australian Dictionary of Biography* in the following occupations: business, finance, industrial relations, retail, wholesale, personal services; for individuals having one of the following terms in the body of the biographical entry: National Party, Nationalist Party, United Australia Party, Consultative Council, National Union or Finance Committee; and those individuals identified in Baiba Beata Berzins Irving's thesis on the Nationalist Party as being members of a Nationalist sponsor organisation that are in the *Australian Dictionary of Biography*.

This politically interested commercial elite was overwhelmingly Protestant, though Jews made up nearly a quarter, and there was no dominant religious denomination. Nor did these individuals share common educational or tertiary backgrounds. Furthermore, military experience was rare, only 15% having served. The lack of military experience was probably an element in the supporting organisations not pressing for a stronger defence. It is supposed their desire for minimal government oversight and low taxation was the critical influence.

COMPETING DEFENCE POLICIES

The defence policy of the conservatives throughout the inter-war period was well encapsulated by Lyons in 1938:

> The defence of Australia and the trade routes between Australia and Great Britain is an essential part of Great Britain's defence policy, forming as it does, part of the "first main effort".[74]

He went on to note that

> Singapore, as a pivotal point of the whole system of naval defence of the Empire, east of Suez, is being provided not only with docks, but also with the most powerful guns and air defences of any port of the Empire.[75]

The undoubted accuracy of these statements notwithstanding, the absence of any reference to local defence is telling. Conservative governments were overly reliant on British naval strength in spite of numerous warnings that the Royal Navy might not be able to always offer immediate protection. Theirs was a blue water strategy which aimed to stop an enemy on the high seas before it reached Australia or Australian territories and was embodied in the Singapore strategy. Conservative governments were reliant on British naval strength. In fact it is argued they were overly reliant, in view of the local defence requirement.

The ALP's defence policy was far more confused. As Hamill put it, the Party needed a policy which could 'satisfy the isolationists, nationalists, anti-imperialists, and pacifist tendencies within the movement'.[76] Consequently, ALP policies were exceedingly vague

NON-CO-OPERATION.

"The Labor policy is a policy of isolation and non-co-operation."—Mr. Hughes.

"Take my part, son—quick!"

"No, Father Bull! I am doing my duty to the family by keeping out of these vulgar brawls."

Norman Lindsay (Sydney *Bulletin*, 12 October 1938) presented the Curtin Labor Opposition as shirking its responsibilities.

to enable the party to accommodate all positions. Defence rarely surfaced in the Caucus and Japan was not mentioned until after Pearl Harbor.[77]

The ALP's defence policy in the 1920s and 1930s consisted of providing adequate home defence against possible foreign aggression, abolishing compulsory military service including compulsory training, allowing civil review of court-martial verdicts, exempting protected services from military service, opposing overseas service without a plebiscite and establishing Commonwealth control of all munitions production.[78]

BLUE WATER TRADE AND BLOCKADES

As we have seen, the defence of Australia involved more than the Australian continent. An island nation's overseas trade had to be protected—as did its interstate trade, which was dependent on coastal shipping. Conservatives such as Hughes, Bruce and Lyons believed in a blue water strategy that aimed 'to ensure that no hostile forces shall be able to cross the seas and impose conquests or inflict serious damage upon the Empire or its principal components', for Australian trade was a key component of the Empire's trade.[79] A blue water strategy would therefore protect Australia by ensuring Japan never achieved naval supremacy over the Pacific and thus could never invade Australia.

Australian defence policy was dictated by Australia's vital interests—its 'Dependence on external markets'.[80] Australia's trade routes were, in the words of Richard Casey, its 'most vulnerable point'.[81] The *Australian Quarterly* correctly noted that the two most important issues in formulating Australian defence policy were 'How could Australia and its trade routes be attacked?' and 'Could Australia be blockaded'?[82] In 1936 Defence Minister Archdale Parkhill described the alternative—'to repel an invader in our own country'—as a 'last resort'.[83] A blue water strategy was therefore also the most economical defence strategy, because the Royal Naval component would be paid for by the British taxpayer. When the strategy appeared to be failing, it would be hardly fair to blame the British.

Trade therefore played a key role in the formulation of Australian defence policy. Several key governmental figures believed trading partners would not attack each other. The most important of these was Frederick Shedden, Secretary of the Department of Defence, who believed that Japan's dependence on overseas trade ensured it would never start a war, for 'Japan would be ruined by the loss of her overseas trade'.[84] He failed to realise, however, that Japan might go to war to protect her trade in resources, and especially to find alternate and secure sources of raw materials.

Sir Frederic Eggleston, a noted Australian intellectual, Victorian state politician and diplomat, accepted the traditional liberal view that free trade would prevent wars.[85] At the 1936 Institute for Pacific Relations Conference he urged the United States to lift its trade restrictions on Japan.[86] In 1935 Ian Clunies Ross, a scientist who had lived and worked in Japan, believed that increased trade between Australia and Japan would 'demonstrate that the supposed conflict of interests of the two countries [Australia and Japan] has no foundation in fact'.[87] Unfortunately Australia's trade was of insufficient importance to affect the policies of Pacific powers. Thus assumptions about regional trade became and remained a defence liability.

An expert on Japan, Edmund Piesse, believed and argued in the Melbourne *Herald* that the RAN could not 'protect Australian trade, coastal trade, or prevent an invasion or even raids'.[88] He correctly saw the inability of Australian naval forces to protect its coastal trade as a serious violation of Australia's local defence responsibility. By the end of 1936, Piesse was of the opinion that Australia should 'give up protecting [its] trade routes' because a 'blockade was unlikely to bring Australia to its knees'.[89] A total blockade of Australia would have been difficult to achieve, but Piesse underestimated the consequences of even a partial blockade on Australia.

The ALP did not accept the strategic importance of trade. Indeed, trade was seen by many in the ALP as merely another cause of war. John West (ALP, East Sydney, NSW) said that as soon as a nation is 'injured in their trade ... there will be trouble'.[90] The Italian invasion of Abyssinia was labelled 'a sordid trade war' by Joseph Clark (ALP, Darling, NSW).[91]

The ALP also rejected a blue water strategy as inherently aggressive. John Curtin responded in 1937 to a UAP statement on the importance of protecting trade:

> The Prime Minister said yesterday that the protection of our sea-borne trade depended upon naval forces. If this be true of Australia, it is also true of New Zealand, of Canada, to a very large extent, and also of South Africa.[92]

The assumption that all Dominion trade routes were equally exposed was patently false and demonstrated a fundamental misunderstanding of Australia's strategic position. New Zealand trade went across the South and Central Pacific through the Panama Canal which greatly reduced the time it was exposed to hostile vessels. Canada's largest trading partner was the United States with whom it shared a long land border. Duncan-Hughes (NAT, Boothby, SA) accurately summed up Canada's position:

> No country be in a safer position than Canada, with the Pacific Ocean on one side, the Atlantic on the other side, and the friendly United States of America on its southern border.[93]

A RELATIVE PACIFICISM

The ALP's pacifism did not reflect the views of the wider community. The lack of widespread public interest in foreign affairs ensured the Peace Movement did not enjoy regular press coverage.[94] The Peace Movement also suffered from internal divisions and was composed of two camps. Some conceded that weapons were necessary and supported collective security, especially the League of Nations, and these were generally found in the League of Nations Union (LNU).[95] The other camp was totally pacifistic. Its members opposed sanctions, all armaments and any sort of military action.[96] One supporter of total disarmament argued for disarmament because: '3/4's of the world, its women and children were compulsorily disarmed and they desire to see the other 1/4 disarmed'.[97]

The two camps did not enjoy close relations. The Peace Movement's largest and most vocal group, the Women's International League of Peace and Freedom (WILPF), was deeply suspicious of the League of Nations and the LNU. The WILPF's leader, Eleanor Moore, believed the League of Nations was doomed to fail because it was based on nation states.[98] Another pacifist claimed that it was 'Deplorable that the League had power to sanction the use of force'.[99]

The disarmament campaign of the outright pacifists enjoyed some public support but the extent of public support was not sufficient to alter elections.[100] Justice Henry Bournes Higgins claimed that the Peace Movement united people of 'all religions and classes'.[101] Perhaps, but the people were few in number. The Australian Government had just signed the Kellogg-Briand Pact and thereby renounced war as an instrument of national policy. In 1928 Higgins told a pacifist meeting in Melbourne that 'We are all agreed upon the folly, futility, and stupidity of war'.[102] One leading pacifist, J.C. Rockwood Proud, later described the Kellogg-Briand Pact as 'An event of outstanding importance in international politics', though by the time he wrote that the Kellogg-Briand Pact had already failed to prevent war in China.[103] The disarmament movement reached its height in 1932 when the League of Nations held a World Disarmament Conference. WILPF presented a petition with 118,000 Australian signatures in favour of global disarmament to the conference. Prime Minister Scullin, several of his Cabinet ministers and Sir John Monash signed the petition.[104] The conference accomplished nothing.

Support for disarmament did not translate into widespread support for the Peace Movement's other activities. Plans to change Armistice Day to Disarmament Day came to nothing.[105] Attempts to initiate Peace Education in the New South Wales School system also failed, and peace rallies held as alternatives to Anzac Day events failed to attract widespread support.[106] The Peace Movement did, however, convince the Scullin Government to distribute World Peace Pact posters to all money order offices.[107]

By the 1930s lack of unity was destroying the Peace Movement,[108] which was struggling to stay relevant in an increasingly dangerous world. By 1929 police agents reported that attendance at meetings was down and funds were running short.[109] The fewer people the Peace Movement attracted, the more bizarre it became. In 1930, for example, E.C. Dyson, who contributed generously to the movement, proposed Australia give New Guinea back to Germany.[110]

By the mid-1930s, the most vocal pacifists were the Communists, though the Spanish Civil War forced them to rethink their pacifism.[111] Their glossy publication, *War! What For?*, later renamed *World Peace*, saw capitalist wars everywhere. The 1934 Centenary was 'a marvellous smokescreen for military preparations'.[112] Australia was to be turned into 'a base for the British drive against Soviet China'.[113] This was only believable if one accepted that 'War is inseparable from capitalism', which the Communists did.[114] *World Peace*, the Communist journal published by the Movement Against War and Fascism, described the Soviet invasion of Poland thus: 'Red Army "Invades" Poland: Half of Poland Saved from Horrors of War'.[115]

LEAGUE OF NATIONS SUPPORT WAVERS

Support for the League of Nations fluctuated throughout the inter-war period and began to seriously falter after the Manchurian crisis. In the immediate postwar period the League of Nations Union provided, as historian Carolyn Rasmussen has written, 'the most dynamic new element in the Peace Movement'.[116] The LNU, however, was very different from other groups in the Peace Movement. It was not on the fringe of political society. Eleanor Moore of the WILPF justifiably lamented the LNU's 'close ties to the government' and that it was so 'well funded'.[117] The LNU was started by a grant from the Nationalist Party.[118] Its early membership reflected its ties to the Nationalists and ALP. One of its main constituents was conservatives attracted by the LNU's British origins.[119] It also appealed to intellectuals and academics more than the absolute pacifism of the WILPF. The historian W.K. Hancock and the intellectual Frederic Eggleston supported the League of Nations in their writings.[120]

Prime Minister 'Billy' Hughes supported the League of Nations at first. In an Armistice Day speech in 1920 he urged the United States to join the League, claiming that 'America would be adjusting

[George] Washington's policy to the circumstances of our time'.[121] He claimed that its objective to preserve world peace was within its capacity.[122] The ALP also initially supported the League, with leader Matthew Charlton lamenting in 1921 that the 'League of Nations is to be allowed to perish'.[123] He would later lament during a debate on the Treaty of Lausanne that

> The very people who talk so much about the League of Nations apparently forget that there is such a thing as a League whenever they are in trouble, because they do not appeal to it, or attempt to put its powers into operation.[124]

Yet when the League did attempt to put its powers into operation in Abyssinia, the ALP vehemently opposed it.

The failure of the United States to join the League of Nations resulted in a decrease of popular and political interest in the League. As W.J. Hudson proposed in his *Australia and the League of Nations*: 'the League now looked altogether too distantly European an institution'.[125] By 1928 the League was so distant that essayist Frederick Gisborne could already pronounce the League a failure because 'Too much idealism and too little common sense prevailed at Paris in 1919, and seems still to haunt the precincts of Geneva'.[126]

Gisborne was premature in his condemnation of the League of Nations. The Australian Government still supported the League officially. Historian W.J. Hudson observes that the Scullin Government was 'vaguely internationalist but qualified in its enthusiasm for a League which was financially expensive and overwhelmingly capitalist in membership'.[127] The LNU's response to Scullin Government ambivalence was to stress the importance of the League as an instrument for world peace and international co-operation. The Secretary General of the LNU, Raymond Watt, urged Australians to 'have faith in the covenant' to prevent massive civilian casualties.[128] Watt's role became increasingly difficult following the outbreak of hostilities in Manchuria which served to remind Australians that neither the United States nor Japan was affected by League pronouncements.[129] Watt was forced to concede that the 'League has failed China'.[130] He argued, however, that 'Without the League a number of essential governmental activities would be hopelessly curtailed'.[131] He cited the League's work combating the slave and drug trades and ensuring food safety.

The League's failure in Manchuria did not immediately strip it of governmental support. Hughes was still willing to address the LNU in 1933. He admitted that the League had its flaws, but 'it has built up an amazing organization which functions smoothly, and which plays an important part in the life of the world'.[132] Two years later, however, Hughes had given up entirely on the League of Nations. He saw Manchuria and Abyssinia as 'proof of the League's impotence'[133] and warned that the League of Nations was 'utterly powerless to protect Australia'.[134]

However prescient Hughes's warning about the League's impotence may have been, it did not conform to government policy. His book *Australia and War To-Day* led to his resignation from the Lyons Cabinet, albeit only temporarily. The UAP still believed that 'Australian security rests in the Covenant of the League of Nations and supplementary treaties'.[135] It is therefore unsurprising that Lyons' UAP Government supported the League of Nations in the Abyssinian crisis and imposed League-mandated sanctions. The UAP proudly proclaimed 'Australia stands by the League of Nations' and pointed out that 'There can be no such thing as "neutrality" unless Australia is prepared to betray the ideals of the League and to repudiate its allegiance to the British Empire'.[136]

The ALP opposed imposing sanctions against Italy. The party's official historian Ross McMullin maintains that during the Abyssinian crisis, John Curtin confirmed 'Labor's perfect loyalty to the League of Nations and support for its high purposes', but the parliamentary debates reveal a party opposed to the League's existence.[137] Langite Jack Beasley bitterly denounced the League of Nations Covenant as having 'been a scrap of paper ever since it was first accepted by the major powers'.[138] Beasley concluded his speech with the demand that 'Australia must withdraw from it [the League]'.[139] It was a view shared by many in the mainstream ALP.

John Curtin, ALP leader from 1935, attempted to hide behind another international treaty, the Kellogg-Briand Pact, by arguing that 'The Covenant of the League is not more binding on Australia than are the provisions of the Kellogg Pact', and that therefore Australia could not enact sanctions, even though Italy's actions had clearly violated the Kellogg-Briand Pact.[140] Australia's decision to apply sanctions and support collective security was described thus by Thomas Sheehan (ALP, Cook, NSW): 'This government … has cut right across the path of peace which the Australian people should follow'.[141] He went on to urge the Government to 'Reject the infamous doctrine of collective security'.[142]

The failure of League-imposed sanctions to halt Italy in Abyssinia robbed the League of Nations of most of its public credibility and political support. The UAP gradually dropped references to the League from its official statements and the Covenant ceased to be a cornerstone of Australian security. Attorney General Robert Menzies averred in 1938 that 'The League of Nations cannot keep the peace'.[143]

In spite of government disillusion with the League of Nations, the LNU continued to advocate reliance on the League, possessing as the Union did 'inexhaustible gullibility'.[144] But its arguments that 'Australia has everything to gain from a strong League' overlooked the vital fact that the League of Nations had never been strong and never would be, whatever Australia did.[145] The LNU's members failed to realise what Hughes had come to understand, that 'The League of Nations has failed, not because the principles for which it stood are wrong, but because words cannot secure peace'.[146]

The Australian defence budget was repeatedly cut during the early inter-war period. The result of these cuts—made by Australian politicians for Australian reasons—was greatly to weaken Australia's defence capability. There was no public opposition to them and even less public support for increased defence spending. Australian conservatives dominated inter-war politics and were the authors of many of these policies. However, it is unfair to blame them alone for Australia's weakened defence capability. It was, as E.F. Harrison (UAP, Bendigo, Victoria) charged, the ALP which had 'emasculated' the Australian military.[147] The UAP realised that the ALP had gone too far and struggled to rearm Australia, but it was hindered by pre-Keynesian orthodoxy and an isolationist opposition which vehemently opposed rearmament. The ALP failed to formulate a realistic alternative defence policy. Fortress Australia was not a viable alternative, for it did not take account of the importance of trade, Australia's reliance on imports, or its lack of industrial capacity. The ALP's naïve attachment to isolationism and the vague notion of a Fortress Australia gave the contrasting policies of their conservative foes an appeal they hardly deserved. The conservatives' rearmament programme was a matter of too little, too late.

CHAPTER 8

THE FAILURE OF AUSTRALIAN LEADERSHIP

The National Characteristic of self-complacency[1]
Archibald A. Montgomery-Massingberd, 30 January 1935

In 1935 Archibald Montgomery-Massingberd, Chief of the Imperial General Staff, wrote in a letter to Sir Maurice Hankey, Secretary to the Committee of Imperial Defence, that when it came to defence, Australia was a complacent nation. The repeated warnings discussed in the preceding chapters had fallen on deaf ears. Australia was a minor power with a small political elite, a developed democracy that had survived the losses of the Great War and the convulsions of two plebiscites on overseas military service. It had avoided political and social disruption threatened from both the extreme right and extreme left in the Great Depression. So why did such a nation seemingly fail to understand its perilous position as the international situation deteriorated from the early 1930s? And what does this say about the quality of Australia's national leadership in the inter-war years? Definitive answers cannot be found in the existing detailed studies surveyed in earlier chapters—as essential as they are. They require some consideration of the Australian political, industrial and military elites and of the relationships within and between them.

THE THEORY AND IMPORTANCE OF ELITES

During years of deteriorating international order Australia did not possess well-integrated elites that could generate and assimilate progressive thinking on Australia's place in the world. Its population was small, less than ten million, and was scattered widely across the continent. Rivalry between the various states and state capitals was still fierce and weakened Australia politically and militarily. The new capital in Canberra, established in 1927, was difficult to reach and many key departments remained in Melbourne. This isolated public servants from their political masters.

Elites are crucial for understanding the formulation of national policies. Historian Harold Perkin observed that

> the study of elites is of vital importance in its own right too. It can throw light on the most searching questions about the past.[2]

Perkin was not the first to posit the notion that elites were important for understanding national history or national issues. The Italian political philosopher Vilfredo Pareto wrote in his 1901 treatise, *The Rise and Fall of Elites*, that the 'History of man is the history of the continuous replacement of certain elites', a conclusion which he based on a study of European political, religious and economic elites.[3] Pareto observed that they 'preserve a certain passive courage, but lack active courage'.[4] They display an unwillingness or inability to enact policies which respond to the challenges facing them as an elite, though they have a general desire to act. Pareto's model of competing elites is useful for understanding Australian inter-war policy formulation, which reflected the competing political, military and industrial elites.

C. Wright Mills expanded on Pareto's work with the idea of a power elite composed of the three principal sub-elites: economic, political, and military.[5] Mills' study of the American power elite in the 1950s revealed that members of the various elites showed similar social origins and were bound by sociometric ties. Further, there was considerable interchange of personnel between the three elites. Mills defined a power elite as one that makes 'decisions having major consequence',[6] but he also observed that 'No one, accordingly, can be truly powerful unless he has access to the command of major institutions'.[7] The lack of an integrated elite therefore severely reduces the power that the elites possess individually and in combination, and precludes them from combining to form a power elite. Australia lacked an integrated elite which, in turn, led to a lack of mutual understanding and coordination within and between the elites. Mills observed that 'their failure to make decisions is itself an act that is often of greater consequence than the decisions they do make'.[8] Because Australian inter-war elites lacked sociometric ties, precluding the development of a power elite, they also lacked 'active courage'. It was often the decisions Australian elites did not or could not make which had the greatest effect on Australian defence policy.

AUSTRALIAN ELITES DEFINED

The historiography of Australian elites is scant. They were first seriously studied in John Higley's *Elites in Australia*, but Higley focused on those in the late 1970s.[9] The only historical observation Higley made about Australian elites was that Australia was forming a 'consensual-unified elite' at Federation, but he does not suggest when this process was completed.[10] This thesis, however, maintains that Australia lacked a unified elite during the inter-war period.

In their study, *The Big End of Town*, Grant Fleming, Simon Ville and David Merrett recently lamented that 'there is no comprehensive identification and investigation of Australian corporate leaders ... in the twentieth century'.[11] Ambitious in scope and covering an entire century, *The Big End of Town* identifies only the largest corporations, but at least it offers a starting point. The political and military elites are equally understudied as elites. Sociologists Robert William Connell and Terence H. Irving in their history of class in Australia, *Class structure in Australian History*, refer to a 'ruling industrial elite' but they do not explore the composition of this elite.[12] Theirs is a narrative-descriptive history of class in Australian society from the beginnings of European settlement. They simply assume that a 'ruling industrial elite' existed and governed Australia from the late 1920s or early 1930s following the end of 'colonial capitalism'.[13]

Therefore, there is little description let alone analysis of who actually composed the 'ruling industrial elite' and little investigation of the links between the industrial and political elites.

Perkin warns that:

> Only empirical research will show whether the elite individuals are recruited from one or more than one social class, how they are socialized by education and training on the job for their particular role, to what extent they are integrated into one or more cohesive groups, how power is distributed within and between elites.[14]

The following empirical research into Australia's inter-war elites adopts an approach commonly adopted by scholars engaged in this sort of study for national elites—a focus on a portion of a country's political, economic and military elites.[15] Their composition varies by country and time period. Here I have attempted to define Australia's inter-war industrial, military and political elites, and to establish their composition in terms of religious affiliation, locale, secondary and tertiary education, occupation(s), military experience, political affiliation and leadership position(s) held during the inter-war period.

The industrial elite is defined as those who made up the boards of directors of Australia's principal manufacturers as listed in *The National Handbook of Australia's Industries*,[16] the Chief Executive Officers, General Managers and Chief Financial Officers of these companies, and members of the Executive of the Victorian Chamber of Manufactures.

The military elite (31 persons) was divided into three sub-elites. The Army elite (14 persons) comprises the Chief of the General Staff and those above the rank of colonel listed in *The Army List of the Australian Military Forces: Active List* and *The Staff and Regimental Lists of the Australian Military Forces*[18] as belonging to the Australian Section of the Imperial General Staff (ASIGS) or the Army Board (AB). The RAAF elite (6 persons) is composed of the heads of the RAAF and those officers of or above the rank of Group Captain as listed in *The Royal Australian Air Force List* of 1927, 1928, 1929,

1930, 1933, 1934 and 1935, the only inter-war years for which RAAF officer lists are available.[19] The RAN elite (11 persons) is composed of the Chief of the Naval Staff and those officers in the Royal Australian Navy, including Royal Navy officers on secondment to the Royal Australian Navy, above the rank of Captain as listed in *The Navy List*.[20] The naval elite does not include those Royal Naval officers in command of Her Majesty's Australian Squadron, as they were not part of the Royal Australian Navy and are only occasionally listed in *The Navy List*.

The political elite (102 persons)[21] was divided by party allegiance: ALP (33 persons), CP (15 persons) and NAT–UAP (58 persons). It comprised those identified in Colin A. Hughes and B.D. Graham's *A Handbook of Australian Government and Politics 1890–1964*[22] as having been a Minister, Treasurer, Attorney General, Treasurer, party leader, assistant/deputy leader or party whip in the six non-caretaker governments between the Hughes Ministry after the end of the Great War and the Menzies Ministry 1939–40. Party leaders, assistant leaders and party whips are identified from Rydon's *A Biographical Register of the Commonwealth Parliament, 1901–1972*.[23] Altogether, the elites comprised some 194 individuals.

INTEGRATION AND LEADERSHIP

The leadership provided by elites is not merely a matter of ascertaining who was in the elite, but of how well the elites were integrated. It could be argued that an integrated elite would have made the same mistakes—or worse—than a non-integrated elite, but the available literature on the subject indicates the opposite.[24] The importance of an integrated elite is that it 'encourages the ascription of legitimacy to group elites' and reinforces shared values.[25] Integration and shared values lead to 'sustained consultation and negotiation' within and between elites. As we shall see, these qualities were absent from Australia's elites.

In *The Comparative Study of Political Elites*, Robert Putnam observes that it is a 'widely shared assumption that a unified elite governs more effectively and more stably than a disunified elite'.[26] A unified elite increases understanding and encourages members of the elite to take complementary actions. Australia's elites lacked the prerequisites—social homogeneity, sociometric ties and similar education backgrounds—to form a unified elite. Putnam does not maintain that elites needed all of these characteristics to be integrated but the absence of any of them among the Australian elites precluded an integrated Australian elite during the inter-war period. The absence of an integrated elite contributed to a failure to appreciate the risks Australia faced and the need to prepare a strong local defence.[27]

The importance of an integrated elite to a nation's defence preparedness can be seen in a brief discussion of the British elites who formed a national government and an all-party government during the Second World War—a level of co-operation unimaginable to members of the Australian political elite. G.C. Peden observed that

> When the test of war came Britain was able to contribute to the Allied cause the world's largest navy, an aircraft industry which out-produced Germany's in 1940, and an army which was just large enough to deny the German Army any decisive advantages in men or quantity of equipment.[28]

Such a statement could not be made about Australian military preparations in 1939 or 1942 in reaction to the defence challenges to national security and defence then apparent.

British elites, benefiting from the small territorial size of the United Kingdom, a well-established class society and the existence in London of what Mills labelled a national city that was 'at once the social center, the political capital, and the financial hub', were very well integrated.[29] Furthermore, elite educational institutions such as Oxford and Cambridge and the 'big six' public schools fostered 'elite integration by ensuring training for a substantial number of elite numbers and by nurturing personal contacts and friendships'.[30]

A NOT-SO-*elite* EDUCATION

W.D. Rubinstein's 'path breaking' research into the British elites[31] reveals that nearly half of British civil servants and industrialists in the inter-war period attended a public school. Oxford and Cambridge educated more of the elite than any other institutions and most of the elite came from London and the surrounding Home Counties.[32] John Scott's research expanded on Rubinstein's research and is even more revealing. His analysis of the top ranks of the armed services in 1939 found that nearly two-thirds of the top Army and RAF officers had attended a public school and 18% of the RAF's high ranking officers had attended Oxford or Cambridge.[33] These factors, in combination with the tradition of military service that existed in many middle- and upper-class British families, ensured that the British military elites were more integrated than their Australian counterparts. As we shall see, Australian elites did not share similar social origins and sociometric ties and there was little interchange between the elites. This prevented the development of an Australian power elite.

The Australian elites were the most educated portion of the Australian population, but how well educated were they? A fifth of the elite had no known secondary education and less than a quarter had any tertiary education. The lack of secondary education of Australian elites, let alone a common secondary education experience, is a telling statistic when compared to the education of the British elites detailed above. Their common primary education experience focused on the past glories of the Empire and seems only to have increased the Australian tendency towards complacency and undue reliance on the Royal Navy.

American Consul J. Pierrepont Moffat lamented in his diary that 'the brainiest type of Australian does not go into politics',[34] though it is unclear just where they went. It was certainly not the military or industry. There was a 'brain drain'. Many of the 'brainiest type' emigrated to the United Kingdom and to other parts of the Empire. New Zealand historian James Belich convincingly demonstrates that this was the case in New Zealand: New Zealanders had leading positions in the British elites and a similar situation in Australia seems just as likely.[35] Those who had tertiary education came from numerous institutions. There was no Oxbridge or Ivy League dominance of the Australian elites and certainly no university college accounting 'for a disproportionate number of elite figures'.[36] The lack of a common educational background made inter-elite communication more difficult and prevented the easy formation of sociometric ties. Such members as had a secondary education came from a wide variety of secondary schools (over 100). In her study of federal parliamentarians, Joan Rydon cautions that 'Many who attended secondary schools did so only for two or three years and did not approach matriculation standard'.[38]

As for those who attended universities and other centres of higher education, Geoffrey Blainey noted that most of those Australian professors elected to chairs in the last quarter of the nineteenth century 'were, with a few exceptions, mediocre men'.[39] These were the men who educated the very best of Australia's elite, but there was 'little scope for oriental studies'.[40] F.B. Smith has observed that

> The history of England, together with the history of the classical world, and the British Empire which encompassed the American and early Australian colonies, formed the staple of history courses from at least the 1870s.[41]

Such an education did not mean university graduates had a sound understanding of the modern world. Arthur Lynch, who studied Civil Engineering, claimed to have found 'only intellectual mediocrity and social snobbery in most professors' at the University of Melbourne.[42] At the end of the nineteenth century and the beginning of the twentieth century, when the elites would have been at university, it was still a classics-based education.[43] Many students were on teacher bursaries and were thus sent to rural locations on graduation which inhibited social interaction and the creation of intellectual and sociometric networks. Furthermore, many intellectuals disliked and distrusted the military.

The political elite, the one most important in the formation of defence policy, had the highest percentage of tertiary-educated members (slightly under 20%). The tertiary-educated were exceptional even amongst their political colleagues, many of whom had been educated solely in 'the school of hard knocks'. Nearly 80% of federal MPs had no tertiary education and nearly a quarter had no known secondary education. Consequently the political elite was reliant on the press for its information about the wider world.

Those who had received only a primary education, that is up to Year Eight or the age of 13 or 14, received an education centred on the British Empire and knew 'all about Wellington, Nelson, and Clive of India and very little else'.[44] They had learned that there was 'One King, one flag and one navy',[45] and to be equally loyal to England and Australia.[46] Students studied the British Empire to learn 'how the English-speaking races have gradually come to hold such an important position in the world'.[47] It was the story of moral and material progress which focused on ideals such as patriotism.[48]

International travel among the political elite was infrequent given Australia's isolation. Those members of the political elite who did travel, did so to attend conferences and invariably went to the United Kingdom first. The United States was generally visited only while returning from the UK, and invariably briefly, such as Lyons' visit to the United States in 1935. Asia was rarely visited by members of any elite, and such visits were often heavily chaperoned, especially in Japan where only approved locales were visited. The shortage of intellectuals in the Australian political elite further precluded any profound debate about the ideas of Australia's relationship with the United Kingdom or defence policy. John Latham, last leader of the Nationalists and Lyons' deputy and foreign minister, was a notable exception.[49]

Intellectuals were notably absent from the ALP, where one might perhaps have expected to find them. Ross McMullin observes in his history of the ALP that

> Practical men predominated in the Australian labour movement, where intellectuals were distrusted as flighty and unreliable and education tended to be downgraded.[50]

The British Labour tradition had a long history of attracting intellectuals, but there was only one Australian Fabian society throughout the inter-war period, a South Australian branch formed in 1939.[51] In his study of Australian Fabians, Race Matthews observes that unlike Britain 'No comparable association of middle-class radicals with labour activists was achieved within the Australian Labor Party until the late 1960s'.[52]

In the 1930s the Australian political elite was also extremely insular. The industrial elite had enjoyed 'direct daily access to Federal ministers' while the government was based in Melbourne.[53] Their interaction with the political elite was focused on improving their financial position. Economic historians Ted Wheelwright and Ken Buckley unsurprisingly noted that for many 'profit was the supreme consideration'.[54] Parliament's 1927 move to Canberra isolated the political elite from the other elites and ensured discussions among political leaders took place with much less direct input from the other elites. There were few members of the other elites in Canberra. Some major industrialists did, however, attempt to enter parliament. H.V. McKay had sought election to the House of Representatives in 1913 but lost and never tried again.[55] He and other major industrialists found they could achieve political influence through lobbyists and peak bodies. It is important to remember, however, as historian Peter Cochrane has observed, that 'Most [industrialists] remained poorly accommodated politically and insecure economically'.[56] Their primary political concern was keeping Labor governments out of power at the state and federal level.

THE POLITICAL ELITE

The composition of the political elite was discussed at length earlier; however, it is worth reiterating that the parliamentary parties' composition reflected urban trade union, rural grazing/farming and urban-industrial middle-class interests and that 'There can be no general picture of the career of a member of parliament'.[57] The ALP was heavily Catholic (over 60% of those in the ALP elite with a known religious affiliation) while the conservative parties were predominantly Protestant with Catholics making up just 12%.

Since most of the returned men who served in parliament did so briefly, military experience within the political elite was rare: less than a quarter had military experience. Military experience was rarest within the ALP (only one member of the ALP elite was a returned soldier), and most common in the Country Party (33.3%). Stanley Melbourne Bruce was the only inter-war Prime Minister with military experience and few Cabinet Ministers had any military experience or deep knowledge of military matters. Only three inter-war defence ministers—Thomas Glasgow, Geoffrey Street and Neville Howse—had military experience. Howse had been a military surgeon.

The absence of veterans from the Australian political elite was in stark contrast to the American political scene where a veteran often had 'value to the ticket as a vote-getter'.[61] The 1930 Congress had 'more veterans than any Congress since the War' and the number only increased.[62] American veterans were not merely back benchers but held 'important places on both sides of the aisle' and in the Cabinet.[63] This may have contributed to American isolationism but it also precluded a pacifist policy being adopted by either major party. The Secretaries of War, the Navy and State in 1930 had all served in frontline combat roles.[64] American President Franklin Roosevelt had been Assistant-Secretary of the Navy, and so he had an intimate knowledge of naval strategy and service requirements. By 1943 more than a third of American Congressmen were members of the American Legion, the American equivalent of the RSL.[65]

The lack of returned men in the Australian House of Representatives ensured the political elite struggled to comprehend fully Australia's defence requirements or the threats posed by new technology on the battlefield. Intra-elite communication was thus also wanting. Richard Casey, himself a member of the political elite, claimed in a 1937 address to the Royal Institute of International Affairs that 'It is always surprising to me that we achieve such a large measure of uniformity of thought such as it was and opinion throughout Australia'.[66] The uniformity of thought was merely a bi-product of poorly informed elites and the shallowness of intellectual debate within Australia. It was also a gross oversimplification, for the ALP did not share the opinions of the conservatives. They were, however, an increasingly marginal party, whose unrealistic policies ensured governmental policies enjoyed widespread support. The uniformity Casey referred to was loyalty to 'the Imperial idea'.[67] The American Consul Moffat observed in September 1937 that 'The general tendency of the present government is to play in strongly with England and to emphasize Imperial unity'.[68]

THE INDUSTRIAL ELITE

Richard Casey's father was the director of several companies, but the younger Casey opted for a career in politics. There is no evidence that he maintained close ties with the industrial elite.[69] One of Casey's harshest criticisms of American society was the dislike he believed American businessman had for public affairs.[70] Australian industrialists, however, were also reluctant to take an interest in public affairs. The Canadian tradition of 'inviting members of the corporate elite to join the federal cabinet' did not exist in Australia.[71]

A section of the commercial elite was interested in politics, primarily in keeping a non-Labor government in power. Herbert Brookes, Alfred Deakin's son-in-law and a member of the industrial elite, was consulted regularly by the political elite before the Great War, but his interest in federal inter-war politics was motivated mainly by a deeply held fear of the influence of Catholics in the ALP.[72] Brookes' papers reveal a man primarily concerned with state political issues after 1919.[73] A fervent personal supporter of Hughes and the Nationalist Party, Brookes is mentioned in Fitzhardinge's biography of Hughes only twice—he hosted a meeting between Hughes and Page (which failed), and Hughes briefly considered making him Australia's trade representative to the United States. Brookes' fervent anti-Catholicism precluded a close relationship with Scullin or Lyons.[74] Less than a third of the industrial elite can be linked to major political parties.[75]

THE MILITARY ELITE

Casey and his colleagues in the political elite did not mix frequently with the military elite either. When a member of the military elite, Thomas Blamey, sought endorsement as the UP candidate for the newly created seat of Deakin, the Party 'gave him little encouragement', thinking him a bad risk.[76] His tenure as Victoria's Commissioner of Police and his lack of social skills meant that he was held in low regard by the other elites. The military elites had little in common with the other elites and had little contact with them. The Australian military elite was educated at nearly 30 secondary institutions with no dominant school, and only two members of it

(6.4%) had attended a civilian tertiary institution. The Australian military elite thus lacked a good foundation for communication let alone integration with other elites. The lack of inter-elite interaction was exacerbated by Parliament's 1927 move to Canberra. The services' headquarters remained in Melbourne which precluded frequent social interaction between the military and political elites. There is no indication that any politician considered any staff officer a personal friend. This ensured that information could not be conveyed to the political elite through informal channels. The lack of informal access to the political elite led the Army to leak documents to the press. These leaks indicate how isolated the Army was from the political elite. Heavily influenced by pacifism and burdened by its anti-conscriptionist past, the ALP deeply distrusted the military. This distrust further restricted the military elite's ability to influence the political debate.

A STRATEGY FOR NON-INTEGRATED ELITES

Lacking sociometric ties or a common background with the political elite, relations between the armed forces and the general public were all-important. The RAN enjoyed the best relations of any service with the political elite—but only with the conservative side of politics. The Navy already enjoyed considerable public support owing to the prominence of naval heroes such as Drake and Nelson in Australian school syllabuses, but the RAN was determined to maintain public support, especially in view of the rise of the soldierly Anzac legend.

As Acting Prime Minister, Earle Page proudly claimed in 1935 that 'Anzac Day has become the personification of the Australian tradition'.[77] However, it was a tradition based on volunteers coming forward to defend the nation and the regular Army therefore enjoyed no increase in public support. Its budget remained much smaller than the RAN's throughout the inter-war period. Speeches at Anzac Day were about memory and honouring the dead: the only references to the Army were phrases such as 'An Army in Mufti',[78] referring to the crowd who were expected to volunteer if there was another war.[79] Indeed, the idea that Australians were natural-born soldiers was central to the rising Anzac myth, which celebrated volunteers coming forward after war broke out. Negating the need for a peacetime military, this myth, as Carl Bridge observes, 'in explaining everything explains virtually nothing about Australia's military endeavours'.[80] The Anzac myth was also based on combat prowess not strategic awareness, which required careful planning rather than mere voluntarism.

Lacking sociometric ties or a common background with the political elite—exacerbated by Parliament's 1927 move to Canberra while the services' headquarters remained in Melbourne—relations between the armed forces and the general public became all important. The RAN engaged in numerous public relations exercises and enjoyed an extremely high profile; its high-ranking officers mixed well, and frequently, with the conservative political elite. They had often served in the Royal Navy and some were on secondment from the British service which conferred on them a greater social cachet.

Throughout the 1920s *Melbourne Punch* published the biographical sketches: 'People We Know' and 'Prominent Personalities'. Naval personnel were the most common military entries with few months going by without at least one naval officer.[81] Most Army officers mentioned were from the Great War rather than officers on active service.[82] The RAN's prominence was ensured by its constant presence at major social events in Melbourne and Sydney. Sir Leslie Wilson was a retired Lieutenant-Colonel and former British MP who had been Parliamentary Assistant Secretary in the War Cabinet in late 1918. Now Governor of Queensland he witheringly described his impressions of the RAN:

> The Royal Australian Navy seldom goes anywhere, except from Sydney to Melbourne, or from Melbourne to Sydney for Cup Days or other festivals, with occasional visits to Tasmania (for the Regatta)! and here [Brisbane] for the Show Week.[83]

But the Navy's presence at social events kept it in the public eye and provided its officers with many opportunities to meet and impress the political elite. On important social occasions RAN officers always wore their dress uniforms.[84] Balls dominated the social calendar in the week before the Melbourne Cup and RAN officers were always prominent. In 1924 numerous senior RAN officers attended the first postwar Naval and Military Club's Ball as did the Governor of Victoria.[85]

The RAN was not content to merely attend balls at private clubs or the Governor's residence. The arrival of HMAS *Australia* in 1928 provided the Navy with an excellent opportunity to show off its newest ship.[86] A thousand guests, including the Governor General and the Governor of Victoria, were invited to enjoy light refreshments and tour the vessel before heading off to a ball hosted by the Governor.[87] In 1936 the RAN hosted a ball or 'At Home' on HMAS *Australia*, which was decorated with 'flags and amber lights' for the event. Several federal and state politicians, the Governor and most of Melbourne's social elite attended.[88] The RAN's ball was so popular that dancing was also 'enjoyed on the decks of HMAS *Sydney*'.[89] There was also a Navy League Ball which the Governor and the American consul attended.[90] The Navy League constantly advocated a stronger navy and their ability to host functions that attracted the political elite facilitated the RAN's communication with the political elite.[91]

Balls provided important opportunities for mixing with members of the various elites, but the RAN also secured wider public support. In 1925 the RAN made its presence felt during the Melbourne Cup with a march through the city in white dress uniforms to attend services at St Paul's Cathedral.[92] The parade was considered worthy of a large photograph by Melbourne's *Herald*. The RAN's numerous parades normally received positive press coverage. The 1936 RAN parade was glowingly described: 'With pipe-clayed caps gleaming and bayonets flashing in the strong sunlight', the evening *Herald* reported, 'a brigade of the Royal Australian Navy passed through the city today on a post-Cup march'.[93] Yes, the sister tabloid opined the next morning, 'They made a fine showing'.[94]

The RAN's greatest public performance was at the 1934 Victorian Centenary celebration when, for a week, the RAN provided a demonstration of naval history and prowess. The life and death of Captain Cook was theatrically portrayed, and the defeat of the

Spanish Armada was re-enacted most impressively with full-size replicas.[95] The Battle of Trafalgar was also recreated, and the Pageant concluded with recreations of the birth of the RAN, the first convoy in the Great War, and HMAS *Sydney* sinking the German raider *Emden*. The *Herald* went so far as to describe the pageant as 'educational', so overwhelmed was the reporter by 'the sight of illuminated frigates and barques sailing through the blackness'.[96] The naval presence at the centenary celebrations also included visits by foreign warships from six foreign nations and the arrival of the Duke of York on HMS *Sussex*.[97]

The RAN was clearly aware of the importance of its vessels' arrival as 'Their spic and span appearance made the ships the centre of attraction at Port Melbourne'.[98] Large photographs of the fleet's arrival were carried in the tabloid press.[99] The arrival of the fleet also provided the press with opportunities for human interest stories, from the disappearance of a ship's pet tortoise[100] to descriptions of 'hundred of sweethearts and wives [who] were down on Prince's Pier early today to greet the Australian Squadron which came in with all flags flying and bands playing'.[101]

All of these events provided the RAN with an opportunity to impress the political elite with the value of their service and the Singapore strategy. They also helped ensure that the RAN remained the preferred service. The Army and the RAAF rarely held such impressive social functions and their uniforms lacked the RAN's braid or stylish cut at civilian functions. There was no Army or RAAF equivalent to the Navy League.

By contrast with the RAN, Army officers were rarely mentioned in Melbourne Cup social columns. General Lavarack, Chief of the General Staff 1935–39, appears to have attended only one Melbourne Cup ball during the entire inter-war period.[102] The Army and RAAF failed to hold any public displays during the social season. In 1927, the Army was the only service not represented at the Governor General's House Party.[103] On the few occasions when Army officers attended such functions they were almost invariably in civilian attire. Army and RAAF officers were conspicuously absent from media accounts.

The Army, which was constantly attempting to change government policy, did not enjoy good relations with the political elite and lacked public support. Unlike the British Army, the men in the Australian Army's senior ranks were predominantly of lower-middle-class origins having joined the Army because it offered secure employment.[104] Consequently, they rarely mixed socially with the political and industrial elites. They were not schooled in the social graces and more than one flirted with extreme politics.[105]

The Army elite also failed to make use of one of its most potent means for inter-elite communication, the Citizen Military Forces (CMF), because intra-elite communication within the Army was poor. The CMF's middle-ranking officers were 'likely to be doctors, lawyers, and accountants',[106] and thus probably more politically connected and astute. They might have had contact or even have been associated with other elites, but 'Permanent staff showed little patience toward most citizen soldiers'.[107] Regular Army officers viewed their CMF counterparts with disdain. General Sir John Monash had not been appointed Inspector General following the Great War in part because the Army Board objected to the prospect of being outranked by a CMF officer.[108] The regular Army's attitude was unfortunate; regular officers were less socially skilled than their counterparts in the CMF who had more social experience with the industrial and political elite.

CMF officers were unimpressed with their professional counterparts. Army Headquarters in Melbourne was 'derisively known as the Hindenburg Line' to CMF officers owing to the difficulty CMF personnel experienced attempting to influence Army policy.[109] The Army elite was determined to ensure that it remained a regular Army elite. Architect and CMF Major-General Sir Charles Rosenthal complained in a letter to the Minister of Defence that the CMF 'has to accept the policy laid down and carry it out without having a voice in its preparation'.[110] Thorby replied three months later, and almost certainly on Army elite advice, that he had carefully considered Rosenthal's letter but had 'reached the same conclusion as my predecessor'.[111] Rosenthal had been a Nationalist member of the New South Wales Legislative Assembly (1922–25) and Legislative

Council (1936–37). His political experience in New South Wales and his subsequent appointment as Administrator of Norfolk Island in 1937 indicates a CMF officer intimate with the political elite.[112] He was ignored by the Army's elite.

Gordon Bennett, a civilian accountant, was scathing in his treatment of the regular army. Bennett had risen to the rank of Major in the CMF before the Great War, and ended the war 'the youngest brigadier in any army of the British Empire'.[113] He firmly believed that CMF officers should be given preferential treatment, arguing in Sydney's *Sunday Sun* that 'Experience has proved that citizen officers can handle our Citizen Army more efficiently than permanent officers'.[114] The army elite disagreed vehemently and wanted to court-martial Bennett.[115] Bennett avoided court martial but was prohibited from writing any more articles.

The failure to use the CMF meant public relations were all important as the Army's contacts with the elite were restricted. The Army's attempts at broader public relations were however unimpressive. The Army's Tattoo at the 1934 Victorian Centenary paled in comparison with the Naval Pageant. It received minimal press coverage for it lasted only one day, whereas the RAN's pageant had lasted an entire week.[116] The Army's lack of social standing was further demonstrated when the Melbourne Club, the club of the social elite—especially those with landed pastoral holdings—refused General Brudenell White's request to hold an Anzac Dinner in 1935. The Club argued that it 'would be entirely against the Committee's and the Club's inclinations' even though White was a former Club president.[117] The Club had hosted several dinners for Army Generals in the immediate aftermath of the First World War. However, Birdwood, Chauvel and Monash were apparently not members of Melbourne's most important club, which would have been of unquestioned value when preparing budgetary requests, as until 1927 Parliament met within blocks of the Club and many politicians were members.[118]

The establishment of the Royal Military College (RMC) in Canberra ensured that professional officers were socially isolated. There was little interaction between cadets and civilians, and certainly not between cadets and the political elite, which was

Canberra's sole elite. Duntroon's cadets lacked family connections with the political or industrial elite, for Australian elite families did not send their sons into the military at the same rate as British parents.[119] Attempts to recruit cadets from the 'Great Public Schools' were unsuccessful.[120] Duntroon's Commandant lamented that the cadets were 'seldom up to that of a good leaving pass'.[121] Cadets were generally from independent schools, but as Coulthard-Clark noted, these schools were not the better ones.[122]

The RAAF enjoyed somewhat higher prestige than the Army but it was so small that its ability to influence the political or industrial elite was minimal. The RAAF's small size meant that its performance at the 1934 Centenary Celebrations in Melbourne had to include the members of a civilian aero club.[123] Any RAAF interaction with the political elite was to ensure it remained an independent service. There was no RAAF presence in Canberra until 1940.[124] In 1930 the RAAF consisted of only 104 officers and 782 other ranks, and the Scullin Government soon shrank the RAAF even more.[125] It was largely composed of part-time pilots serving in the Citizen Air Force (CAF) and the CAF had the air of a social club, attracting the sons of state governors and even Prime Minister Lyons.[126] CAF pilots, however, averaged only 15 flying hours a month.[127]

The RAAF's status as a new service ensured political curiosity but not governmental support. The RAAF's want of professionalism was severely criticised in the 1928 Salmond Report. Air Marshal Sir John Salmond noted that the RAAF was unable to undertake bombing, reconnaissance and fleet or army co-operation.[128] Attempts by the RAAF to demonstrate its value to the political elite by crop dusting and making aerial surveys—even of fish—were often dreadful failures.[129] An attempt to fly a seaplane to Samoa was completed only after the plane was repaired in Rabaul—at a Japanese-owned shipyard.[130] A 1934 strategic exercise was halted when it became apparent that the RAAF was unable to protect Port Moresby from an invasion or stop a mock Japanese invasion fleet heading for Queensland.[131]

The lack of sufficient flying time coupled with a devil-may-care attitude produced a dreadful safety record, although the RAAF rarely reprimanded pilots for reckless behaviour.[132] The former RAF Chief of Air Staff, Sir Edward Ellington, noted in his 1938 report that the RAAF's accident rate was 'definitely worse than in the United Kingdom'.[133] There were frequent crashes which often killed RAAF aircrew.[134] Some of the RAAF's accidents were spectacular, such as the 1927 crash at the grand opening of Parliament House in Canberra which did nothing to ingratiate the RAAF with the political elite.[135] The RAAF had been quick to claim that it believed in 'Safety First', asserting that the type of plane involved in the accident was 'considered to be the safest' flying in Australia.[136] Such statements could not disguise the fact that the aircraft of Australia's exceedingly small RAAF were obsolete.

THE INDUSTRIAL ELITE

The industrial elite did not have a common position on defence or foreign policy either, although their members were deeply affected by international developments and should therefore have played a key role in defining an effective Australian defence policy. The industrial elite, crucial if Australia was to meet its Imperial defence obligation of self-sufficiency 'in terms of materiel at all levels except for the heaviest equipment',[137] was poorly placed to take part in Australian defence. Australia's industrial sector consisted of a large number of concerns, 'by and large, very small operations using primitive and outmoded machinery, lacking financial collateral'.[138] Furthermore, few in the industrial elite had military experience, only 10 (16.3%) having served in the military. The industrial elite was primarily concerned with preserving their own interests, a time-consuming preoccupation. There is no indication that any member of the industrial elite or the political elite realised the key role assigned to Australian industry under Imperial defence. The industrial elite's primary concern was preserving and expanding their industries, many of which were relatively new, and unsurprisingly they were primarily concerned with making money—the primary goal of any industrialist.

Admittedly, a section of the industrial elite was greatly concerned by the lack of Australian preparedness, including Herbert Gepp of the Australian Explosives and Chemical Company and later the Zinc Corporation. He believed in publicly campaigning for a stronger defence and told the Mining and Metallurgical Institute of Australasia in 1923 that Australia must become independent in terms of defence production. Gepp argued that war meant 'mobilising means of production'.[139] Joseph Lyons, then the Premier of Tasmania, endorsed Gepp's views.[140] Gepp visited Japan in 1931 and was also alarmed by what he saw. In the mid-1930s Gepp warned that 'Australia may have to fight for its existence'.[141] Therefore, he argued, the nation must take steps to prevent attack. He believed this could best be done with a strong air force, though he also argued for a stronger army and believed that compulsory training, if not conscription, was necessary.

Gepp became more concerned about the need to rearm as European crises intensified. In July 1935 he urged the establishment of an 'economic general staff'.[142] However, neither the political elite nor his fellow industrialists responded to Gepp's pleas. Gepp may have been ignored because he advanced a long list of problems facing Australia which included

> The danger of birth control and of the declining birth rate, particularly among the higher educated sections of the community, and the higher birth rate among the improvident; our haphazard human breeding and perpetuation of the unfit and our refusal to apply sterilisation to the unfit.[143]

He listed defence as a problem only above 'the effects of malnutrition'.[144] Following the Munich crisis, Gepp wrote two articles for the *Argus* warning that

> We know or should know of the inability—at least for the next few years—of Britain to help Australia with ships or men if a European war were imminent or actual.[145]

Gepp noted that Australia could not consider itself prepared for war until the industrial elite and the unions were 'working in their own spheres side by side with the personnel directing the fighting forces'.[146]

Essington Lewis, general manager of the iron and steel manufacturer BHP, then Australia's largest company, was also worried about Australia's defence. Lewis knew many federal and state ministers, but according to his biographer took little part in politics as a private citizen until the approach of war.[147] He had a very low opinion of the ALP and during the Scullin Government imprudently let slip his view that 'A short-lived dictatorship under which ministers were appointed according to their ability would not be altogether a bad thing for Australia'.[148]

In 1934 Lewis embarked on a world tour that included Japan. The BHP director was impressed by the patriotism, energy and industriousness of the Japanese.[149] For the first time on an overseas trip, however, Lewis was not allowed to see everything he wanted to and was followed by the police wherever he went.[150] On departing, he announced 'Japan may be described as a big gun powder magazine and the people as fanatics and any day the two might connect and there will be an explosion'.[151] He warned that 'The Army and Navy will assume such tremendous proportions that the populace will be impatient to get some results'.[152] A visit to Singapore where Essington Lewis saw the nearly complete naval base 'did nothing to reassure him'.[153]

On his return to Australia, Lewis immediately committed BHP's resources to building up Australian defences and increasing its industrial capacity in those areas with military applications. He decided that BHP ore carriers would be constructed in Australia to ensure a domestic shipbuilding capability. In addition, Lewis had BHP stockpile iron ore and other strategic raw materials.[154] Pig iron, however, was not stockpiled and BHP continued to export it to Japan to finance BHP's other defence preparations.[155] Lewis did not publicly campaign for a stronger Australian defence, believing that the Government would soon grasp how dire the situation was and also realise that BHP was well placed to satisfy government rearmament demands.

Lewis was the most important industrialist to advocate stronger defence, but he did not appeal to the wider public or to his fellow industrialists.[156] He and Gepp were exceptions among Australian industrialists. Gepp's ability to influence his fellow industrialists was further reduced by his leaving the Collins House Group,[157] which along with BHP 'dominated manufacturing development throughout the period between the wars'.[158]

Peter Cochrane observes that BHP and the Collins House Group, while separate entities, 'were far more interdependent than their financial and administrative separateness indicated'.[159] The Collins House Group was composed of the key Australian businessmen whose economic power had been markedly increased by the Great War that had 'engendered the demand that launched the metals and engineering industries'.[160] W.L. Baillieu, a Melbourne financier, was the Group's primary point of contact with the political elite.[161] He knew many state and federal politicians well, but approached the political elite only 'when politics and Group business overlapped'.[162] The Collins House Group's primary objective was 'risk minimization' which ensured that their interest in defence policy was minimal.[163] Risk minimisation ensured that the Collins House Group 'did not move hastily into a wide-range of manufacturing in Australia'.[164] Unfortunately, this prudence, though financially sound, did not assist Australia's defence forces. The industrial elite faced the added problem that 'depression in the manufacturing sector was evident as early in 1927', weakening the industrial base needed to build up the nation's defences.[165]

The Melbourne Chamber of Commerce took little note of Asian affairs or of Lewis' and Gepp's warnings. A proposal by Alexander Clifford Vernon Melbourne of the University of Queensland to take members of the Chamber on a tour of Japan, Korea and Manchuria was cancelled owing to Japanese governmental indifference.[166] Neither this cancellation nor Japan's 1931 and 1937 invasions of China provoked discussion within the Chamber of Commerce.

The *Monthly Journal of the Melbourne Chamber of Commerce* reveals an industrial elite little concerned with foreign policy. Aside from reprinting an article from *The Times* on the Abyssinian crisis,[167] and the tour of Japan (that never eventuated), foreign events were not discussed.[168] The only international news stories regularly featured trade statistics and potential export markets. Stanley Melbourne Bruce was the only politician to have a speech to the

Chamber reprinted in its *Journal*, and his speech centred on trade preferences and the 1932 Ottawa Conference.[169]

The failure to develop heavy industry[170] meant that Australia could not be self-sufficient in armaments production to the level mandated by Imperial defence. Throughout the inter-war period primary production was always the largest component of the nation's GDP. While manufactured goods never reached 19% of GDP, primary production never fell below 19% and was normally between a quarter and a fifth of Australian GDP.[171] Australia was therefore heavily reliant on imported steel which was essential in most defence industries.[172] The Great War had 'launched the metals and engineering industries',[173] but the Australian market was too small to support a viable steel industry without extremely high tariffs—there was no opportunity to export Australian steel.[174] Economic historians Pat Brown and Helen Hughes have observed that 'The iron and steel industry [was] unable to compete with imports throughout the 1920s, and many steel products continued to be at a disadvantage until the Second World War'.[175] 'Repetitive slumps and world overproduction' plagued Australian metal industries throughout the inter-war period,[176] and metal industries were a crucial element in defence industries.

Risk minimisation also ensured that the Australian industrial elite responded unfavourably to early attempts to establish an aviation industry in Australia. Occasionally defence force figures attempted to influence major industrialists in defence matters. In October 1933 RAAF Wing Commander A.T. Cole visited Lewis to urge him to create 'a new company to manufacture planes', but Lewis demurred.[177] An attempt by the RAAF a few months later to convince Laurence Hartnett of General Motors Holden to enter aviation production, as its American parent company was doing, also failed.[178] Lewis eventually changed his opinion of aviation and would persuade Hartnett to support aviation production.

The industrial elite was not entrepreneurial[179] and was reluctant to embark on new technologies such as aviation. Therefore a proposal by the world's largest maker of commercial aircraft, Douglas Aviation Corporation, for an Australian factory was met with indifference in industrial and political circles.[180] *The Australasian Manufacturer: Special Industrial Annual* lists only two companies concerned with aviation.[181] Neither of these companies was large or had significant defence potential. Having been formed to defend its members' financial position, the Collins House Group was inherently inward-looking. It was not a body designed for risks or business gambles. Consequently, the industrial elite was unwilling to urge radical changes in governmental policy, especially if that policy did not directly benefit them. Members of the industrial elite were concerned primarily with making money, and less interested in strengthening Australian industry or aiding Australia's defence position.[182] They were particularly supportive of high tariffs which they saw as a means to enhance profits. When one considers that 'The presence of large numbers of small producers is the most distinctive feature of the scale of manufacturing in Australia between the wars',[183] their focus on their own bottom line is understandable.

***

Elites were and are crucial for the development of defence policy. For elites to function well, however, they need to be integrated, a process facilitated by sociometric ties, a truly national capital and common educational backgrounds. Certainly Australia's small and scattered population meant the elites were not closely integrated. The nation's new national capital was too recent, isolated and empty to facilitate inter-elite or even intra-elite communication. The military elite was unable to come to a common position on the preferred defence for Australia while the industrial elite was focused almost exclusively on the bottom line. The political elite was forced to respond to the Great Depression while still divided and reacting to the Great War. Consequently, Australia's political, military and industrial elites lacked a common outlook.

These facts prevented a clear appreciation of the dangers facing the nation and the need for local defence to complement the Singapore strategy. Rather than encouraging inter-elite communication, the elites' smallness may have made them more insular and contributed to the lack of inter-elite communication that accompanied divergent social, educational, religious and military backgrounds. The 1927 move to Canberra only served to further isolate the various elites from each other and this insularity ensured that Australian defence and foreign policy was uninformed. Ultimately, the political, military and industrial elites were primarily accountable for Australia's lack of defence preparedness. This analysis renders hollow the notion that Britain was somehow responsible for Australia's lamentable defence position. The Australian elites were too insular to adequately appreciate and communicate the risks Australia faced as the international situation deteriorated in the 1930s.

CHAPTER 9

CONCLUSION

Erle Cox's 1939 novel *Fool's Harvest* described an Asian invasion of Australia following the destruction of the Royal Navy at Singapore. Sydney suffered several intense air raids and a prolonged naval bombardment. The RAN was destroyed at the quayside on 'Bloody Sunday'[1] and with the entire population of Sydney 'either dead, injured or panic stricken',[2] the invader landed near Port Stephens virtually unopposed and rapidly advanced inland taking no prisoners and slaughtering civilians. That these events never occurred is perhaps a moot point. The Australian Government in 1942 certainly believed that invasion was imminent and it is clear that Australia was a highly vulnerable and defenceless target had an aggressor chosen to pursue it.

The Road to Singapore has demonstrated that Australia was unprepared for the Pacific War and for the invasion feared both by the Australian public and Government. Australian unpreparedness cannot be blamed on British betrayal. Australia's defence and foreign policies had complex origins but their shortcomings were mainly Australian in origin. Imperial defence and the Singapore strategy were misunderstood during the inter-war period. Imperial defence did not mean that the Royal Navy would protect Australia come what may, and it did not mean that the Singapore naval base was the key component of Australia's local defence as Curtin claimed.[3] A thorough understanding of Imperial defence would have prevented over-reliance on the Royal Navy and precluded any notion of betrayal. It is possible to argue that Britain betrayed Australia only if one does not appreciate the nuances of Imperial defence.

Australia's key political, military and industrial elites were wholly responsible for shaping Australian defence and foreign policy and are the primary reason that Australia was so unprepared for the outbreak of war. These elites—fragmented, self-centred and uncommunicative—misunderstood Imperial defence and were largely focused on serving their own interests at the expense of understanding developments in Europe, Asia and the Pacific and their relevance to Australia's future. Their failure to understand Imperial defence fully ensured Australia's impotence in the international arena and meant that successive governments were poorly placed to assess the scale, form or likelihood of an attack by Japan on the Australian continent.

The inability of the elites to agree on Australia's vulnerability and defence sprang, at least in part, from a failure to appreciate the significance of the rise of fascism in Italy and Spain, Nazism in Germany and Japanese militarism, all of which embarked on expansionist and aggressive policies that threatened to lead to European and Asian wars. In spite of numerous attempts by concerned citizens, the Australian Government and public failed to appreciate the significance of the major inter-war international crises. There was both a failure of imagination, and a failure to appreciate the dangers posed to Australia by events around the world. The warnings that did emanate were too diverse, fragmented and inconsistent to be a prescription for Australian defence policy. However, they did at least indicate the potential threat Australia faced.

The failure of the elites to appreciate the dangers Australia faced was exacerbated by Australian domestic politics. Australian political parties had a major effect on Australian defence policy and the ALP, although in opposition for most of the inter-war period, had a significant role in shaping Australian policy, albeit mainly a negative one. The ALP's anti-conscriptionist past and pacifist and isolationist leanings ensured it objected to increased defence spending and non-isolationist foreign policies. These conditions made an already cautious and conservative Government even more cautious and conservative, and negated the need for a long-term approach to defence. This caution left Australia dangerously exposed and ultimately unprepared for a war that it had to fight.

Complete self-sufficiency in armaments production was an impossibility owing to Australia's small industrial base and its small population. However, self-sufficiency in armaments was not required for Australia to be prepared. Imperial defence offered Australia a measure of protection, but it did not absolve Australia from taking measures to ensure its own local defence. Indeed Imperial defence required local defence, but as we have seen there was a persistent misreading and misinterpretation of Imperial defence by Australian governments and elites; they repeatedly failed to understand that Imperial defence also placed obligations on the various Dominions. Australia's obligation was not merely to provide soldiers to fight in Europe or the Middle East, but also to defend Australia until the Royal Navy could arrive in the Pacific. However, Australia's defence was reduced too drastically following the Great War for it to meet its local defence obligations, and the failure of elite communication prevented a defence build-up.

In order to meet its local defence obligations Australia needed trained men. Compulsory militia training, as had existed prior to the Great War, would have resolved the issue without—and contrary to ALP thinking—implying an aggressive intent. Even the staunchly isolationist United States initiated a peacetime draft more than a year before it entered the war. Australia only made militia service compulsory eight months after the event and there were strict limitations on where militiamen could be sent. A peacetime compulsory militia had been politically impossible in Australia, which had endured two divisive plebiscites on conscription during the Great War; the ALP remained opposed to conscription in any form—even universal training—as did UAP Prime Minister Joseph Lyons, a former ALP Minister and Treasurer.

Trained men require armaments, armaments which Australia could not produce but which Australia could have purchased and should have begun purchasing as early as the Manchurian crisis (1931), if not before. It did not. Small arms were cheaper and did not become obsolete as quickly as equipment such as aircraft, vehicles and tanks. Small arms could also have been stockpiled, so relatively small purchases throughout the inter-war period would have ensured Australia entered the Second World War with sufficient small arms to equip its defenders.

Aircraft could also have been purchased before the war began, though they could not have so easily been stockpiled owing to their increasing complexity and the risk of obsolescence. Airfields and airstrips, however, could have been prepared around the continent in preparation for war throughout the early inter-war period, which would have also supported the development of civil and commercial aviation. This would have saved the RAAF valuable time and resources in creating new facilities once war began. Large purchases of aircraft should have been made from the mid-1930s as the threat of war increased markedly. The Spanish Civil War and the Sino-Japanese War both demonstrated the effect of air raids on large cities and the need for large air forces to intercept bombing raids.

Unfortunately, however, defence was a low priority in inter-war budgets and the RAAF lacked political clout or support. Australia's aircraft purchase in the mid-1930s was subsequently 10 Hawker Demons, an outdated biplane-fighter that had originally been conceived of as a bomber, whose ability to protect Australia was minimal. More modern fighters were available at that time; Britain ordered 900 Hawker Hurricanes and Submarine Spitfires in the same year.[4] British manufacturers would have struggled to meet large British and Australian orders simultaneously, but American aircraft more modern than the Demon were available. However, when American aircraft were purchased they were merely trainers. John Curtin did propose a defence strategy based almost entirely on the RAAF, but local defence required in-depth defence, coordinated among all three services. A much enlarged RAAF required not just planes but a vast assortment of support personnel and, most importantly, trained pilots. For the part-time pilots who made up the inter-war RAAF lacked experience, were few in number and were unsuitable for serious defence purposes.

The Road to Singapore has attempted to explain why Australia misinterpreted Imperial defence and was so unprepared for the Second World War. The popular and populist assumption of a British betrayal is superficially attractive but deeply flawed. The betrayal argument excuses the failure of Australian governments to develop a system of local defence, a failure made possible by the Opposition's desire to avoid debate on defence and a general failure of imagination on the part of most of Australia's elites.

The betrayal argument remains popular, for it feeds on latent anti-British feelings and open hostility towards the British Empire. David Day, the leading proponent of the betrayal thesis, bases his criticism of Australian inter-war defence policy and of Australian wartime policies on his outright opposition to Australian participation in the Second World War. An arch Republican, Day makes much of the fact that Australia considered itself at war immediately following Britain's declaration, 'unlike Canada or South Africa where the declaration of war was left to the respective parliaments to deliberate on'.[5] The Australian declaration of war may have been unique, but the effect was not. Even though they had enacted the Statute of Westminster, every Dominion except Ireland declared war on Germany.

Day objects not just to Australia's automatic declaration of war, but to Australia's entry into the war. Recently Day asked rhetorically: 'Would the world have been a better place had Britain and France not rushed to war when Germany invaded Poland?'[6] According to Day, the obvious answer is 'yes' because 'it might have prevented a world war'[7] and also the Holocaust, because 'the total war that was fought against Germany provided the conditions that allowed the genocide to happen'.[8] Moreover, Day has blamed Churchill for wanting total war.[9] It is an absurd argument that reveals the ridiculousness of the betrayal argument. Britain is seen as betraying Australia by upholding its obligation to Poland and declaring war on the world's most horrendous regime, which we are supposed to believe became even more horrendous simply because Britain declared war on it.

According to Day, if Britain and France had allowed Hitler to seize Poland unopposed, Australia would not have been threatened because

> it would probably have ensured that Japan was not able to launch its attacks against the countries of Southeast Asia, since there could have been a British fleet at Singapore, a French fleet at Saigon and a much stronger US fleet in the Pacific.[10]

In reality it is highly unlikely that Britain would have sent its fleet around the world while a major continental war raged, even if confined to Eastern Europe. Indeed the British Chiefs of Staff had written in June 1937 that even while at peace with Germany, Britain 'must retain in home waters a fleet sufficient to neutralise the German fleet'.[11] There is no reason to think Hitler would not have attacked France and the United Kingdom even had they not declared war on Germany. Hitler attacked the Soviet Union in spite of a non-aggression pact and the Netherlands, Denmark and Norway, and in spite of those countries' declarations of neutrality. Furthermore, it should be remembered that the presence of the British and French navies in European waters did not stop Germany or Italy from attacking them.

The idea that it is preferable to do nothing and wait for other nations to defeat the aggressors fails to consider what the victors would have thought of a nation that owed its continued independence to their sacrifices—sacrifices which Australia had been unwilling to make for itself. The idea that Australia could (and can) expect a free ride from the world's major powers indicates a continuing failure to understand international relations.

If the attitude 'She'll be right' continues to dominate public and political thinking about defence, Australia runs the risk of being terribly unprepared for any future war. The Left's belief that wars can be avoided, at least by Australia, only increases the chance that Australia will be unprepared. Unpreparedness for war leads to unnecessary and higher casualties. It is not too late for the lessons of the inter-war period to be learned, but they are difficult lessons that require attention from both sides of politics and the public at large. The notions of betrayal that inform popular thinking about Australia in the Second World War do nothing to assist our understanding of the past or prepare for the future, based as they are on overly simplistic interpretations. Those with a simplistic understanding of the past are surely condemned to misunderstand the complexities of the present.

NOTES

INTRODUCTION

1 Benjamin Rhodes, 'The Image of Britain in the United States, 1919–1929', in *Anglo-American Relations in the 1920's: The Struggle for Supremacy*, ed. B.J.C. McKercher (Hampshire: Macmillan, Houndmills, Basingstoke, 1991), 194.

2 John Howard Morrow, *The Great War: An Imperial History* (London: Routledge, 2004), 285.

3 Frederick William Peabody and Frederick E. Coe, *Honour or Dollars: A Critical Examination of the Moral Obligations of America to Her Former Allies* (Sydney: Angus and Robertson, 1929), v.

4 *Ibid.*

5 Imperial Conference, *1926—Inter-Imperial Relations Committee—Report, proceedings and memoranda*, report, October–November 1926, NAA A4640/1, 32.

6 Neville Meaney, *Fears & Phobias: E.L. Piesse and the Problem of Japan* (Canberra: National Library of Australia, 1996), 27.

7 Paul Hasluck, *The Government and the People, 1939–1941*, vol. 1 of *Australia in the War of 1939–1945: Series 4, Civil* (2 vols) (Canberra: Australian War Memorial, 1952), 9–10.

8 Karl Hack and Kevin Blackburn, *Did Singapore Have to Fall? Churchill and the Impregnable Fortress* (London: Routledge Curzon, 2003), 154.

9 Stephen Howarth, *Morning Glory: A History of the Imperial Japanese Navy* (London: Arrow, 1985), 145.

10 G. Swinburne *et al.,* Recommendations by the Council of Defence, report, 1920, Papers of Sir Frederick Shedden, NAA A5954, 1209/5.

11 *Ibid.*

12 David Horner, 'Australian Army Strategic Planning between the Wars', in *Serving Vital Interests: Australia's Strategic Planning in Peace and War: Proceedings of the Australian Army History Conference Held at the Australian War Memorial, 30 September 1996*, ed. Peter Dennis and Jeffrey Grey (Canberra: Australian Defence Force Academy, 1996), 77.

13 G. Swinburne *et al.*, Recommendations by the Council of Defence.

14 *Ibid.*

15 Albert Palazzo, *The Australian Army: A History of Its Organisation 1901–2001*, Australian Army History Series (South Melbourne: Oxford University Press, 2001), 95.

16 General G.R. Campbell, 'Australian Defence Policy', in *Studies in Australian Affairs* (Melbourne: Macmillan, 1928), 180.

17 Malcolm Murfett, 'Defending Australia in 1942', *War & Society* 11, no. 1 (1993): 79-80.

18 E.M. Andrews, *The Writing on the Wall: The British Commonwealth and Aggression in the East 1931–1935* (Sydney: Allen & Unwin, 1987), 30.

19 Ian Hamill, 'An Australian Defence Policy?: The Singapore Strategy and the Defence of Australia', *Australian National University Historical Journal* 10–11 (1973–74): 15.

20 *Ibid.*

21 Australia. House of Representatives 1931, *Debates*, vol. HR132, 14 October 1931, p. 709.
22 John Robertson, *J.H. Scullin: A Political Biography* (Nedlands, WA: University of Western Australia Press, 1974), 213.
23 *Ibid.*, 216.
24 Australia. House of Representatives 1934, *Debates*, vol. HR144, 31 July 1934, p. 915.
25 Robertson, *J.H. Scullin*, 82.

PROLOGUE

1 John Curtin, 'Prime Minister's Broadcast', 24 January 1942, *Digest of Decisions and Announcements and Important Speeches by the Prime Minister*, vol. 1, no. 16 (Canberra: Commonwealth Government Printer, 1942), 12.
2 John Curtin, 'Facing 1942', 27 December 1941, *Digest of Decisions and Announcements and Important Speeches by the Prime Minister*, vol. 1, no. 13 (Canberra: Commonwealth Government Printer, 1941), 11.
3 John Curtin, 'Prime Minister's Speech to House', 16 December 1941, *Digest of Decisions and Announcements and Important Speeches by the Prime Minister*, vol. 1, no. 11 (Canberra: Commonwealth Government Printer, 1941), 19.
4 Curtin, 'Facing 1942', 11.
5 Broadcast Message by Mr. R.G. Menzies, 3 September 1939, *Documents on Australian Foreign Policy 1937–49*, ed. R.G. Neale *et al.*, vol. II, doc. 189 (Canberra: Australian Government Publishing Service, 1976), 221.
6 John Curtin, 'The Task Ahead', *Herald*, 27 December 1941, p. 10.
7 'Australia Looks to America', *Australian Worker*, 31 December 1941, p. 8.
8 Casey to Menzies, Fifth Progress Report, cable, 25 February 1941, NAA A1196/6, 12/501/59.
9 Major General S.D. Embick and Rear-Admiral R.L. Ghormley, report to Australian Legation in Washington as part of United States–British Staff Conversations, 27 March 1941, Papers of Sir Frederick Shedden, NAA A5954/69, 567/2.
10 H.E.B., 'Jap Strategy: May Be Craftily Designed to Mislead us as to Their Intention to Invade Australia', *Australian Worker*, 25 March 1942, 3.
11 John Beasley, 'Need for Support for Australia', 23 January 1942, *Digest of Decisions and Announcements and Important Speeches by the Prime Minister*, vol. 1, no. 16 (Canberra: Commonwealth Government Printer, 1942), 9 & 10.
12 John Curtin, 'Prime Minister's Broadcast', 24 January 1942, *Digest of Decisions and Announcements and Important Speeches by the Prime Minister*, vol. 1, no. 16 (Canberra: Commonwealth Government Printer, 1942), 12.
13 *Ibid.*, 15.
14 Francis Forde, 'Possibility of Invasion', 29 January 1942, *Digest of Decisions and Announcements and Important Speeches by the Prime Minister*, vol. 1, no. 16 (Canberra: Commonwealth Government Printer, 1942), 7.
15 John Curtin, 'Fall of Singapore', 16 February 1942, *Digest of Decisions and Announcements and Important Speeches by the Prime Minister*, vol. 1, no. 19 (Canberra: Commonwealth Government Printer, 1942), 7.
16 United States–British Commonwealth Joint Basic War Plan, agreement, April 1941, Papers of Sir Frederick Shedden, NAA A5954/67, 567/2.
17 John Curtin, 'Prime Minister's Speech', 17 February 1942, *Digest of Decisions and Announcements and Important Speeches by the Prime Minister*, vol. 1, no. 18 (Canberra: Commonwealth Government Printer, 1942), 6.
18 David Horner, *Defence Supremo: Sir Frederick Shedden and the Making of Australian Defence Policy* (Sydney: Allen & Unwin, 2000), 137.
19 Quoted in David Day, *The Politics of War* (Sydney: Harper Collins, 2003), 270. He does not provide the source.
20 *Ibid.*, 269.

21 John Curtin, 'Attack on Darwin', 19 February 1942, *Digest of Decisions and Announcements and Important Speeches by the Prime Minister,* vol. 1, no. 19 (Canberra: Commonwealth Government Printer, 1942), 9.
22 Henry Frei, *Japan's Southward Advance and Australia: From Sixteenth Century to World War II* (Honolulu: University of Hawaii Press, 1991), 133.
23 John Curtin, 'Relations with America', 14 March 1942, *Digest of Decisions and Announcements and Important Speeches by the Prime Minister,* vol. 1, no. 22 (Canberra: Commonwealth Government Printer, 1942), 12.
24 *Ibid.*
25 John Curtin, 'Prime Minister's Broadcast', 17 June 1942, *Digest of Decisions and Announcements and Important Speeches by the Prime Minister*, vol. 2, no. 32 (Canberra: Commonwealth Government Printer, 1942), 11.
26 Henry Frei, *Japan's Southward Advance and Australia: From Sixteenth Century to World War II* (Honolulu: University of Hawaii Press, 1991), 149.
27 Peter Stanley, 'The Invasion that Wasn't', *Wartime: Official Magazine of the Australian War Memorial,* Issue 19 (July 2002): 7.
28 Graham Freudenberg, *Churchill and Australia* (Sydney: Macmillan, 2008), 359.
29 For example, Geoffrey Grey, observing that the Pacific war exposed 'the inability of the British to defend Australia, and the necessity for Australians to defend themselves', maintains: 'Despite two years of war Australia was in no way prepared for the Japanese onslaught when it came, and the legacy of inter-war neglect was paid for by young militiamen, poorly trained and equipped, in New Guinea in 1942.' Furthermore, Australian survival of the 1941–42 emergency 'owed nothing to the defence preparations of the preceding twenty years'. Geoffrey Grey, *A Military History of Australia,* 3rd ed. (Melbourne: Cambridge University Press, 2008), 165.
30 Mr John Curtin, Prime Minister, to Mr Winston Churchill, U.K. Prime Minister, Cablegram Johcu 21, 23 January 1942, in *Documents on Australian Foreign Policy 1937–49,* ed. W.J. Hudson *et al.*, vol. V, doc. 293 (Canberra: Australian Government Publishing Service, 1982), 463.
31 The historiography of Australian elites is discussed in chapter 8.

CHAPTER 1 **UNARMED AND UNREADY**

1 Andrew Ross, 'The Arming of Australia: The Politics and Administration of Australia's Self Containment Strategy for Munitions Supply 1901–1945' (PhD diss., University of New South Wales, Australian Defence Forces Academy, 1986), 1.
2 Andrew Ross, *Armed and Ready: The Industrial Development & Defence of Australia, 1900–1945* (Sydney: Turton & Armstrong, 1995), 280.
3 J.K. Jensen, Chapter 10 in 'Defence Production in Australia: Planning for Total War—1938–1940', unpublished 1964, NAA MP956/2 Box 6.
4 Lionel Wigmore, *The Japanese Thrust*, vol. 4 of *Australia in the War of 1939–1945: Series 1, Army* (7 vols) (Canberra: Australian War Memorial, 1957), 114.
5 Stephen Howarth, *Morning Glory: A History of the Imperial Japanese Navy* (London: Arrow, 1985), 382.
6 C. Hartley Grattan, *Introducing Australia* (New York: John Day, 1942).
7 Henry Frei, *Japan's Southward Advance and Australia: From Sixteenth Century to World War II* (Honolulu: University of Hawaii Press, 1991), 149.
8 *Ibid.*, 161.
9 David Horner, 'Australian Estimates of the Japanese Threat, 1905–1941', in *Estimating Foreign Military Power*, ed. Philip Towle (London: Croom Helm, 1982), 165.
10 Frei, *Japan's Southward Advance and Australia*, 163.
11 *Ibid.*
12 *Ibid.*, 164.

13 Lieutenant-General Sir H.G. Chauvel *et al.*, Report on the Military Defence of Australia by a Conference of Senior Officers of the Australian Military Forces, report, 22 January – 6 February 1920, Papers of Sir Frederick Shedden, NAA A5954/69, 797/1.
14 Army, Overseas Plan 401, plan, 1923–1926, NAA MP826/1, 54 Copy 30.
15 Frei, *Japan's Southward Advance and Australia*, 109.
16 Defence Committee, War in the Pacific—appreciation by Defence Committee, appreciation, 1928, NAA MP1185/8, 1846/363.
17 Karl Hack and Kevin Blackburn, *Did Singapore Have to Fall? Churchill and the Impregnable Fortress* (London: Routledge Curzon, 2003), 32.
18 Army, Strategic Concentration Formation Areas, plan, 1929, AWM 54, 243/6/159.
19 *Ibid.*
20 *Ibid.*
21 Lieutenant-Colonel V.A.H. Sturdee, Lecture on the Plan of Concentration, lecture, 1933, AWM 54, 243/6/150.
22 *Ibid.*
23 David Horner, 'Australian Army Strategic Planning between the Wars', in *Serving Vital Interests: Australia's Strategic Planning in Peace and War: Proceedings of the Australian Army History Conference Held at the Australian War Memorial, 30 September 1996*, ed. Peter Dennis and Jeffrey Grey (Canberra: Australian Defence Force Academy, 1996), 88.
24 *Ibid.*
25 Paul Burns, *The Brisbane Line Controversy: Political Opportunism Versus National Security, 1942–45, Army Military History Series. Issues* (St Leonards, NSW: Allen & Unwin, 1998), 27.
26 Lieutenant-Colonel V.A.H. Sturdee, Lecture on the Plan of Concentration, lecture, 1933, AWM 54, 243/6/150.
27 *Ibid.*
28 Army Board, Appreciation—The Concentration of the Australian Land Forces in Time of War, appreciation, 6 January 1931, AWM 54, 243/6/6.
29 Horner, 'Australian Estimates of the Japanese Threat', 148.
30 *Ibid.*
31 J.H. Bruche, Memorandum by the Chief of the General Staff on report on certain aspects of Australian defence, memorandum 1935, Papers of the Cabinet, Public Records Office (London), PRO CAB 21/397.
32 Horace Robertson, The Defence of Australia, draft article, April 1935, Papers of Sir Frederick Shedden, NAA A5954/69, 1025/6.
33 Chief of the Naval Staff, The Invasion Bogey, minute paper, 14 February 1935, Papers of Sir Frederick Shedden, NAA A5954, 1018/7.
34 *Ibid.*
35 Vice Admiral G.F. Hyde, Australian Defence Policy, memorandum, 3 April 1935, Papers of the Cabinet, Public Records Office (London), PRO CAB 21/397.
36 *Ibid.*
37 Ernle Chatfield, C.J. Deverell and E.L. Ellington, Report on 1937 Imperial Conference relating to questions raised by Australian delegation, report, 10 December 1937, Papers of the Cabinet, Public Records Office (London), PRO CAB 21/2525.
38 *Ibid.*
39 *Ibid.*
40 *Ibid.*
41 *Ibid.*
42 *Ibid.*
43 Tota Ishimaru, *Japan Must Fight Britain*, trans. G.V. Rayment (London: Hurst & Blackett, 1936).
44 Horner, 'Australian Estimates of the Japanese Threat', 150.

45 Chiefs of Staff, War in the Pacific. Defence of Australia and adjacent areas—Chiefs of Staff Appreciation, appreciation, December 1941, Papers of Sir Frederick Shedden, NAA A5954/69, 555/10.

46 David Horner, *Defence Supremo: Sir Frederick Shedden and the Making of Australian Defence Policy* (Sydney: Allen & Unwin, 2000), 35.

47 Chiefs of Staff, War in the Pacific. Defence of Australia and adjacent areas—Chiefs of Staff Appreciation, appreciation, December 1941, Papers of Sir Frederick Shedden, NAA A5954/69, 555/10.

48 *Ibid.*

49 John Beasley, 'Need for Support for Australia', 23 January 1942, *Digest of Decisions and Announcements and Important Speeches by the Prime Minister,* vol. 1, no. 16 (Canberra: Commonwealth Government Printer, 1942), 9.

50 H.V. Evatt, 'External Affairs Statement', 25 February 1942, *Digest of Decisions and Announcements and Important Speeches by the Prime Minister,* vol. 1, no. 20 (Canberra: Commonwealth Government Printer, 1942), 11.

51 Peter Stanley, 'The Invasion That Wasn't', *Wartime*, July 2002, p. 8.

52 Chiefs of Staff, The Defence of Australia Following the Collapse of the Malay Barrier, appreciation, 27 February 1942, Papers of Sir Frederick Shedden, NAA A5954/69, 769/7.

53 Chiefs of Staff, War in the Pacific. Defence of Australia and adjacent areas—Chiefs of Staff Appreciation, appreciation, December 1941, NAA A5954/69, 555/10.

54 Craig Wilcox, *For Hearths and Homes: Citizen Soldiering in Australia, 1854–1945* (St Leonards, NSW: Allen & Unwin, 1998), 86.

55 *Ibid.*, 93.

56 Geoffrey Whiskard to Malcolm MacDonald (Secretary of State for Dominion Affairs), letter, 7 May 1936, PRO DO35/182/6.

57 Horace Robertson, 'The Defence of Australia', article, April 1935, Papers of Sir Frederick Shedden, NAA A5954/69, 1025/6.

58 Maurice Hankey to Sir General Archibald A. Montgomery-Massingberd (Chief of the Imperial General Staff), letter, 31 January 1935, Papers of the Cabinet, Public Records Office (London), PRO CAB 21/386.

59 Peter Dennis *et al.*, 'Citizen Military Forces (CMF)', in *The Oxford Companion to Australian Military History*, ed. Peter Dennis (Melbourne: Oxford University Press, 2008), 133.

60 Robert Menzies, *Prime Minister on War Programme* (Canberra: Government Printer, 1940), 17.

61 Philip Hart, 'J.A. Lyons: A Political Biography' (PhD diss., Australian National University, 1967), 248.

62 Geoffrey Whiskard, British High Commissioner in Canberra, to Malcolm MacDonald, Secretary of State for Dominion Affairs, letter, 7 May 1936, PRO DO35/182/6.

63 'Where Australia Lies Open to Attack', *Herald*, 25 September 1933.

64 Laurence Frederic Fitzhardinge, *The Little Digger, 1914–1952: William Morris Hughes, a Political Biography*, vol. 2 (Sydney: Angus & Robertson, 1979), 649.

65 Will Donald, 'Voluntary Enlistment', *Australian Worker*, 16 November 1938, p. 11.

66 H.E.B., 'Why the Unions Won't Help Lyons to Implement His 'Defence' Policy', *Australian Worker*, 20 July 1938, p. 1.

67 Wilcox, *For Hearths and Homes*, 104.

68 Dudley McCarthy, *South-West Pacific Area—First Year: Kokoda to Wau* (Canberra: Australian War Memorial, 1959), 11.

69 Albert Palazzo, *The Australian Army: A History of Its Organisation 1901–2001*, Australian Army History Series (South Melbourne: Oxford University Press, 2001), 148.

70 *Ibid.*

71 Australian Army, Australian Army Unit Training Assessment, report, July 1942, NAA MP729/6, 42/401/142.

72 David Horner, *The Gunners: A History of Australian Artillery* (St Leonards, NSW: Allen & Unwin, 1995), 191.
73 Robert Rayner, *The Darwin Detachment* (Wollongong: Rudder Press, 2002), 159.
74 Minutes of War Cabinet Meeting, 13 June 1940, War Cabinet Minutes, vol. 2, NAA A2673/1.
75 Horner, *The Gunners*, 189.
76 *Ibid.*, 289.
77 *Ibid.*,, 207.
78 *Ibid.*, 289.
79 *Ibid.*, 303.
80 Australia. House of Representatives 1934, Debates, vol. HR144, 31 July 1934, p. 915.
81 Horner, 'Australian Army Strategic Planning between the Wars', 93.
82 Henry Chauvel and T.W. Glasgow, Local Defence of Australian Ports, report, May 1927, NAA B197/0, 1856/4/592.
83 Douglas Gillison, *Royal Australian Air Force, 1939–42*, vol. 1 of *Australia in the War of 1939–1945: Series 3, Air* (4 vols) (Canberra: Australian War Memorial, 1954), 11.
84 C.D. Coulthard-Clark, *The Third Brother: The Royal Australian Air Force 1921–39* (North Sydney: Allen & Unwin, 1991), 9.
85 *Ibid.*, 184.
86 Chiefs of Staff, War in the Pacific. Defence of Australia and adjacent areas—Chiefs of Staff Appreciation, appreciation, December 1941, NAA A5954/69, 555/10.
87 *Ibid.*
88 Coulthard-Clark, *The Third Brother*, 448.
89 Gillison, *Royal Australian Air Force, 1939–42*, 739.
90 *Ibid.*, 719.
91 *Ibid.*, 354.
92 Coulthard-Clark, *The Third Brother*, 455.
93 Chiefs of Staff, War in the Pacific. Defence of Australia and adjacent areas—Chiefs of Staff Appreciation, appreciation, December 1941, Papers of Sir Frederick Shedden, NAA A5954/69, 555/10.
94 Rayner, *The Darwin Detachment*, 13.
95 Committee of Imperial Defence, Defence of Ports at Home and Abroad—Australian Ports, 1925, NAA MP826/1, 6.
96 Frei, *Japan's Southward Advance and Australia*, 132.
97 *Ibid.*
98 Gillison, *Royal Australian Air Force, 1939–42*, 715–16.
99 John Robertson, *Australia at War 1939–1945* (Melbourne: Heinemann, 1981), 102.
100 Peter Grose, *A Very Rude Awakening: The Night the Japanese Midget Subs Came to Sydney Harbour* (Sydney: Allen & Unwin, 2007), 6.
101 Horner, *The Gunners*, 307.
102 Grose, *A Very Rude Awakening*, 149.
103 *Ibid.*, 216.
104 *Ibid.*, 215.
105 *Ibid.*, 149.
106 *Ibid.*, 5.
107 Joseph Lyons, Re-armament is a long process, speech, November 1938, Papers of Sir Frederick Shedden, NAA A5954/69, 1090/2.
108 B.N Primrose, 'Equipment and Naval Policy 1919–1942', *Australian Journal of Politics and History* 23, no. 2 (1977): 163.
109 Ross, 'The Arming of Australia', 385.
110 Andrew Ross, 'The Rise of Australian Defence Industry and Science 1901–1945', in *Arming the Nation*, ed. Frank Cain (Canberra: Australian Defence Studies Centre, 1999), 24.
111 'Behind the Guns: Making Munitions in Australia', *Castlemaine Mail*, 9 March 1934, p. 1.

112 *Ibid.*
113 Joan Beaumont, *Australian Defence: Sources and Statistics, The Australian Centenary History of Defence* (Melbourne: Oxford University Press, 2001), 30. MSB funding was never more than 9% in any year between 1920/21 and 1938/39, usually less and more commonly 6–7%. In the period 1922–24 the MSB received nothing.
114 Sydney James Butlin, *War Economy 1939–1942* (Canberra: Australian War Memorial, 1955), 351.
115 Robertson, *Australia at War 1939–1945*, 266.
116 Chiefs of Staff, War in the Pacific. Defence of Australia and adjacent areas—Chiefs of Staff Appreciation, appreciation, December 1941, Papers of Sir Frederick Shedden, NAA A5954/69, 555/10.
117 *Ibid.*
118 Ross, *Armed and Ready*, 50.
119 C.D. Coulthard-Clark, *Breaking Free: Transforming Australia's Defence Industry* (Melbourne: Australian Scholarly Publishing, 1999), 28.
120 J.H. Bruche, Memorandum by the Chief of the General Staff on Report on Certain Aspects of Australian Defence, memorandum, 1935, Papers of the Cabinet, Public Records Office (London), PRO CAB 21/397.
121 Ross, *Armed and Ready*, 352.
122 Even Ross concedes this: see *ibid.*, 29.
123 Ross, *Armed and Ready*, 228.
124 Essington Lewis to Frederick Shedden (Secretary of the Department of Defence), letter, 17 March 1938, Papers of Sir Frederick Shedden, NAA A5954/69, 913/1.
125 Geoffrey Blainey, *Jumping over the Wheel* (St Leonards, NSW: Allen & Unwin, 1993), 171.
126 Beaumont, *Australian Defence: Sources and Statistics*, 30.
127 E.M. Andrews, *Australia and China: The Ambiguous Relationship* (Melbourne: Melbourne University Press, 1985), 66.
128 Coulthard-Clark, *Breaking Free*, 29.
129 Australia. House of Representatives 1933, Debates, vol. HR141, 4 October 1933, p. 3220.
130 Butlin, *War Economy 1939–1942*, 1.
131 Australia. House of Representatives 1933, Debates, vol. HR142, 16 November 1933, p. 4715.
132 *Ibid.*, p. 4716.
133 *Ibid.*, p. 4718.
134 Australia. House of Representatives 1933, Debates, vol. HR141, 6 October 1933, p. 3385.
135 Australia. House of Representatives 1933, Debates, vol. HR141, 17 November 1933, p. 4741.
136 Carl Bridge, 'Appeasement and After: Towards a Re-Assessment of the Lyons and Menzies Governments' Defence and Foreign Policies 1931–41', *Australian Journal of Politics and History* 51, no. 3 (2005): 337.
137 Australia. House of Representatives 1937, Debates, vol. HR154, 25 August 1937, p. 104.
138 *Ibid.*
139 Coulthard-Clark, *The Third Brother*, 180.
140 Australia. House of Representatives 1937, Debates, vol. HR154, 25 August 1937, p. 113.
141 Paul Hasluck, *The Government and the People, 1939–1941*, vol. 1 of *Australia in the War of 1939–1945: Series 4, Civil* (2 vols) (Canberra: Australian War Memorial, 1952), 73.
142 United Australia Party, 'New Defence Programme: Increased Expenditure of Nearly 25 Millions', *United Australia Party Monthly Bulletin* III, no. 2 (1938): 19.
143 Joseph Lyons, 'Defence of Australia: New Programme of National Defence', radio broadcast script, April 1938, Papers of the Cabinet, Public Records Office (London), PRO CAB 21/2526.
144 Beaumont, *Australian Defence: Sources and Statistics*, 30.

145 Hasluck, *The Government and the People, 1939–1941*, 102.
146 Andrew May, 'Fortress Australia', in *Between Empire and Nation: Australia's External Relations from Federation to the Second World War*, ed. Carl Bridge and Bernard Attard (Melbourne: Australian Scholarly Publishing, 2000), 218.
147 W.F.A., 'Some Problems That Demand Attention but Joseph Lyons Says Not a Word About Them', *Australian Worker*, 26 October 1938, 1.
148 George Jones, *From Private to Air Marshal: The Autobiography of Air Marshal Sir George Jones KB CB DFC* (Melbourne: Greenhouse, 1988), 35.
149 Coulthard-Clark, *The Third Brother*, 174.
150 Hasluck, *The Government and the People, 1939–1941*, 43. It would have been uneconomic for the government to have sponsored an aviation industry earlier than 1936.
151 Archdale Parkhill, Aircraft Manufacture in Australia, Department of Defence Minute Paper, July 1935, Papers of Sir Frederick Shedden, NAA A5954/69, 873/1.
152 Stewart Wilson, 'Glory Days: Australian Aircraft Production in WWII', *Aero Australia*, January–March 2004, 41.
153 Archdale Parkhill, Aircraft Manufacture in Australia, Department of Defence Minute Paper, July 1935.
154 United Australia Party, 'Aircraft Manufacture', *United Australia Party Monthly Bulletin* II, no. 2 (1937): 24.
155 H.F. King, 'Home Production', *The BHP Review* XVI, no. 1 (1938): 8.
156 'Achievement! Commonwealth Aircraft Corporations No.1 Wirraway Makes First Flight', *The BHP Review* XVI, no. 3 (1939): 4.
157 Kathy Haenke, 'The Boomerang Story', ed. John Haenke (Nomad Television Productions, 1994).
158 *Ibid.*
159 Ross, *Armed and Ready*, 322.
160 Laurence Hartnett and John Veitch, *Big Wheels and Little Wheels* (Melbourne: Lansdowne, 1964), 78.
161 Robert Conlon, *Wheels and Deals: The Automotive Industry in Twentieth Century Australia* (Sydney: Ashgate, 2001), 30.
162 Ross, *Armed and Ready*, 192.
163 Conlon, *Wheels and Deals*, 42.
164 Blainey, *Jumping over the Wheel*, 174.
165 *Ibid.*, 180.
166 Ross, *Armed and Ready*, 381.
167 Robertson, *Australia at War 1939–1945*, 190.
168 *Ibid.*, 381.
169 Day, *The Politics of War*, 269–70; Gavin Long, *The Six Years War: A Concise History of Australia in the 1939–45 War* (Canberra: Australian War Memorial and the Australian Government Publishing Service, 1973), 164–5.
170 Robert Menzies, 'Men and Munitions', radio broadcast script, 16 June 1940, Papers of Robert G. Menzies, NLA MS 4936 2000 Addition Box 580 Folder 16.
171 *Ibid.*
172 Robert Menzies, 'Munitions', radio broadcast script, 22 August 1940, Papers of Robert G. Menzies, NLA MS 4936 2000 Addition Box 580 Folder 15.
173 *Ibid.*

CHAPTER 2 **THE HISTORIOGRAPHY OF AUSTRALIAN INTER-WAR DEFENCE AND FOREIGN POLICY**

1 R. MacGregor Dawson, *The Development of Dominion Status, 1900–1936* (London: Frank Cass, 1965).
2 The chapter by Greenwood himself on 'Development in the Twenties, 1919–29', and that by P.H. Partridge, 'Depression and War, 1929–1950'.
3 E.M. *Andrews, Isolationism and Appeasement in Australia: Reactions to the European Crises, 1935–1939* (Canberra: Australian National University, 1970).

4 *Ibid.*, 101.

5 E.M. Andrews, *The Writing on the Wall: The British Commonwealth and Aggression in the East 1931–1935* (Sydney: Allen & Unwin, 1987).

6 W.J. Hudson and M.P. Sharp, *Australian Independence: Colony to Reluctant Kingdom* (Melbourne: Melbourne University Press, 1988), 4.

7 *Ibid.*

8 *Ibid.*, 5.

9 P.G. Edwards, *Prime Ministers and Diplomats: The Making of Australian Foreign Policy, 1901–1949* (Melbourne: Oxford University Press in association with the Australian Institute of International Affairs, 1983), vii.

10 *Ibid.*, 191.

11 Douglas Gillison, *Royal Australian Air Force, 1939–42*, vol. 1 of *Australia in the War of 1939–1945: Series 3, Air* (4 vols.) (Canberra: Australian War Memorial, 1954); Gavin Long, *To Benghazi*, vol. 1 of *Australia in the War of 1939–1945: Series 1, Army* (7 vols.) (Canberra: Australian War Memorial, 1952); Lionel Wigmore, *The Japanese Thrust*, vol. 4 of *Australia in the War of 1939–1945: Series 1, Army* (7 vols.) (Canberra: Australian War Memorial, 1957).

12 Paul Hasluck, *The Government and the People, 1939–1941*, vol. 1 of *Australia in the War of 1939–1945: Series 4, Civil* (2 vols.) (Canberra: Australian War Memorial, 1952), 5.

13 John McCarthy, *Australia and Imperial Defence 1918–39: A Study in Air and Sea Power* (St Lucia: University of Queensland Press, 1976).

14 *Ibid.*, 150.

15 McCarthy, *Australia and Imperial Defence 1918–39*, 148.

16 *Ibid.*, 46.

17 Imperial defence was a complex strategy that is explained in detail in the next chapter.

18 Andrew Ross, 'The Arming of Australia: The Politics and Administration of Australia's Self Containment Strategy for Munitions Supply 1901–1945' (PhD diss., University of New South Wales, Australian Defence Forces Academy, 1986), 385.

19 David Horner, *Defence Supremo: Sir Frederick Shedden and the Making of Australian Defence Policy*. (Sydney: Allen & Unwin, 2000).

20 Jeffrey Grey, *A Military History of Australia* (Melbourne: Cambridge University Press, 1990).

21 *Ibid.*, 125.

22 *Ibid.*, 140.

23 David Day, *The Great Betrayal: Britain, Australia and the onset of the Pacific war, 1939–42* (First published North Ryde, NSW: Angus & Robertson, 1988).

24 David Day, *Menzies and Churchill at War: A Controversial New Account of the 1941 Struggle for Power* (Sydney: Angus & Robertson, 1986), 1.

25 Day, *The Great Betrayal*, 10.

26 Mr John Curtin, Prime Minister, to Mr Winston Churchill, U.K. Prime Minister, 23 January 1942, in *Documents on Australian Foreign Policy 1937–49*, ed. W.J. Hudson and H.J.W. Stokes, vol. V, doc. 294 (Canberra: Australian Government Publishing Service, 1982), 463, 464.

27 Day, *The Great Betrayal*, 354.

28 *Ibid.*, 356.

29 David Day, *Reluctant Nation: Australia and the Allied Defeat of Japan 1942–45* (Melbourne: Oxford University Press, 1992).

30 Paul Keating, 'Foreword', in David Day, *Reluctant Nation*, iii.

31 *Ibid.*, iv.

32 Australia. House of Representatives 1992, *Debates,* vol. HR182, 27 February 1993, p. 374.

33 *Ibid.*

34 Paul Keating, 'Foreword', in David Day, *Reluctant Nation*, iv.

35 James Curran, *The Power of Speech: Australian Prime Ministers Defining the National Image* (Melbourne: Melbourne University Press, 2004), 12.

36 Paul Keating speaking on 7 April 1992 to the Asia–Australia Institute, in Paul Keating, *Paul Keating, Prime Minister: Major Speeches of the First Year* (Canberra: Australian Labor Party, 1993), 35–6.

37 See for example: Cameron Hazlehurst, 'David Day, Menzies and Churchill at War', *Politics: Journal of the Australasian Political Studies Association* 22, no. 2 (1987): 131; Paul Addison, 'Menzies and Churchill at War', *Journal of Imperial and Commonwealth History* 19, no. 1 (1991): 108; Douglas Johnson, 'Kangeroo Shadow-Boxing' [*sic*], *History Today* 37, no. 5 (1987): 56.

38 *The Great Betrayal* was reviewed overseas: Phillip Knightley, 'Victim of the Colonial Mentality', *The Sunday Times*, 17 July 1988; 'Recent Books on International Relations', *Foreign Affairs* 68, no. 3 (1989); Christopher Thorne, 'Book Reviews', *The Journal of Imperial and Commonwealth History* 17, no. 3 (1989).

39 See for example: David Day, 'Curtin Led us out of Dark Days into a Golden Age', *Australian*, 5 July 2005; David Day, 'Farewell to the Old Country', *Australian*, 15 August 2005; David Day, 'The Horrors and Legacy of World War II', *Australian*, 15 August 2005; David Day, 'How the ALP Will Make Its Mark', *Australian*, 2 December 2003; David Day, 'Me-Too Gulf Adventurism Will Exact a Heavy Price', *Australian*, 28 January 2003; David Day, 'Shooting at Shadows', *Australian*, 26 April 2004; David Day, 'VP Day', *Australian*, 16 August 2005.

40 See for example: Peter Butt, 'Our Darkest Hour', in *When the War came to Australia* (Australia: ABC, 1991); Ray Connolly and Bob Wilson, *Cruel Britannia: Britannia Waives the Rules* (Belmont, NSW: R. Connolly and B. Wilson, 1994); David Day, *Claiming a Continent: A New History of Australia* (Pymble, NSW: Angus & Robertson, 1997).

41 Peter Hastings, 'Britain's Great Betrayal', *Sydney Morning Herald*, 25 April 1988, p. 9.

42 Dust jacket, David Day, *The Great Betrayal*, 2nd ed.

43 Roland Quinault, 'Churchill and Australia: The Military Relationship, 1899–1945', *War & Society* 6, no. 1 (1988): 41.

44 John McCarthy, 'The "Great Betrayal" Reconsidered: An Australian Perspective', *Australian Journal of International Affairs* 48, no. 1 (1994): 54–62.

45 David Day, *The Politics of War* (Sydney: Harper Collins, 2003).

46 Brian Farrell, *The Defence and Fall of Singapore 1940–1942* (London: Tempus, 2005); Ian Hamill, *The Strategic Illusion: The Singapore Strategy and the Defence of Australia and New Zealand, 1919–1942* (Singapore: Singapore University Press, 1981); W. David McIntyre, *The Rise and Fall of the Singapore Naval Base, 1919–1942* (Hamden, Ct.: Archon Books, 1979); Malcolm Murfett, 'Reflections on an Enduring Theme: The "Singapore Strategy" at Sixty', in *Sixty Years On: The Fall of Singapore Revisited*, ed. Brian Farrell and Sandy Hunter (Singapore: Eastern Universities Press, 2002); Malcolm Murfett *et al.*, *Between Two Oceans: A Military History of Singapore from First Settlement to Final British Withdrawal* (Singapore: Marshall Cavendish, 2005); James Neidpath, *The Singapore Naval Base and the Defence of Britain's Eastern Empire, 1919–1941* (Oxford: Oxford University Press, 1981).

47 Graham Freudenberg, *Churchill and Australia* (PanMacmillan Australia: Sydney, 2008), vii.

48 *Ibid.*, quoting the philosopher Isiah Berlin, 2–3.

49 Freudenberg, *Churchill and Australia*, 6.

50 *Ibid.*, 7.

51 John Gooch, 'The Politics of Strategy: Great Britain, Australia and the War against Japan, 1939–1945', *War in History* 10, no. 4 (2003): 447.

52 *Ibid.*, 426.

53 *Ibid.*, 447.

54 John Robertson, *Australia at War 1939–1945* (Melbourne: Heinemann, 1981), 99.

CHAPTER 3 **AUSTRALIA, THE EMPIRE AND IMPERIAL DEFENCE**

1 Australia. House of Representatives 1923, Debates, vol. HR104, 1 August 1923, p. 1952.

2 Donald C. Gordon, *The Dominion Partnership in Imperial Defense, 1870–1914* (Baltimore: Johns Hopkins Press, 1965), 24.

3 John Bach, *The Australia Station: A History of the Royal Navy in the South West Pacific, 1821–1913* (Kensington, NSW: New South Wales University Press, 1986), 171–2.

4 The best account of Australia and Imperial defence in the pre- and early federation period is found in L.D. Atkinson, 'Australian Defence Policy: A Study of Empire and Nation (1897–1910)' (PhD diss., Australian National University, 1964).

5 Luke Trainor, *British Imperialism and Australian Nationalism: Manipulation, Conflict, and Compromise in the Late Nineteenth Century, Studies in Australian History* (Melbourne: Cambridge University Press, 1994), 21, 23.

6 *Ibid.*, 21.

7 Robert K. Massie, *Dreadnought: Britain, Germany, and the Coming of the Great War* (New York: Random House, 1991), 608.

8 *Ibid.*

9 Tom Frame, *No Pleasure Cruise: The Story of the Royal Australian Navy* (Crows Nest, NSW: Allen & Unwin, 2004), 91.

10 Albert Palazzo, 'The Australian Army: A History of Its Organisation 1901–2001', *Australian Army History Series* (South Melbourne: Oxford University Press, 2001), 47.

11 Frame, *No Pleasure Cruise*, 91.

12 C.D. Coulthard-Clark, 'Formation of the Australian Armed Services, 1901–1914', in *Australia, Two Centuries of War & Peace*, ed. Michael McKernan and Margaret Browne (Canberra, ACT: Australian War Memorial in association with Allen & Unwin Australia, 1988), 134.

13 *Ibid.*

14 Frame, *No Pleasure Cruise*, 94.

15 Quoted in *ibid.*

16 Palazzo, *The Australian Army*, 49.

17 John Leonard Mordike, *We Should Do This Thing Quietly: Japan and the Great Deception in Australian Defence Policy 1911–1914* (Canberra: Aerospace Centre, 2002), 33.

18 *Ibid.*

19 *Ibid.*, 39.

20 Neville Meaney, *The Search for Security in the Pacific, 1901–14* (Sydney: Sydney University Press, 1976), 1.

21 *Ibid.*, 11.

22 Gordon, *The Dominion Partnership in Imperial Defense, 1870–1914*, 277.

23 Ian McGibbon, *Blue-Water Rationale: The Naval Defence of New Zealand 1914–1942* (Wellington: Government Printer, 1981), 35.

24 Ian Hamill, *The Strategic Illusion: The Singapore Strategy and the Defence of Australia and New Zealand, 1919–1942* (Singapore: Singapore University Press, 1981), 19.

25 'Lord Jellicoe Embarrassed', *Times*, 4 June 1919, p. 11.

26 Henry Frei, Japan's Southward Advance and Australia: From Sixteenth Century to World War II (Honolulu: University of Hawaii Press, 1991), 19.

27 John Rushworth Jellicoe, *The Jellicoe Papers: Selections from the Private and Official Correspondence of Admiral of the Fleet Earl Jellicoe of Scapa*, ed. A. Temple Patterson and J.E.T. Harper (London: Spottiswoode Ballantyne for the Navy Records Society, 1966).

28 'Imperial and Foreign News Items', *Times*, 9 September 1919, 9.

29 'Australian Naval Defence: Lord Jellicoe's Report', *Times*, 23 October 1919, p. 11.

30 *Ibid.*

31 *Ibid.*

32 These debates are found in: United Kingdom. House of Commons 1919, Debates, vol. HC.122, 10 December 1919, cols. 1367–1497.

33 E.M. Andrews, 'The Broken Promise—Britain's Failure to Consult Its Commonwealth on Defence in 1934, and the Implications for Australian Foreign and Defence Policy', *The Australian Journal of Defence Studies* 2, no. 2 (1978), 104.

34 William Morris Hughes, *The Splendid Adventure: A Review of Empire Relations within and without the Commonwealth of Britannic Nations* (London: Ernest Benn Limited, 1929), 72.
35 Laurence Frederic Fitzhardinge, *The Little Digger, 1914–1952: William Morris Hughes, a Political Biography*, vol. 2 (Sydney: Angus & Robertson, 1979), 458.
36 Hughes, *The Splendid Adventure*, 115.
37 *Ibid.*, 237.
38 John S. Galbraith, 'The Imperial Conference of 1921 and the Washington Conference', *The Canadian Historical Review* XXIX, no. 2 (1948): 145.
39 R. MacGregor Dawson, *The Development of Dominion Status, 1900–1936* (London: Frank Cass, 1965), 64.
40 *Ibid.*, 39.
41 *Ibid.*, 64.
42 David Walder, *The Chanak Affair* (London: Hutchinson, 1969).
43 Peter M. Sales, 'W.M. Hughes and the Chanak Crisis of 1922', *The Australian Journal of Politics and History* XVII, no. 3 (1971): 393.
44 Dawson, *The Development of Dominion Status, 1900–1936*, 54.
45 Sales, 'W.M. Hughes and the Chanak Crisis of 1922', 394.
46 Hughes, *The Splendid Adventure*, 242–4.
47 Paul Bartrop, *Bolt from the Blue: Australia, Britain and the Chanak Crisis* (Sydney: Halstead Press, 2002), 98.
48 Sales, 'W.M. Hughes and the Chanak Crisis of 1922', 404.
49 *Ibid.*, 400.
50 Fitzhardinge, *The Little Digger, 1914–1952*, 458. A resident minister would have kept Hughes better informed but would not have had official input into British policy.
51 Sales, 'W.M. Hughes and the Chanak Crisis of 1922', 401.
52 Dawson, *The Development of Dominion Status, 1900–1936*, 69.
53 I.M. Cumpston, *Lord Bruce of Melbourne* (Melbourne: Longman, 1989), 71.
54 Richard Gardiner Casey, *My Dear P.M.: R.G. Casey's Letters to S.M. Bruce, 1924–1929*, ed. W.J. Hudson and J. North (Canberra: Australian Government Publishing Service, 1980), 39.
55 *Ibid.*, for Casey's letters to Bruce from London.
56 Gwendolen M. Carter, *The British Commonwealth and International Security: The Role of the Dominions, 1919–1939* (Toronto: Ryerson Press, 1947), 73.
57 Christopher Waters, *The Empire Fractures: Anglo–Australian Conflict in the 1940s* (Melbourne: Australian Scholarly Publishing, 1995), 6.
58 W. Macmahon Ball, 'Australian Press and World Affairs', in *Press, Radio and World Affairs*, ed. W. Macmahon Ball (Melbourne: Melbourne University Press, 1938), 13.
59 Waters, *The Empire Fractures*, 6.
60 John Darwin, 'A Third British Empire? The Dominion Idea in Imperial Politics', in *The Twentieth Century*, ed. William Roger Louis, Judith M. Brown and Alaine Low (Oxford: Oxford University Press, 1999), 69.
61 Lorna Lloyd, 'Loosening the Apron Strings: The Dominions and Britain in the Interwar Years', *The Round Table*, no. 369 (2003): 279.
62 See for example, *Conference of Prime Ministers and Representatives of the United Kingdom, the Dominions, and India* (London: J.J. Keliher & Co., 1921); *Imperial Conference, 1923: Summary of Proceedings* (Canberra: Commonwealth Government Printer, 1924); *Imperial Conference, 1926: Summary of Proceedings* (Canberra: Commonwealth Government Printer, 1927); *Imperial Conference, 1937: Summary of Proceedings* (Canberra: Commonwealth Government Printer, 1937).
63 'Hush-a-Bye, Baby', *Herald*, 1 November 1926, 1.
64 Darwin, 'A Third British Empire? The Dominion Idea in Imperial Politics', 73.
65 Lionel Curtis, *The Problem of the Commonwealth* (Toronto: Macmillan, 1916), 75.
66 W.J. Hudson and M.P. Sharp, *Australian Independence: Colony to Reluctant Kingdom* (Melbourne: Melbourne University Press, 1988), 81.
67 Dawson, *The Development of Dominion Status, 1900–1936*, 93.
68 Hudson and Sharp, *Australian Independence*, 76.

69 Darwin, 'A Third British Empire? The Dominion Idea in Imperial Politics', 69.

70 Imperial Conference, 1926—Inter-Imperial Relations Committee—Report, proceedings and memoranda, report, October–November 1926, NAA A4640/1, 32.

71 Hudson and Sharp, *Australian Independence*, 94.

72 Hughes, *The Splendid Adventure*, 149.

73 *Ibid.*, 228.

74 John Darwin, 'Imperialism in Decline? Tendencies in British Imperial Policy between the Wars', *The Historical Journal* 23, no. 3 (1980): 667.

75 Hudson and Sharp, *Australian Independence*, 115.

76 John Robertson, *J.H. Scullin: A Political Biography* (Nedlands, WA: University of Western Australia Press, 1974), 83.

77 David Day, *The Politics of War* (Sydney: Harper Collins, 2003), 10.

78 'The Imperial Conference', *The Round Table* XX, no. 80 (1930).

79 Leonie Foster, *High Hopes: The Men and Motives of the Australian Round Table* (Melbourne: Melbourne University Press, 1986), 98.

80 John Latham, *Australia and the British Commonwealth, The John Murtagh Macrossan Lectures; 1928* (London: Macmillan and Co., 1929), 24.

81 Andrews, 'The Broken Promise', 111.

82 Norman Hilmer, 'The Foreign Office, the Dominions and the Diplomatic Unity of the Empire, 1925–29', in *Retreat from Power: Studies in Britain's Foreign Policy of the Twentieth Century*, ed. David Dilks (London: Macmillan, 1981), 75.

83 Graham Freudenberg, *Churchill and Australia* (Pan Macmillan Australia: Sydney, 2008), 6–7.

84 Franklyn A. Johnson, *Defence by Committee: The British Committee of Imperial Defence* (London: Oxford University Press, 1960), 353.

85 David Horner, Defence Supremo: Sir Frederick Shedden and the Making of Australian Defence Policy (Sydney: Allen & Unwin, 2000), 21.

86 A.R. Selby, 'The Association of the Dominions in the Direction of War', *Army Quarterly* XI, no. 1 (1925): 29.

87 Edward Miller, *War Plan Orange: The U.S. Strategy to Defeat Japan, 1897–1945* (Annapolis: Naval Institute Press, 1991).

88 T.B. Millar, *Australia in Peace and War* (Canberra: Australian National University Press, 1991), 121.

89 John Malcolm McCarthy, 'The Imperial Commitment 1939–41', *Australian Journal of Politics and History* 23, no. 2 (1977): 181.

90 The history of the Singapore Naval base is described in Ian Hamill (1981), *The Strategic Illusion*; W. David McIntyre (1979), *The Rise and Fall of the Singapore Naval Base, 1919–1942* (Hamden, Ct.: Archon Books, 1979); James Neidpath (1981), *The Singapore Naval Base and the Defence of Britain's Eastern Empire, 1919–1941* (Oxford: Oxford University Press, 1981).

91 Brian Farrell, *The Defence and Fall of Singapore 1940–1942* (London: Tempus, 2005), 20.

92 David McIntyre, *The Rise and Fall of the Singapore Naval Base, 1919–1942*, 35.

93 Quoted in I.M. Cumpston, *Lord Bruce of Melbourne* (Melbourne: Longman, 1989), 39.

94 'The Imperial Conference of 1923', in *Colonial and Imperial Conferences from 1887–1937*, ed. Maurice Olliver (Ottawa: Queen's Printer and Controller of Stationery, 1954), 13.

95 J. Ramsay MacDonald, *National Defense* (London: George Allen, 1917), 73.

96 United Kingdom. House of Commons 1924, Debates, vol. HC.169, 13 February 1924, col. 835.

97 *Ibid.*

98 United Kingdom. House of Commons 1924, Debates, vol. HC.171, 18 March 1924, cols. 288–289.

99 *Ibid.*, cols. 306–307.

100 *Ibid.*, col. 321.

101 'Mr Bruce and Singapore', *Times*, 21 March 1924, 12.

102 *Caucus Minutes 1917–1931*, ed. Patrick Weller, vol. 2 (Melbourne: Melbourne University Press, 1975), 202.

103 Paul Hasluck, The Government and the People, 1939–1941, vol. 1 of Australia in the War of 1939–1945: Series 4, Civil (2 vols.) (Canberra: Australian War Memorial), 30.

104 *Ibid.*, 34.

105 Farrell, *The Defence and Fall of Singapore 1940–1942*, 20.

106 Winston S. Churchill to Stanley Baldwin, 13 December 1924, ed. Martin Gilbert, *Winston S. Churchill: The Exchequer Years 1922–1929*, vol. V Companion Part 1 (London: Heinemann, 1979), 306.

107 Robert Rayner, *The Darwin Detachment* (Wollongong: Rubber Press, 2002), 8, 15.

108 'Empire Defence: Policy of the Dominions', *Times*, 3 December 1926, 9.

109 *Ibid.*

110 United Kingdom. House of Commons 1929–1930, Debates, vol. HC.232, 20 November 1929, col. 463.

111 *Ibid.*

112 Jeffrey Grey, *A Military History of Australia* (Melbourne: Cambridge University Press, 1990), 140. The inter-war period is covered briefly in one relatively short chapter.

113 The 1999 monograph was reissued in a substantially expanded edition in 2006.

114 McIntyre, *The Rise and Fall of the Singapore Naval Base, 1919–1942*, 53.

115 Paul Haggie, *Britannia at Bay: The Defence of the British Empire against Japan 1931–1941* (Oxford: Clarendon Press, 1981), 146. Additionally, Britain did not know herself what forces she would be able to send to the East.

116 Hamill, *The Strategic Illusion.*

117 Neidpath, *The Singapore Naval Base and the Defence of Britain's Eastern Empire, 1919–1941*. This conclusion precludes the investigation of the various strategies to be employed once a fleet arrived at Singapore.

118 Malcolm Murfett *et al.*, *Between Two Oceans: A Military History of Singapore from First Settlement to Final British Withdrawal* (Singapore: Marshall Cavendish, 2005), 193.

119 *Ibid.*, 10.

120 Murfett *et al.*, *Between Two Oceans*, viii.

121 *Ibid.*, 56.

122 Andrew Ross, *Armed and Ready: The Industrial Development & Defence of Australia, 1900–1945* (Sydney: Turton & Armstrong, 1995), 45. However, Ross offers scant evidence for his claim and admits that 'Nobody has discovered any significant action by Hughes or Bruce which stemmed from their doubts on the Blue Water strategy'.

123 John Malcolm McCarthy, *Australia and Imperial Defence 1918–39: A Study in Air and Sea Power* (St Lucia: University of Queensland Press, 1976), 9.

124 David Horner, 'Australian Estimates of the Japanese Threat', in *Serving Vital Interests: Australia's Strategic Planning in Peace and War: Proceedings of the Australian Army History Conference Held at the Australian War Memorial*, 30 September 1996, ed. Peter Dennis and Jeffrey Grey (Canberra: Australian Defence Force Academy, 1996), 75–101; David Horner, *High Command: Australia and Allied Strategy, 1939–45* (Canberra: Australian War Memorial, 1982).

125 Freudenberg, *Churchill and Australia*, 173.

126 *Ibid.*, 330

127 Malcolm Murfett, 'Living in the Past: A Critical Re-Examination of the Singapore Naval Strategy 1918–1941', *War & Society* 11, no. 1 (1993): 77.

128 Day, *The Politics of War*, 4.

129 McCarthy, *Australia and Imperial Defence 1918–39*, 132.

130 John Malcolm McCarthy, 'Australia and Imperial Defence: Co-Operation and Conflict 1918–1939', *Australian Journal of Politics and History* XVII, no. 1 (1971): 28.

131 Ernle Chatfield, C.J. Deverell and E.L. Ellington, Appreciation of the Situation in the Far East, 1937, by the Chiefs of Staff Sub-Committee, appreciation, 14 June 1937, Papers of the Cabinet, Public Records Office (London), PRO CAB 16/182.

132 Admiralty to High Commission Canberra, cable, 1 April 1939, Papers of the Foreign Office, Public Records Office (London), PRO FO371/22791.

133 Committee of Imperial Defence, Despatch of a Fleet to the Far East in the event of war with Japan, appreciation, April 1939, Papers of the Prime Minister's Office, Public Records Office (London), PRO PREM 1/309.

134 Malcolm Murfett *et al.*, *Between Two Oceans*, 193.

135 Day, *The Politics of War*, 1.

136 *Ibid.*, 49.

137 *Ibid.*, 38.

138 Lord Caldecote, U.K. Secretary of State for Dominion Affairs, to Sir Geoffrey Whiskard, U.K. High Commissioner in Australia for Prime Minister, 12 August 1940, ed. W.J. Hudson *et al.*, *Documents on Australian Foreign Policy 1937–49* (Canberra: Australian Government Publishing Service, 1975), vol. IV Canberra 1980, doc. 64, 84–5.

139 Day, *The Politics of War*, 173.

140 *Ibid.*, 205.

141 *Ibid.*, 10.

142 Imperial Conference 1923: Summary of Proceedings and Conclusions, Memoranda on Naval Policy, Report of Meetings, November 1923, NAA A981, IMP 111.

143 Hasluck, *The Government and the People, 1939–1941*, 17.

144 McCarthy, *Australia and Imperial Defence 1918–39*, 1.

145 Australia. House of Representatives 1936, Debates, vol. HR152, 5 November 1936, p. 1545.

146 *Ibid.*

147 *Ibid.*

148 G.C. Peden, 'The Burden of Imperial Defence and the Continental Commitment Reconsidered', *The Historical Journal* 27, no. 2 (1984): 415.

149 *Ibid.*

150 Robert Hyslop, *Australian Naval Administration 1900–1939* (Melbourne: Hawthorn Press, 1973), 41.

151 Vice Admiral G.F. Hyde, Australian Defence Policy, memo, 3 April 1935, Papers of the Cabinet, Public Records Office (London), PRO CAB 21/397.

152 *Ibid.*

153 Lieutenant-Colonel V.A.H. Sturdee, Lecture on the Plan of Concentration, lecture, 1933, AWM 54, 243/6/140.

154 David Horner, 'Australian Army Strategic Planning between the Wars', in Serving Vital Interests: Australia's Strategic Planning in Peace and War: Proceedings of the Australian Army History Conference Held at the Australian War Memorial, 30 September 1996, ed. Peter Dennis and Jeffrey Grey (Canberra: Australian Defence Force Academy, 1996), 83.

155 See for example, War Establishments. Overseas Plan – 401, memo, 1938, NAA MP826/1.

156 See for example, J.D. Lavarack, 'The Defence of the British Empire with Special Reference to the Far East and Australia', *Army Quarterly XXV* (1933); Horace Robertson, 'The Empire and Modern War', article, July 1933, NAA A5954/69, 1025/6.

157 C.D. Coulthard-Clark, *The Third Brother: The Royal Australian Air Force 1921–39* (North Sydney: Allen & Unwin, 1991), 97.

158 Squadron Leader A.A. Walser, 'Aircraft and Imperial Defence', *Army Quarterly* V, no. 1 (1922): 40.

159 Hugh Trenchard, The Defence of Australia, memo, November 1925, NAA A981, DEF 261.

160 For examples of British proposals see: Trenchard, The Defence of Australia; F.L. Field, G.F. Milne, and J.M Salmond, The Defence of Australia, Committee of Imperial Defence memo, 2 June 1932, AWM 113, MH 1/43; Air Vice-Marshal R. Williams, The Defence of Australia, memo, 3 May 1935. Papers of the Cabinet, Public Records Office (London), PRO CAB 21/397.

161 Neville Meaney, *Fears & Phobias: E.L. Piesse and the Problem of Japan* (Canberra: National Library of Australia, 1996).
162 Warren Perry, 'The Late Sir Frederick Shedden: An Appreciation', *Victorian Historical Magazine* 42, no. 3 (1971): 635.
163 Horner, *Defence Supremo*, 48.
164 E.M. Andrews, *Isolationism and Appeasement in Australia: Reactions to the European Crises, 1935–1939* (Canberra: Australian National University, 1970), 4.
165 Horner, *Defence Supremo*, 22.
166 Herbert Richmond, 'Australian Defence Policy', article, February 1936, Papers of Sir Frederick Shedden, NAA A5954/69, 1025/6.
167 Herbert Richmond, 'Imperial Defence: Australian Defence Policy', article, October 1933, NAA Papers of Sir Frederick Shedden, A5954/69, 1025/6.
168 Herbert Richmond, 'Australian Defence Policy', article, February 1936, Papers of Sir Frederick Shedden, NAA A5954/69, 1025/6.
169 Herbert Richmond, 'Australia's Defences', *Journal of the Royal United Service Institution* LXXXI, no. 521 (1936).
170 Richmond, 'Australian Defence Policy', February 1936.
171 Horner, *Defence Supremo*, 25.
172 Frederick Shedden, Imperial Defence College Exercise: Principles of Imperial Defence, personal notes, 1927–1928, Papers of Sir Frederick Shedden, NAA A5954/69, 20/1.
173 Frederick Shedden, War with Japan in 1938, Imperial Defence College exercise, 1931, Papers of Sir Frederick Shedden, NAA A5954/69, 19/5.
174 Horner, *Defence Supremo*, 26.
175 Ross McMullin, *The Light on the Hill: The Australian Labor Party, 1891–1991* (Melbourne: Oxford University Press, 1992), 186.
176 See for example, ALP parliamentary statements in: Australia. House of Representatives 1923, Debates, vol. HR104, 1 August 1923, pp. 1965–6.
177 E.M. Andrews, 'Australian Labour and Foreign Policy 1935–1939', *Labour History* 9 (1965): 22.
178 See for example, Archdale Parkhill, *Statement of the Government's Policy Regarding the Defence of Australia* (Canberra: Commonwealth Government Printer, 1935).
179 E.M. Andrews, *The Writing on the Wall: The British Commonwealth and Aggression in the East 1931–1935* (Sydney: Allen & Unwin, 1987), 55.
180 *Ibid.*, 57.
181 McCarthy, *Australia and Imperial Defence 1918–39*, 132.
182 McCarthy, 'Australia and Imperial Defence', 28.

CHAPTER 4 **AUSTRALIAN RESPONSES TO INTER-WAR CRISES**

1 Australia. House of Representatives 1931, Debates, vol. HR132, 9 January 1931, p. 709.
2 David Walker, *Anxious Nation: Australia and the Rise of Asia 1850–1939* (St Lucia: University of Queensland, 1999), 4.
3 *Ibid.*, 108.
4 Phillips Payson O'Brien, *British and American Naval Power: Politics and Policy, 1900–1936* (Westport, CT: Praeger, 1998), 160.
5 Robert Thornton, 'Australia and the Abrogation of the Anglo-Japanese Alliance' (MA thesis, University of Melbourne, 1975), 92.
6 E.L. Piesse, The Anglo-Japanese Alliance: Japan an unworthy ally, memo, 1921, Piesse Papers, National Library of Australia, MS 882 Series 5 Folder 3.
7 Charles Nelson Spinks, 'The Termination of the Anglo-Japanese Alliance', *Pacific Historical Review* VI, no. 4 (1937): 334.
8 Thornton, 'Australia and the Abrogation of the Anglo-Japanese Alliance', 129.
9 John Galbraith, 'The Imperial Conference of 1921 and the Washington Conference', *The Canadian Historical Review* XXIX, no. 2 (1948), 150.

10 Australia. House of Representatives 1921, Debates, vol. HR97, 4 October 1921, p. 11716.

11 Neville Meaney, 'Australia and the World', in *Under New Heavens: Cultural Transmission and the Making of Australia*, ed. Neville Meaney (Melbourne: Heinemann Educational, 1989), 314.

12 Galbraith, 'The Imperial Conference of 1921 and the Washington Conference', 152.

13 Meaney, 'Australia and the World', 321.

14 George Foster Pearce, *Carpenter to Cabinet* (Melbourne: Hutchinson, 1951), 161.

15 Australia. House of Representatives 1922, Debates, vol. HR99, 26 July 1922, p. 794.

16 *Ibid.*

17 E.M. Andrews, *Australia and China: The Ambiguous Relationship* (Melbourne: Melbourne University Press, 1985), 56.

18 Ian Nish, 'Relations with Japan', in *Between Empire and Nation: Australia's External Relations from Federation to the Second World War*, ed. Carl Bridge and Bernard Attard (Melbourne: Australian Scholarly Publishing, 2000), 160.

19 Jacqui Murray, *Watching the Sun Rise: Australian Reporting of Japan, 1931 to the Fall of Singapore* (New York: Lexington Books, 2004), 1.

20 John McCarthy, *Australia and Imperial Defence 1918–39: A Study in Air and Sea Power* (St Lucia: University of Queensland Press, 1976), 19.

21 Bradford A. Lee, *Britain and the Sino-Japanese War, 1937–1939: A Study in the Dilemmas of British Decline* (Stanford: Stanford University Press, 1973), 20.

22 W. Macmahon Ball, 'Australian Press and World Affairs', in *Press, Radio and World Affairs*, ed. W. Macmahon Ball (Melbourne: Melbourne University Press, 1938), 13.

23 Murray, *Watching the Sun Rise*, 2.

24 Philip Hart, 'J.A. Lyons: A Political Biography' (PhD diss., Australian National University, 1967), 262.

25 David Bird, 'J.A. Lyons, the Tame Tasmanian: A Study in Australian Foreign and Defence Policy, 1932–39' (PhD diss., University of Melbourne, 2004), 71.

26 *Ibid.*, 8.

27 *Ibid.*, 299.

28 David Carlton, 'The Dominions and British Policy in the Abyssinian Crisis', *Journal of Imperial and Commonwealth History* I, no. 1 (1972): 59.

29 Bird, 'J.A. Lyons, the Tame Tasmanian', 398.

30 *Ibid.*, I.

31 See, for example, Minister for Co-Ordination of Defence, Australia and New Zealand Naval Defence, note, 23 November 1939, PRO ADM 1/11062.

32 Carl Bridge, 'Australia and the Italo-Abyssinian Crisis of 1935–6', *Journal of the Royal Australian Historical Society* 92, no. 1 (2006): 1.

33 Bird, 'J.A. Lyons, the Tame Tasmanian', 135.

34 C.J. Lloyd, 'The Formation and Development of the United Australia Party, 1929–37' (PhD diss., Australian National University, 1984), 235 and 42.

35 Bridge, 'Australia and the Italo-Abyssinian Crisis of 1935–6', 11.

36 *Ibid.*, 4.

37 Jay Pierrepont Moffat, diary entry, 2 October 1935, Diaries of Jay Pierrepont Moffat, US Consul-General to Australia, 1935–37, National Library of Australia, MFM G7251.

38 'Isolation is Suicide', *Herald*, 11 October 1937, p. 5.

39 Bridge, 'Australia and the Italo-Abyssinian Crisis of 1935–6', 4.

40 Australia. House of Representatives 1935, Debates, vol. HR147, 23 September 1935, p. 35.

41 *Ibid.*, p. 36.

42 Australia. House of Representatives 1935, Debates, vol. HR147, 9 October 1935, pp. 565–7.

43 For examples of the ALP's opinions on the Abyssinian crisis, see Australia. Senate 1935, Debates, vol. HR147, 24 September 1935, p. 80; Australia. House of Representatives 1935, Debates, vol. HR147, 10 October 1935, pp. 629–47.

44 Australia. Senate 1935, Debates, vol. HR147, 24 September 1935, p. 84.

45 Australia. House of Representatives 1935, Debates, vol. HR147, 24 September 1935, p. 39.
46 *Ibid.*
47 Australia. House of Representatives 1921, Debates, vol. HR97, p. 1163.
48 'Where Labor Stands: Statement by Federal Leader Curtin', *Australian Worker*, 9 October 1935, p. 8.
49 Australia. House of Representatives 1935, Debates, vol. HR147, pp. 1257–74.
50 Michael Howard, 'British Military Preparations for the Second World War', in *Retreat from Power: Studies in Britain's Foreign Policy of the Twentieth Century*, ed. David Dilks (London: Macmillan, 1981), 103.
51 Lyons to Parkhill, cable, 12 September 1935, Papers of Archdale Parkhill, NAA A981/4, ABY46.
52 Bridge, 'Australia and the Italo-Abyssinian Crisis of 1935–6', 4.
53 E.M. Andrews, *Isolationism and Appeasement in Australia: Reactions to the European Crises, 1935–1939* (Canberra: Australian National University, 1970), 52.
54 *Ibid.*, 4.
55 Bridge, 'Australia and the Italo-Abyssinian Crisis of 1935–6', 7.
56 See for example, Australia. House of Representatives 1936, Debates, vol. HR150, 30 April 1936, p. 1093; Australia. House of Representatives 1936, Debates, vol. HR150, 8 May 1936, p. 1461; Australia. House of Representatives 1936, Debates, vol. HR150, 12 May 1936, p. 1521.
57 'Overseas Trade: Italy', *Monthly Journal of The Melbourne Chamber of Commerce* XII, no. 7 (1935): 128.
58 Australia. House of Representatives 1935, Debates, vol. HR147, 7 November 1935, p. 1394.
59 'The New Peace Proposals', *The Advocate*, 19 December 1935, p. 17.
60 Pauline Kneipp, 'Australian Catholics and the Abyssinian War', *The Journal of Religious History* 10, no. 4 (1979): 423.
61 *Ibid.*: 422.
62 *Ibid.*: 419.
63 *Ibid.*: 421.
64 *Ibid.*
65 Pauline Kneipp, 'A Comparative Study of American and Australian Catholic Reaction to European Diplomatic Crises: 1935 to 1939' (PhD diss., University of Sydney, 1974), 125.
66 Andrews, *Isolationism and Appeasement in Australia*, 60.
67 Australia. House of Representatives 1936, Debates, vol. HR149, 26 March 1936, p. 590.
68 Ross McMullin, *The Light on the Hill: The Australian Labor Party, 1891–1991* (Melbourne: Oxford University Press, 1992), 197.
69 Australia. House of Representatives 1937–38, Debates, vol. HR155, 27 April 1938, p. 540.
70 Andrews, *Isolationism and Appeasement in Australia*, 95.
71 Australia. House of Representatives 1937–38, Debates, vol. HR155, 1 December 1937, p. 88.
72 Amirah Inglis, *Australians in the Spanish Civil War* (Sydney: Allen & Unwin, 1987), 35.
73 United Australia Party, 'The European Crisis—Narration of Events', *United Australia Party Monthly Bulletin* III, no. 8 (1938): 118.
74 Bird, 'J.A. Lyons, the Tame Tasmanian', 256.
75 Ritchie Ovendale, *"Appeasement" and the English Speaking World: Britain, the United States, the Dominions, and the Policy of "Appeasement" 1937–1939* (Cardiff: University of Wales Press, 1975), 147.
76 Bird, 'J.A. Lyons, the Tame Tasmanian', 285.
77 Menzies to Lord Halifax (British Foreign Minister), letter, 6 August 1938, Menzies Papers, National Library of Australia, MS 4936 Box 598 Folder 3.
78 Andrews, *Isolationism and Appeasement in Australia*, 143.

79 Australia. House of Representatives 1938, Debates, vol. HR157, 28 September 1938, p. 326.

80 'Australia and the Czech Crisis', in *Australian Commentaries: Select Articles from the 'Round Table' 1911–1942*, ed. L.L. Robson (Melbourne: Melbourne University Press, 1975), 179.

81 E.M. Andrews, 'The Australian Government and Appeasement', *Australian Journal of Politics and History* 13 (1967): 43.

82 Australia. House of Representatives 1937–38, Debates, vol. HR155, 28 April 1938, p. 599.

83 J.A. Lyons, Honourable J.A. Lyons, Prime Minister: Speech on International Situation, radio broadcast, 28 September 1938, NFSA 244260.

84 Bird, 'J.A. Lyons, the Tame Tasmanian', 307.

85 'Hard to Invade, Hughes Holds', *Daily Telegraph*, 12 December 1938, p. 5.

86 David Horner, 'Australian Army Strategic Planning between the Wars', in *Serving Vital Interests: Australia's Strategic Planning in Peace and War: Proceedings of the Australian Army History Conference Held at the Australian War Memorial, 30 September 1996*, ed. Peter Dennis and Jeffrey Grey (Canberra: Australian Defence Force Academy, 1996), 94.

87 Richard Gardiner Casey, 'Speech to the Boston Chamber of Commerce', in *Speeches in America* (Washington: 1940–41), 4.

88 Australia. House of Representatives 1938, Debates, vol. HR157, 2 November 1938, p. 1100.

89 E.M. Andrews, 'Australian Labour and Foreign Policy 1935–1939', *Labour History* 9 (1965): 23.

90 Australia. House of Representatives 1938, Debates, vol. HR157, 5 October 1938, p. 400.

91 Australia. House of Representatives 1931, Debates, vol. HR132, 14 October 1931, p. 709.

92 See for example, Department of Defence, Manchuri—Situation in, Secretariat Report, 1931–34, Papers of Department of Defence, NAA B197/0, 1877/7/59.

93 E.L. Piesse, The Anglo-Japanese Alliance: Japan an unworthy ally, MS 882, Series 5 Folder 3.

94 Ruth Megaw, 'The Australian Goodwill Mission to the Far East in 1934 and the Evolution of Australian Foreign Policy', *Journal of Royal Australian Historical Society* 59, no. 4 (1973): 253.

95 E.M. Andrews, 'The Great Temptation: The Australian Government and the Sale of Arms to China During the Manchurian Crisis, 1931–33', *Australian Journal of Politics and History* XXIII, no. 3 (1977): 347.

96 For a detailed account of the Army's plans to sell weapons to the Chinese, see *ibid.*

97 Examples of this view are found in Australia. House of Representatives 1932, Debates, vol. HR136, 26 October 1932, p. 1628. For further examples of this attitude see: Australia. Senate 1932, Debates, vol. HR136, 3 November 1932, p. 1823; Australia. House of Representatives 1933, Debates, vol. HR142, 17 November 1933, p. 4744; Australia. House of Representatives 1933, Debates, vol. HR142, 21 November 1933, p. 4833; Australia. Senate 1933, Debates, vol. HR143, 6 December 1933, p. 5601.

98 E.M. Andrews, *The Writing on the Wall: The British Commonwealth and Aggression in the East 1931–1935* (Sydney: Allen & Unwin, 1987), 55.

99 John Sleeman, *White China: An Austral–Asian Sensation* (Sydney: J.H.C. Sleeman, 1933), 9.

100 C.D. Coulthard-Clark, *The Third Brother: The Royal Australian Air Force 1921–39* (North Sydney: Allen & Unwin, 1991), 447–8.

101 Murray, *Watching the Sun Rise*, 163.

102 Antony Best, *British Intelligence and the Japanese Challenge in Asia, 1914–1941* (2002: Palgrave, 2002), 138.

103 Department of External Affairs, 'The Far East', *Current Notes* VI (1939): 377.

104 Robert Menzies and George Foster Pearce, 'International Situation-Ministerial Statement', *Current Notes* III (1937): 210.

105 These reports are found in: Foreign Office, Japan—internal situation (Military Coup d'etat), report, 1934–1937, Papers of the Department of Defence, NAA A816/1, 19/304/121.
106 See for example, A.G. Colley, 'Australia's Enemies', *The Australian Quarterly* IX, no. 4 (1937): 86-87.
107 J. Pierrepont Moffat, *Moffat Papers: Selections from the Diplomatic Journals of Jay Pierrepont Moffat, 1919–1943*, ed. Nancy Hooker (Cambridge: Harvard, 1956), 130.
108 Australia. House of Representatives 1935, Debates, vol. HR147, 11 October 1935, p. 712.
109 Australia. House of Representatives 1937–38, Debates, vol. HR155, 29 April 1938, p. 668.
110 For examples of pacifist writings on the Sino-Japanese Wars see Rupert Hornabrook, *Japan and Ourselves: Humanity Cries for Peace* (Melbourne: Stillwell, 1939); International Peace Research Committee, *Crisis in the Pacific: The Coming Anglo-Japanese-American Conflict* (Melbourne: Ruskin Press, 1937).
111 Canberra, 'Pacific Chessboard', *The Australian National Review* 5, no. 27 (1939): 12.
112 Norman Angell, *The Defence of the Empire* (London: H. Hamilton, 1937), 104.
113 Nish, 'Relations with Japan', 161.
114 Bird, 'J.A. Lyons, the Tame Tasmanian', 11.
115 Andrews, *Australia and China*, 66.
116 Nish, 'Relations with Japan', 162.
117 *Ibid.*, 169.
118 Bird, 'J.A. Lyons, the Tame Tasmanian', 123.
119 John Latham, *The Australian Eastern Mission, 1934: Report of the Rt. Hon. J.G. Latham, Leader of the Mission* (Canberra: Government Publisher, 1934).
120 Nish, 'Relations with Japan', 161.
121 Andrews, *Australia and China*, 79.
122 Lionel Dennis, *Australia since 1890* (Melbourne: Addison, Wesley, and Longman, 1996), 123.
123 David Day, *The Politics of War* (Sydney: Harper Collins, 2003), 10.
124 *Ibid.*, 60.
125 Nish, 'Relations with Japan', 165.
126 Hart, 'J.A. Lyons', 271.
127 Ruth Megaw, 'Undiplomatic Channels: Australian Representation in the United States, 1919–1939', *Historical Studies* 15, no. 60 (1973): 623.
128 Bird, 'J.A. Lyons, the Tame Tasmanian', 140.
129 Megaw, 'Undiplomatic Channels', 623.
130 Nish, 'Relations with Japan', 165.
131 Harper, *A Great and Powerful Friend: A Study of Australian American Relations between 1900 and 1975* (St Lucia: University of Queensland Press, 1987), 92.
132 Vigilis and Vera Shepel (trans.), 'Security in the Pacific Ocean', *Izvestiya*, 21 May 1937.
133 'All Eyes on the Pacific', *World Peace* 2, no. 7 (1937): 99.
134 'Australia Demands Pacific Pact', *World Peace* 4, no. 6 (1939): 62.
135 Bridge, 'Poland to Pearl Harbor', in *Munich to Vietnam: Australia's Relations with Britain and the United States since the 1930s*, ed. Carl Bridge (Melbourne: Melbourne University Press, 1991), 40.
136 Hart, 'J.A. Lyons', 272.
137 Jay Pierrepont Moffat, diary entry, October 1935, Diaries of Jay Pierrepont Moffat, US Consul-General to Australia, 1935–1937, National Library of Australia, MFM G7251.
138 E.L. Piesse, 'Australia's Duty to Herself', *Austral–Asiatic Bulletin* 1, no. 2 (1937): 6.
139 Day, *The Politics of War*, 68.
140 Marylin Bender and Selig Altschul, *The Chosen Instrument: Pan Am, Juan Trippe, the Rise and Fall of an American Entrepreneur* (New York: Simon and Schuster, 1982), 13.
141 *Ibid.*, 15.

142 Ruth Megaw, 'The Scramble for the Pacific Anglo-United States Rivalry in the 1930s', *Historical Studies* 17, no. 69 (1977): 458.
143 Robert Daley, *American Saga: Juan Trippe and His Pan Am Empire* (New York: Random House, 1980), 191.
144 Bruce Brown, *Gatty: Prince of Navigators* (Hobart: Libra Books, 1997), 177.
145 Cordell Hull (US Secretary of State) to Walter Nash New Zealand Prime Minister, letter, 13 August 1937, PRO CO 323/1455/32.
146 Bender and Altschul, *The Chosen Instrument.*
147 Meaney, 'Australia and the World', 613.
148 These reports are found in United States. Annual reports, reports, 1920–1940, NAA A981, UNI 9 Parts 1 and 2.
149 W.J. Hudson, *Casey* (Melbourne: Oxford University Press, 1986), 116.
150 Harper, *A Great and Powerful Friend*, 56.
151 United States Annual Report—Economic, report, April 1938, NAA A981/4.
152 Hudson, *Casey*, 113.
153 David Reynolds, *The Creation of the Anglo-American Alliance, 1937–41: A Study in Competitive Co-Operation* (Chapel Hill: University of North Carolina Press, 1982), 12.
154 Richard Gardiner Casey, 'Australia in World Affairs', *International Affairs* 16, no. 5 (1937): 708.
155 Cyrill Wynne to J. Pierrepont Moffat, 25 July 1936, in *Australia through American Eyes*, ed. P.G. Edwards (St Lucia: University of Queensland Press, 1979), 38.
156 Jay Pierrepont Moffat, diary entry, 5 April 1936, Diaries of Jay Pierrepont Moffat, US Consul-General to Australia, 1935–1937, National Library of Australia, MFM G7251.
157 R.G. Menzies, diary, 15 August 1941, Menzies Papers, National Library of Australia, MS 4936 Series 13 Box 589 Folder 8.
158 'The Decline of Americano-Mania', *Bulletin*, 23 February 1922, p. 6.
159 *Ibid.*
160 Philip Bell and Roger J. Bell, *Implicated: The United States in Australia, Australian Retrospectives.* (Melbourne: Oxford University Press, 1993), 77.
161 William Hughes, *The Splendid Adventure: A Review of Empire Relations within and without the Commonwealth of Britannic Nations* (London: Ernest Benn Limited, 1929), 277.
162 P.R. Stephensen, *Mental Rubbish from Overseas* (Sydney: Cultural Defence Committee, 1935), 4.
163 Jill Julius Matthews, 'Which America', in *Americanization and Australia*, ed. Roger J. Bell and Philip Bell (Sydney: University of New South Wales Press, 1998), 26.
164 Travel writer Willard Price described American policy in Asia with 'America retires – Ungracefully'. Jay Pierrepont Moffat, diary entry, October 1935, Diaries of Jay Pierrepont Moffat, US Consul-General to Australia, 1935–37, National Library of Australia, MFM G7251.
165 Matthews, 'Which America', 28.
166 Philip Bell and Roger Bell, *Implicated: The United States in Australia, Australian Retrospectives* (Melbourne: Oxford University Press, 1993), 47.
167 *Ibid.*
168 *Ibid.*
169 *Ibid.*, 71.
170 L.G. Churchward, *Australia & America, 1788–1972, an Alternative History* (Chippendale, NSW: Alternative Publishing, 1979), 137.
171 Bell and Bell, *Implicated*, 71.
172 *Ibid.*, 82.
173 Clarence Gauss, 'C.E. Gauss to the Secretary of State, 1 December 1940', in *Australia through American Eyes*, ed. P.G. Edwards (St Lucia: University of Queensland Press, 1979), 60.
174 Edward Miller, *War Plan Orange: The U.S. Strategy to Defeat Japan, 1897–1945* (Annapolis: Naval Institute Press, 1991), 6–7.
175 Glen St James Barclay, 'Singapore Strategy: The Role of the United States in Imperial Defense', *Military Affairs* 39, no. 2 (1975): 55.

176 Miller, *War Plan Orange*, 36.
177 Henry Burrell, *Mermaids Do Exist* (South Melbourne: Macmillan, 1986), 298.
178 See for example, Singapore Defence Conference, conference report, 8 November 1940, AWM 113, MH1/95.
179 Stanley Melbourne Bruce, Visit to the United States, report, May 1939, Papers of Stanley Melbourne Bruce, NAA M104/1, 7/4.
180 'Tame Tasmanian', *Time*, 8 July 1935, p. 19.
181 Enid Muriel Lyons, *So We Take Comfort* (London: Heinemann, 1965), 241.
182 'Premier J.A. Lyons of Australia Here', *New York Times*, 7 July 1935, p. 43.
183 'Premier J.A. Lyons of Australia Here', p. 43.
184 Lyons, *So We Take Comfort*, 243.
185 Megaw, 'Undiplomatic Channels', 623.
186 *Ibid.*, 624.
187 *Ibid.*
188 Carl Bridge, 'R.G. Casey, Australia's First Washington Legation, and the Origins of the Pacific War, 1940–42', *Australian Journal of Politics and History* 28, no. 2 (1982): 182.
189 Carl Bridge, *Casey and the Americans: Australian War Propaganda in the United States, 1940–41* (London: Australian Studies Centre Institute of Commonwealth Studies, 1988), 11.
190 *Ibid.*, 12.
191 *Ibid.*, 5.
192 Richard Gardiner Casey, 'Speech to Mid-Day Luncheon Club at Springfield Illinois', in *Speeches in America* (Washington: 1940–41).
193 Bridge, *Casey and the Americans*, 7.
194 Richard Gardiner Casey, 'America's Second Fight for Freedom', in *Speeches in America* (Washington: 1940–41).
195 See for example, Casey, 'Speech to Mid-Day Luncheon Club at Springfield Illinois'.
196 Richard Gardiner Casey, 'Australia and the War', in *Speeches in America* (Washington: 1940–41).
197 Bridge, 'R.G. Casey, Australia's First Washington Legation, and the Origins of the Pacific War', 1940–42', 183.
198 Bridge, *Casey and the Americans*, 3.
199 Casey to Menzies, Fifth Progress Report, cable, 25 February 1941, Papers of the Department of Air, NAA A1196/6, 12/501/59.
200 Sumner Welles, Australia, minute of conversation with Casey, 16 May 1940, Franklin D. Roosevelt Presidential Library, Hyde Park, Box 161 Folder 1.
201 Raymond Esthus, *From Enmity to Alliance: US–Australian Relations, 1931–1941* (Seattle: University of Washington Press, 1964), 85.

CHAPTER 5 **CRITICS OF COMPLACENCY AND THEIR RECEPTION**

1 'Australia's Frontiers', *Argus*, 17 February 1940, p. 6.
2 Neville Meaney, *Fears & Phobias: E.L. Piesse and the Problem of Japan* (Canberra: National Library of Australia, 1996), 45.
3 Laurence Fitzhardinge, *The Little Digger, 1914–1952: William Morris Hughes, a Political Biography*, 2 vols., vol. 2 (Sydney: Angus & Robertson, 1979), 615.
4 '"Watch the East": Mr. Hughes's Warning', *Sydney Morning Herald*, 14 April 1933, p. 15.
5 William Morris Hughes, 'Defence: A Policy for the Times', *Sydney Morning Herald*, 7 August 1933, p. 8.
6 *Ibid.*
7 C.G. Armitage, 'Defence of Australia', *Sydney Morning Herald*, 9 August 1933, p. 9; 'Defence of Australia', *Sydney Morning Herald*, 8 August 1933, p. 8; Frederick

Jones, 'Defence of Australia', *Sydney Morning Herald*, 10 August 1933, p. 4; Once AIF, 'Strengthen the Navy', *Sydney Morning Herald*, 8 August 1933, p. 6.

8 See for example, 'Britain Sea Strength Weaker Than for Decades', *Sydney Morning Herald*, 14 August 1933, p. 9; 'Loan Destroyers: Three May Be Kept in Reserve', *Sydney Morning Herald*, 11 August 1933, p. 12; 'Weakness of the Navy', *Sydney Morning Herald*, 15 August 1933, p. 8.

9 Fitzhardinge, *The Little Digger, 1914–1952*, 619.

10 'Defence: Warning Note', *Sydney Morning Herald*, 9 September 1933, p. 13.

11 'Duty Imposed by Civilisation', *Sydney Morning Herald*, 11 September 1933, p. 12.

12 'Vulnerable Sydney: What an Enemy Would Do', *Sydney Morning Herald*, 12 September 1933, p. 9.

13 'League's Critics', *Sydney Morning Herald*, 16 September 1933, p. 16.

14 ' Alarmist Propaganda Decried', *Sydney Morning Herald*, 4 October 1933, p. 14.

15 Fitzhardinge, *The Little Digger, 1914–1952*, 619.

16 William Morris Hughes, *Australia and War to-Day: The Price of Peace* (Sydney: Angus & Robertson, 1935).

17 Hughes, *Australia and War To-Day*, 1–2.

18 *Ibid.*, 115.

19 Fitzhardinge, *The Little Digger, 1914–1952*, 626.

20 Hughes, *Australia and War To-Day*, 24, 31.

21 *Ibid.*, 114.

22 *Ibid.*

23 *Ibid.*, 150.

24 The role and influence of this journal will be discussed later in this chapter.

25 Lewis Charles Wilcher, 'Australia and War To-Day (W.M. Hughes)', *The Australian Rhodes Review* 2 (1936): 126.

26 William Morris Hughes, 'Australia and War To-Day—Notes, 1935', Papers of William Morris Hughes, National Library of Australia, NLA MS 1538 Series 35 Subseries 2 Box 169 Folder 10.

27 Fitzhardinge, *The Little Digger, 1914–1952*, 633.

28 *Ibid.*

29 William Morris Hughes, Labor's Defence Policy, speech, 1937, Papers of William Morris Hughes, National Library of Australia, NLA MS 1538 Series 35 subseries 1.

30 *Ibid.*

31 Philip Hart, 'J.A. Lyons: A Political Biography' (PhD diss., Australian National University, 1967), 251.

32 Fitzhardinge, *The Little Digger, 1914–1952*, 649.

33 Meaney, *Fears & Phobias*, 17.

34 *Ibid.*, 29.

35 E.L. Piesse, 'Japan and Australia', *Foreign Affairs* IV, no. 3 (1926): 488.

36 Leonie Foster, *High Hopes: The Men and Motives of the Australian Round Table* (Melbourne: Melbourne University Press, 1986), 92.

37 E.L. Piesse, *Japan and the Defence of Australia* (Melbourne: Robertson & Mullens, 1935).

38 E.L. Piesse to R.G. Menzies, letter, 16 November 1935, Papers of E.L. Piesse, National Library of Australia, NLA MS 882 Series 9 Folder 1.

39 Meaney, 'Australia and the World', in *Under New Heavens: Cultural Transmission and the Making of Australia*, ed. Neville Meaney (Melbourne: Heinemann Educational, 1989), 415.

40 'Australia and Japan', *Argus*, 2 November 1935.

41 Meaney, *Fears & Phobias*, 48.

42 R.G. Menzies to E.L. Piesse, letter, 15 November 1935, Papers of E.L. Piesse, National Library of Australia, NLA MS 882 Series 9 Folder 1.

43 Piesse, *Japan and the Defence of Australia*, 4.

44 *Ibid.*, 36.

45 *Ibid.*, 31.

46 *Ibid.*, 37.

47 E.L. Piesse to R.G. Menzies, letter, 16 November 1935, Piesse Papers, National Library of Australia, MS 882 Series 9 Folder 1.

48 E.L. Piesse, 'Mr Wentworth's Demand for Defence', *The Australian Quarterly* XI, no. 1 (1939): 54.

49 See for example, E.L. Piesse, 'More Planes Urged for Defence', *Morning Herald*, 25 October 1935.

50 E.L. Piesse, 'Australian Defence: Coastal Defence', *Age*, 21 March 1936; E.L. Piesse, 'Australian Defence: Factors Affecting Local Decisions', *Age*, 19 March 1936; E.L. Piesse, 'Australian Defence: Suggested Practicable Plan', *Age*, 24 March 1936; E.L. Piesse, 'Australian Defence: Survey of World Position', *Age*, 18 March 1936; E.L. Piesse, 'Australian Defence: The Militia Army', *Age*, 20 March 1936; E.L. Piesse, 'Australian Defence: The Navy and Air Force', *Age*, 23 March 1936.

51 Piesse, 'Australian Defence: Survey of World Position'.

52 'Imperial Defence: Australian Apathy', *Age*, 29 April 1936, p. 3

53 Warren Perry, 'Wynter, Henry Douglas', in *Australian Dictionary of Biography* (Melbourne: Melbourne University Press, 2002), 599.

54 Warren Perry, 'Lieutenant General Henry Douglas Wynter: An Officer of the Australian Staff Corps', *Victorian Historical Magazine* 43, no. 1 (1972): 837.

55 *Ibid.*

56 Horner, *Defence Supremo: Sir Frederick Shedden and the Making of Australian Defence Policy* (Sydney: Allen & Unwin, 2000), 48.

57 Perry, 'Lieutenant General Henry Douglas Wynter', 848.

58 H.D. Wynter, 'The Strategical Inter-Relationship of the Navy, the Army, and the Air Force: An Australian View', *Army Quarterly* XIV (1927): 24.

59 *Ibid.*, 31.

60 For an example of the influence of this legacy see E. George Marks, *Pacific Peril, or, Menace of Japan's Mandated Islands* (Sydney: Wynyard Book Arcade, 1933); Herbert Richmond, 'Australia's Defences', *Journal of the Royal United Service Institution* LXXXI, no. 521 (1936): 61–5; Herbert Richmond, 'An Outline of Imperial Defence', *Army Quarterly* XX IV (1932): 260–79.

61 This lecture found in H.D. Wynter, Defence of Australia and its relation to Imperial Defence, lecture, 3 July and 22 August 1935, Papers of the Cabinet, Public Records Office (London), PRO CAB 21/2525.

62 *Ibid.*

63 *Ibid.*

64 *Ibid.*

65 Chiefs of Staff, Defence of Australia and its relation to Imperial Defence—COS Response, memo, 17 June 1937, Papers of the Cabinet, Public Records Office (London), PRO CAB 21/2525.

66 *Ibid.*

67 Minister for Defence, Speech in Parliament on Defence Estimates on 5 November, 1936 by the Hon J. Curtin MP, minute, 16 December 1936, Papers of Sir Frederick Shedden, NAA A5954/69, 886/1.

68 Our Military Writer, 'How We Can Defend Australia', *Daily Telegraph*, 3 April 1936, p. 6.

69 *Ibid.*

70 *Ibid.*

71 This regulation is found in Minister for Defence, Observations on Colonel Wynter's Explanation and the Military Board's Report, minute, 16 December 1936, Papers of Sir Frederick Shedden, NAA A5954/69, 886/1.

72 Archdale Parkhill, Case of Colonel H.D. Wynter, minute, 16 November 1937, Papers of Sir Frederick Shedden, NAA A5954/69, 886/1.

73 C.B. Laffan, Article in *Daily Telegraph*, letter to Minister of Defence, 9 April 1936, Papers of Sir Frederick Shedden, A5954/69, 886/1.

74 Archdale Parkhill, Article in *Daily Telegraph*, comment on letter, 16 April 1936, Papers of Sir Frederick Shedden, A5954/69 886/1.

75 David Day and Gavin Long offer different views on how Curtin obtained Wynter's lectures and Peter Dennis does not comment on it, but as we will see

it is clear that they did reach Curtin. David Day, *John Curtin: A Life* (Pymble, NSW: Harper Collins, 1999), 350; Peter Dennis, 'Australia and the Singapore Strategy', in *Sixty Years On: The Fall of Singapore Revisited*, ed. Brian Farrell and Sandy Hunter (Singapore: Eastern Universities Press, 2002), 31–9; Gavin Long, *To Benghazi*, vol. 1 of *Australia in the War of 1939–1945: Series 1, Army* (7 vols.) (Canberra: Australian War Memorial, 1952), 19.

76 Archdale Parkhill to Lavarack, Speech in Parliament on Defence Estimates by the Hon J. Curtin, leader of the Opposition, letter, 3 December 1936, Papers of Sir Frederick Shedden, NAA A5954/69, 886/1.

77 Australia. House of Representatives 1936, Debates, vol. HR152, 5 November 1936, p. 1548.

78 *Ibid.*, p. 1553.

79 C.B. Laffan, Speech in Parliament on Defence Estimates on 5 November, 1936, by the Hon J. Curtin, MP, memo, NAA A5954/69, 886/1.

80 *Ibid.*

81 H.D. Wynter to CGS, letter, 11 December 1936, Papers of Sir Frederick Shedden, NAA A5954/69, 886/1.

82 *Ibid.*

83 *Ibid.*

84 Archdale Parkhill, minute, 17 December 1936, Papers of Sir Frederick Shedden, NAA A5954/69, 886/1.

85 *Ibid.*

86 H.G. Butler to Archdale Parkhill, minute, 21 December 1936, Papers of Sir Frederick Shedden, NAA A5954/69, 886/1.

87 H.D. Wynter to CGS, Court Martial Request, letter, 7 April 1937, Papers of Sir Frederick Shedden, NAA A5954/69, 886/1.

88 Personal notes for Minister on appeal of Colonel H.D. Wynter, minute, 27 January 1937, Papers of Sir Frederick Shedden, NAA A5954/69, 886/1.

89 Minister for Defence, Speech in Parliament on Defence Estimates on 5 November, 1936, by the Hon J. Curtin, MP, minute by Minister, 15 January 1937, Papers of Sir Frederick Shedden, NAA A5954/69, 886/1.

90 Dennis, 'Australia and the Singapore Strategy', 38.

91 Horace Robertson, *Defence of Australia* (Sydney: Smith & Lane, 1934).

92 *Ibid.*, 1.

93 *Ibid.*, 6.

94 *Ibid.*, 19.

95 Horace Robertson, The Defence of Australia, draft article, April 1935, Papers of Sir Frederick Shedden, NAA A5954/69, 1025/6.

96 Thomas Blamey, 'The Sentinel', radio broadcast script, 19 February 1939, AWM 3DRL/16643 Wallet 7.

97 E.M. Andrews, *Isolationism and Appeasement in Australia: Reactions to the European Crises, 1935–1939* (Canberra: Australian National University, 1970); Jacqui Murray, *Watching the Sun Rise: Australian Reporting of Japan, 1931 to the Fall of Singapore* (New York: Lexington Books, 2004).

98 C.J. Lloyd, 'The Development and Organisation of the Federal Parliamentary Press Gallery, 1901–1978' (MA thesis, Australian National University, 1979), 33.

99 *Ibid.*, 51.

100 *Ibid.*, 62.

101 *Ibid.*, 51.

102 Some of these articles have been discussed in reference to Billy Hughes and Edmund Piesse's attempts to inform Australians of the danger facing them.

103 'Defence Proposals', *Argus*, 28 June 1924, p. 37.

104 'Sea Power: Why It Is the Basis of Defence', *Argus*, 1 August 1935, p. 9.

105 'Australia Must Rearm', *Argus*, 31 March 1937, p. 9.

106 See for example, 'Britain Sea Strength Weaker Than for Decades', *Sydney Morning Herald*, 14 August 1933, p. 9; 'Japan Issues: Approves Huge Arms Plans', *Herald*, 20 November 1936, p. 36; 'Japan's Aims and Australia: Opinion in the East', *Herald*, 2 February 1939, p. 11; 'Sea Power Still Main Guardian', *Herald*, 23 July

1936, p. 14; 'Weakness of the Navy', *Sydney Morning Herald*, 15 August 1933, p. 8.
107 Observer, 'Australian Defence Policy', *The Australian Quarterly* VII, no. 2 (1935): 65–74.
108 *Ibid.*, 72.
109 J.G. Crawford, 'Australia as a Pacific Power' in *Australia's Foreign Policy*, ed. W.G.K. Duncan, D.A.S. Campbell and Australian Institute of Political Science (Sydney: Angus and Robertson, 1938), 99.
110 Neil Harcourt MacNeil, 'A Case for National Defence', *The Australian Rhodes Review* 4 (1939): 50.
111 *Ibid.*, 52.
112 E. George Marks, *Pacific Peril, or, Menace of Japan's Mandated Islands* (Sydney: Wynyard Book Arcade, 1933); E. George Marks, *Watch the Pacific!: Defenceless Australia* (Sydney: Coles Book Arcade, 1924). The Navy League was founded during the naval arms race before the Great War to lobby for a stronger Royal Navy with branches around the Empire.
113 *Ibid.*, 53.
114 Marks, *Watch the Pacific*, 18.
115 *Ibid.*, 143.
116 Marks, *Pacific Peril.*
117 *Ibid.*, 160.
118 *Ibid.*, 74.
119 J.M. Fowler, *Australia's Perils: Real and Imaginary* (Melbourne: Brown, Prior & Company, 1926).
120 *Ibid.*, 8.
121 *Ibid.*, 9.
122 *Ibid.*, 15.
123 *Ibid.*, 19.
124 *Ibid.*, 39.
125 *Ibid.*, 44.
126 W.C. Wentworth, *Demand for Defence: Being a Plan to Keep Australia White and Free* (Sydney: W.C. Wentworth, 1939), 11.
127 *Ibid.*, 1.
128 *Ibid.*, 24.
129 *Ibid.*, 32.
130 *Ibid.*, 167.
131 Gerald Packer, 'Demand for Defence', *The Australian Quarterly* XI, no. 2 (1939): 97.
132 *Ibid.*
133 Quoted in Lesley Johnson, *The Unseen Voice: A Cultural Study of Early Australian Radio* (London: Routledge, 1988), 48.
134 *Ibid.*, 163.
135 Philip Geeves and Oam Frahs, *The Dawn of Australia's Radio Broadcasting* (Alexandria: Electronics Australia, 1993), 63.
136 *Ibid.*, 67.
137 Lloyd, 'The Development and Organisation of the Federal Parliamentary Press Gallery, 1901–1978', 68.
138 Alan Thomas, *Broadcast and Be Damned: The ABC's First Two Decades* (Melbourne: Melbourne University Press, 1980), 38.
139 Johnson, *The Unseen Voice*, 52.
140 Thomas, *Broadcast and Be Damned*, 38.
141 *Ibid.*
142 *Ibid.*
143 Lloyd, 'The Development and Organisation of the Federal Parliamentary Press Gallery, 1901–1978', 66.
144 *Ibid.*, 68.
145 Johnson, *The Unseen Voice*, 166.
146 Thomas, *Broadcast and Be Damned*, 78.

147 Alan Thomas, 'Political Pressure in the ABC', in *Stay Tuned: An Australian Broadcasting Reader*, ed. Albert Moran (Sydney: Allen and Unwin, 1992), 66.
148 Johnson, *The Unseen Voice*, 182.
149 Thomas, 'Political Pressure in the ABC', 67.
150 Andrews, *Isolationism and Appeasement in Australia*, 5.
151 Murray, *Watching the Sun Rise*, 121.
152 I.A. Hudgson to Raymond Watt, World Peace Congress (Brussels Sept. 3–6 1936), letter, 13 October 1936, Watt Papers, National Library of Australia, MS 1923 Box 5.
153 K.S. Inglis and Jan Brazier, *This is the ABC: The Australian Broadcasting Commission, 1932–1983* (Melbourne: Melbourne University Press, 1983), 63.
154 G.L. Mann (Daughter of E.A. Mann) to E.M. Andrews, letter, 14 April 1965, Papers of E.A. Mann, National Library of Australia, NLA MS 1955.
155 E.A. Mann, 'The Watchman', radio broadcast script, 15 November 1937, Papers of E.A. Mann, National Library of Australia, NLA MS 1955.
156 E.A. Mann, Arrows in the Air: A Selection from Broadcasts by "The Watchman" (Melbourne: S. John Bacon, 1944), 29–30.
157 Inglis and Brazier, *This is the ABC*, 63.
158 Thomas, 'Political Pressure in the ABC', 67.
159 Thomas, *Broadcast and Be Damned*, 91.
160 E.L. Piesse, 'Australia and Imperial Defence', radio broadcast script 3LR, 29 November 1936, National Library of Australia, NLA MS 882 Series 9 Folder 4.

CHAPTER 6 **WHY THE WARNINGS WERE IGNORED**

1 Gerald Packer, 'Demand for Defence', *The Australian Quarterly* XI, no. 2 (1939): 97.
2 David Day, *The Politics of War* (Sydney: Harper Collins, 2003), 7.
3 Clarence Gauss, 'C.E. Gauss to the Secretary of State, 1 December 1940', in *Australia through American Eyes*, ed. P.G. Edwards (St Lucia: University of Queensland Press, 1979), 61.
4 John Curtin, *To Build and Defend a Happy and Self-Reliant Australia: Policy Speech of the Australian Labor Party* (Sydney: 1937), 17.
5 James Curran, *The Power of Speech: Australian Prime Ministers Defining the National Image* (Melbourne: Melbourne University Press, 2004), 22.
6 Stuart Macintyre, 'Annihilation of the Annals', *Australian*, 20 May 2005, p. 15.
7 Ross McMullin, *The Light on the Hill: The Australian Labor Party, 1891–1991* (Melbourne: Oxford University Press, 1992), 186.
8 Australia. House of Representatives 1923, Debates, vol. HR104, 31 July 1923, p. 1885.
9 Australia. House of Representatives 1936, Debates, vol. HR152, 5 November 1936, p. 1564.
10 C.J. Lloyd, 'The Formation and Development of the United Australia Party, 1929–37' (PhD diss., Australian National University, 1984), 293.
11 Australia. House of Representatives 1923, Debates, vol. HR104, 31 July 1923, p. 1888.
12 Australia. House of Representatives 1937, Debates, vol. HR154, 25 August 1937, p. 121.
13 'Our Silent Defence', *Argus*, 5 August 1938, p. 8.
14 'The Course of Empire', *Time*, 9 February 1942, p. 15.
15 David Day, 'Labor Must Be No Party to War Cry', *Australian*, 4 October 2002, p. 11.
16 E.M. Andrews, *Isolationism and Appeasement in Australia: Reactions to the European Crises, 1935–1939* (Canberra: Australian National University, 1970), 8.
17 Australia. House of Representatives 1937–1938, Debates, vol. HR155, 1 December 1937, p. 59.
18 Labor Anti-War Committee, *Labor's Case against War and Fascism* (Melbourne: 1935), 1.
19 Solomon Brigg, 'Australia Must Be Neutral: Policy of War Resistance', *Labor Daily*, 14 September 1935, 11.

20 Australia. House of Representatives 1935–1936, Debates, vol. HR151, 17 September 1936, p. 268.

21 Australia. House of Representatives 1935–1936, Debates, vol. HR151, 11 September 1936, p. 70.

22 'Lyons Budget Does Not Give Anything to Anybody: Huge Defence Vote', *Labor Daily*, 24 September 1935, p. 1.

23 Australia. House of Representatives 1936, Debates, vol. HR149, 26 March 1936, p. 590.

24 Curtin, *To Build and Defend a Happy and Self-Reliant Australia*, 17.

25 Australia. House of Representatives 1937–1938, Debates, vol. HR155, 28 April 1938, p. 600.

26 Australia. House of Representatives 1937, Debates, vol. HR154, 25 August 1937, p. 108.

27 See for example, Australia. Senate 1937–1938, Debates, vol. HR155, 2 December 1937, p. 113.

28 John Edwards, *Curtin's Gift: Reinterpreting Australia's Greatest Prime Minister* (Crows Nest, NSW: Allen & Unwin, 2005), 22–3.

29 Australia. House of Representatives 1937–38, Debates, vol. HR155, 27 April 1938, p. 543.

30 *Ibid.*

31 Malcolm Murfett, 'The Singapore Strategy', in *Between Empire and Nation: Australia's External Relations from Federation to the Second World War*, ed. Carl Bridge and Bernard Attard (Melbourne: Australian Scholarly Publishing, 2000), 231.

32 Captain P.D. Winter, 'Comparing the "Singapore Strategy" and "Fortress Australia": Concepts for Australia's Defence in the 1930s', *Defence Force Journal*, no. 65 (1987): 37.

33 Ian Hamill, 'An Australian Defence Policy?: The Singapore Strategy and the Defence of Australia', *Australian National University Historical Journal* 10–11 (1973–74): 12.

34 Jason Sears, '1929–1939: Depression and Rearmament', in *The Royal Australian Navy*, ed. David Stevens (Oxford: Oxford University Press, 2001), 92.

35 Karl Hack and Kevin Blackburn, *Did Singapore Have to Fall? Churchill and the Impregnable Fortress* (London: Routledge Curzon, 2003), 32.

36 Sir Maurice Hankey to CID, Report by Sir Maurice Hankey, Secretary to the Committee of Imperial Defence on certain aspects of Australian Defence, cable, 15 November 1934, Papers of the Cabinet, Public Records Office (London), PRO CAB 21/386.

37 *Ibid.*

38 An appreciation of an attack on Singapore from the Japanese point of view, 1935, Papers of the War Office, Public Records Office (London), PRO WO 106/5698.

39 Ernle Chatfield, C.J. Deverell, E.L. Ellington, Report on 1937 Imperial Conference relating to questions raised by Australian delegation, report, 10 December 1937, Papers of the Cabinet, Public Records Office (London), PRO CAB 21/2525.

40 *Ibid.*

41 *Ibid.*

42 Leo Amery to R.G. Menzies, letter, 6 May 1939, Menzies Papers, National Library of Australia, NLA MS 4936 Box 579 Folder 9.

43 Quoted in Christopher Bell, 'Winston Churchill, Pacific Security, and the Limits of British Power, 1921–1941', in *Churchill and Strategic Dilemmas before the World Wars*, ed. John H. Maurer (London: Frank Cass, 2003), 70–1.

44 United Australia Party, 'Defence Policy', *United Australia Party Monthly Bulletin*, no. 17 (1936): 245.

45 Australia. House of Representatives 1936, Debates, vol. HR152, 5 November 1936, p. 1545.

47 Australia. House of Representatives 1934, Debates, vol. HR144, 31 July 1934, p. 915.

48 Empire and Local Defence from the Australian Aspect, report, 1937, Papers of Sir Frederick Shedden, NAA A5954/69, 1812/10.

49 Frederick Shedden, An outline of the principles of Imperial defence with special reference to Australian defence, Imperial Defence College exercise, 1929, Papers of Sir Frederick Shedden, NAA A5954/69, 38/4.

50 'Should the Airforce Be Strengthened: Its Role in Our Defence Forces', *Herald*, 30 October 1934, p. 6.

51 Jeffrey Grey, *The Australian Army* (Melbourne: Oxford University Press, 2001), 93.

52 Archdale Parkhill, Australian Defence with particular reference to the security problem of small nations, speech to the Constitutional Club Sydney, 11 May 1936, Papers of the Department of Defence, NAA A664/1, 534/401/72.

53 Australia. House of Representatives 1936, Debates, vol. HR152, 5 November 1936, p. 1541.

54 J.V. Fairbairn, 'Australia's Defence', *The Australian National Review* 4, no. 23 (1938): 16.

55 Robert Hyslop, *Australian Naval Administration 1900–1939* (Melbourne: Hawthorn Press, 1973), 38.

56 *Ibid.*

57 Frederick Shedden, Minute by Defence Committee at meeting held on Monday 5 November 1934, minute of meeting with Sir Maurice Hankey, 5 November 1934, Papers of the Cabinet, Public Records Office (London), PRO CAB 21/397.

58 David Horner, 'Australian Army Strategic Planning between the Wars', in *Serving Vital Interests: Australia's Strategic Planning in Peace and War: Proceedings of the Australian Army History Conference Held at the Australian War Memorial, 30 September 1996*, ed. Peter Dennis and Jeffrey Grey (Canberra: Australian Defence Force Academy, 1996), 90.

59 Horace Robertson, The Defence of Australia, draft article, April 1935, Papers of Sir Frederick Shedden, NAA A5954/69, 1025/6.

60 Director Naval Operations Western Australia to Navy Department Melbourne, Local Naval Defence Schemes, memo, 9 January 1922, Papers of the Navy Office, NAA MP1049/1, 1921/0765.

61 J.H. Bruche, Memorandum by the Chief of the General Staff on Report on certain aspects of Australian Defence, memo, 1935, Papers of the Cabinet, Public Records Office (London), PRO CAB 21/397.

62 Council of Defence Agenda: Australian Army Organization, agenda, 1935, Papers of the Cabinet, Public Records Office (London), PRO CAB 21/397.

63 J.D. Lavarack, Memorandum by Colonel J.D. Lavarack on report on certain aspects of Australian Defence, memo, 14 March 1935, Papers of the Cabinet, Public Records Office (London), PRO CAB 21/397.

64 A.B. Lodge, *Lavarack: Rival General* (Sydney: Allen & Unwin, 1998), 46.

65 Horner, 'Australian Army Strategic Planning between the Wars', 90.

66 Lodge, *Lavarack: Rival General*, passim.

67 Horner, 'Australian Army Strategic Planning between the Wars', 83.

68 Australian Army, The Defence of Australia: Future Policy, memo on CID report, 1932, AWM 113, MH 1/43.

69 J.D. Lavarack, 'The Defence of the British Empire with Special Reference to the Far East and Australia', *Army Quarterly* XXV (1933): 210.

70 Andrew Ross, *Armed and Ready: The Industrial Development & Defence of Australia, 1900–1945* (Sydney: Turton & Armstrong, 1995), 136.

71 Horner, 'Australian Estimates of the Japanese Threat, 1905–1941', in *Estimating Foreign Military Power*, ed. Philip Towle (London: Croom Helm, 1982), 145.

72 For Examples of the RAAF position see Chief of Air Staff, Memorandum on the defence of Australia, memo, 3 May 1935, Papers of the Council of Defence, NAA A9787/1, Attachment 13, Air Vice-Marshal R. Williams; The Defence of Australia, memo, 3 May 1935, Papers of the Cabinet, Public Records Office (London), PRO CAB 21/397.

73 Australia. House of Representatives 1924, Debates, vol. HR106, 28 March 1924, p. 126.

74 Horner, 'Australian Army Strategic Planning between the Wars', 90.
75 'Should the Airforce Be Strengthened: Its Role in Our Defence Forces', *Herald*, 30 October 1934, p. 24.
76 Day, *The Politics of War*; Ross, *Armed and Ready*.
77 John Curtin, 'Defending Australia', *Herald*, 30 July 1937, p. 2.
78 Joan Beaumont, *Australian Defence: Sources and Statistics, The Australian Centenary History of Defence* (Melbourne: Oxford University Press, 2001), 30.
79 John Malcolm McCarthy, *Australia and Imperial Defence 1918–39: A Study in Air and Sea Power* (St Lucia: University of Queensland Press, 1976), 22.
80 Geoffrey Serle, 'Great Britain and Australia, 1919–39' (DPhil diss., Oxford, 1949), 51.
81 G.L. Kristianson, *The Politics of Patriotism: The Pressure Group Activities of the Returned Servicemen's League* (Canberra: Australian National University Press, 1966), 36.

CHAPTER 7 **DOMESTIC POLITICS AND AUSTRALIAN DEFENCE**

1 'Mr. Bruce's Task', *Times*, 24 May 1923, p. VII.
2 Australia. House of Representatives 1935, Debates, vol. HR147, 7 November 1935, p. 1382.
3 David Day, 'The Politics of War', *The Sydney Papers* 15, no. 1 (2003): 128.
4 Herbert Richmond, 'Australian Defence Policy', article, February 1936, Papers of Sir Frederick Shedden, NAA A5954/69, 1025/6.
5 *Ibid.*
6 Bird's views, discussed earlier, are found in David Bird,' J.A. Lyons, the Tame Tasmanian: A Study in Australian Foreign and Defence Policy, 1932–39' (PhD diss., University of Melbourne, 2004).
7 Brian Costar and Peter Vlahos, 'Sir Earle Page', in *Australian Prime Ministers* (Sydney: New Holland, 2000), 170.
8 Joan Rydon, 'The Conservative Electoral Ascendancy between the Wars', in *Australian Conservatism: Essays in Twentieth Century Political History*, ed. Cameron Hazlehurst (Canberra: Australian National University Press, 1979), 56.
9 Joan Rydon, *A Federal Legislature: The Australian Commonwealth Parliament, 1901–1980* (Melbourne: Oxford University Press, 1986), 22.
11 Rydon, *A Federal Legislature*, 173.
12 Rydon, 'The Conservative Electoral Ascendancy between the Wars', 52.
13 C.J. Lloyd, 'The Formation and Development of the United Australia Party, 1929–37' (PhD diss., Australian National University, 1984), 294.
14 *Ibid.*, 293.
15 C.J. Lloyd, 'The Rise and Fall of the United Australia Party', in *Liberalism and the Australian Federation*, ed. J.R. Nethercote (Annandale, NSW: Federation Press, 2001), 134.
16 Carl Bridge, 'Appeasement and After: Towards a Re-Assessment of the Lyons and Menzies Governments' Defence and Foreign Policies 1931–41', *Australian Journal of Politics and History* 51, no. 3 (2005): 373.
17 Judith Brett, *The Australian Liberals and the Moral Middle Class: From Alfred Deakin to John Howard* (Port Melbourne: Cambridge University Press, 2003), 13.
20 Kim E. Beazley Sr., 'Labour and Foreign Policy', *Australian Outlook* 20, no. 2 (1966): 129. Kim Beazley Sr. (1917–2007) entered the House of Representatives in 1945 and was Minister of Education in the Whitlam Government from 1972–75.
22 C.D. Coulthard-Clark, *Soldiers in Politics: The Impact of the Military on Australian Political Life and Institutions, Army Military History Series. Issues.* (St Leonards, NSW: Allen & Unwin, 1996), 123.
23 Rydon, *A Federal Legislature*, 106.
25 Rydon, *A Federal Legislature*, 107.

26 Coulthard-Clark, *Soldiers in Politics*, 126.
27 *Ibid.*, 125.
28 *Ibid.*
29 *Ibid.*, 203.
30 Bede Nairn, *The 'Big Fella': Jack Lang and the Australian Labor Party 1891–1949* (Melbourne: Melbourne University Press, 1986), 228.
31 Ross McMullin, *The Light on the Hill: The Australian Labor Party, 1891–1991* (Melbourne: Oxford University Press, 1992), 171.
32 Nairn, *The 'Big Fella'*, 229.
33 L.F. Crisp, *The Australian Federal Labour Party, 1901–1951* (Melbourne: Longmans, 1955), 42.
34 McMullin, *The Light on the Hill*, 177.
35 Nairn, *The 'Big Fella'*, 252.
36 McMullin, *The Light on the Hill*, 183.
37 Crisp, *The Australian Federal Labour Party, 1901–1951*, 43.
38 McMullin, *The Light on the Hill*, 198.
39 H.E.B., 'A Great Labor Crusade against Dictatorship', *Australian Worker*, 29 June 1938, 1.
40 Stuart Macintyre, *The Reds: The Communist Party of Australia from Origins to Illegality* (Sydney: Allen & Unwin, 1998), 392.
41 McMullin, *The Light on the Hill*, 204.
42 Macintyre, *The Reds*, 92.
43 *Ibid.*, 93.
44 *Ibid.*, 416.
45 *Ibid.*, 386.
46 Lloyd, 'The Formation and Development of the United Australia Party, 1929–37', 229.
47 *Ibid.*, 234.
48 Geoffrey Sawer, *Australian Federal Politics and Law, 1929–1949* (Melbourne: Melbourne University Press, 1963), 99.
49 Henry Mayer, 'Pressure Groups in Australia', in *Australian Politics: A Reader*, ed. Kurt Mayer (Melbourne: Cheshire, 1966), 209.
50 Lex Watson, 'The United Australia Party and Its Sponsors', in *Australian Conservatism: Essays in Twentieth Century Political History*, ed. Cameron Hazlehurst (Canberra: Australian National University Press, 1979), 71.
51 Lloyd, 'The Formation and Development of the United Australia Party, 1929–37', iii.
52 This is an unsubmitted thesis found in the NLA catalogue as: Berzins, Baiba. 'The Nationalist Party, 1919–1930: Organisation and Ideology'. The actual thesis claims to be written by Baiba Beata Berzins Irving and is referred to hereafter as, Baiba Beata Berzins Irving, 'The Nationalist Party, 1919–1930: Organisation and Ideology' (PhD diss., University of Sydney, 1972), 118.
53 'Mr. Bruce Faces Crisis of His Career: People's Mandate or Orders of the Moneybags?', *Smith's Weekly*, 20 February 1926, p. 1.
54 'What Nationalists Spent on 15 Federal Candidates: Sensational Disclosures', *Smith's Weekly*, 6 March 1926, p. 3.
55 J.A. McCallum, 'The Economic Bases of Australian Politics', in *Trends in Australian Politics*, ed. Maurice Blackburn and W.G.K. Duncan (Sydney: Angus & Robertson in conjunction with the Australian Institute of Political Science, 1935), 67.
56 *Ibid.*, 69.
57 Irving, 'The Nationalist Party', 149.
58 Philip Hart, 'The Piper and the Tune', in *Australian Conservatism: Essays in Twentieth Century Political History*, ed. Cameron Hazlehurst (Canberra: Australian National University Press, 1979), 116.
59 R.S. Parker, 'Group Interests and the Non-Labour Parties since 1930', in *Readings in Australian Government*, ed. Colin A. Hughes (St Lucia: University of Queensland Press, 1968), 385.

60 Lloyd, 'The Formation and Development of the United Australia Party, 1929–37', 225.
61 *Ibid.*
62 Irving, 'The Nationalist Party, 1919–1930: Organisation and Ideology', 118.
63 Parker, 'Group Interests and the Non-Labour Parties since 1930', 388.
64 Irving's analysis is based on the only known membership list, compiled at a meeting before 1920, and some people are only identified by initials.
65 Irving, 'The Nationalist Party, 1919–1930: Organisation and Ideology', 136.
66 *Ibid.*
67 Watson, 'The United Australia Party and Its Sponsors', 86.
68 Hart, 'The Piper and the Tune', 113.
69 *Ibid.*, 123.
70 *Ibid.*
71 Watson, 'The United Australia Party and Its Sponsors', 85.
72 Irving, 'The Nationalist Party, 1919–1930: Organisation and Ideology', 159.
74 United Australia Party, 'Britain's Defence Policy: Protection of Overseas Possessions', *United Australia Party Monthly Bulletin* III, no. 2 (1938): 18.
75 *Ibid.*
76 Hamill, *The Strategic Illusion: The Singapore Strategy and the Defence of Australia and New Zealand, 1919–1942* (Singapore: Singapore University Press, 1981), 151.
77 Judging from the record of proceedings: *Caucus Minutes 1932–1949*, ed. Patrick Weller, vol. 3 (Melbourne: Melbourne University Press, 1975).
78 Australian Labor Party, Defence Policy of the Australian Labor Party, ALP policy platform presented at ALP Conference, July 1936, Papers of Sir Frederick Shedden, NAA A5954 885/2.
79 Australian Army, Defence of Australia and its relation to Imperial Defence, memorandum, 17 June 1937, Papers of the Cabinet, Public Records Office (London), PRO CAB 21/2525.
80 H.L. Harris, *Australia's National Interests and National Policy* (Melbourne: Melbourne University Press, 1938), 124.
81 'Where Australia Lies Open to Attack', *Herald*, 25 September 1933, p. 17.
82 Observer, 'Australian Defence Policy', *The Australian Quarterly* VII, no. 2 (1935): 67.
83 Archdale Parkhill, Australian Defence with particular reference to the security problem of small nations, speech to the Constitutional Club, Sydney, 11 May 1936, Papers of the Department of Defence, NAA A664/1, 534/401/72.
84 Frederick Shedden, Imperial Defence College Exercises: Principles of Imperial Defence, notes, 1927–28, Papers of Sir Frederick Shedden, NAA A5954, 20/1.
85 F.W. Eggleston, *Search for a Social Philosophy* (Melbourne: Melbourne University Press, 1941), 287.
86 Warren Osmond, *Frederic Eggleston: An Intellectual in Australian Politics* (Sydney: George Allen & Unwin, 1985), 184.
87 Ian Clunies Ross, 'Factors Influencing the Development of Australia's Trade with Japan', in *Australia and the Far East*, ed. I. Clunies Ross (Sydney: Angus and Robertson in conjunction with The Australian Institute of International Affairs, 1935), 201.
88 E.L. Piesse, 'More Planes Urged for Defence', *Morning Herald*, 25 October 1935, p. 6.
89 E.L. Piesse, 'Australia and Imperial Defence', radio broadcast script, 13 December 1936, Papers of E.L. Piesse, NLA, MS 882 Series 9 Folder 4.
90 Australia. House of Representatives 1922, Debates, vol. HR100, 17 August 1922, p. 1506.
91 Echoing Dr. Daniel Mannix's alleged description of the Great War: Australia. House of Representatives 1935, Debates, vol. HR147, 11 October 1935, p. 711.
92 Australia. House of Representatives 1937, Debates, vol. HR154, 25 August 1937, p. 105.
93 Australia. Senate 1937–38, Debates, vol. HR155, 4 May 1938, p. 765.

94 Carolyn Rasmussen, *The Lesser Evil? Opposition to War and Fascism in Australia, 1920–1941*, Melbourne University History Monographs, No. 15 (Melbourne: History Department University of Melbourne, 1992), 96.

95 This movement is discussed below in relation to the League of Nations.

96 Malcolm Saunders, *Quiet Dissenter: The Life and Thought of an Australian Pacifist: Eleanor May Moore 1875–1949*, Monograph/Peace Research Centre, No. 12 (Canberra: Peace Research Centre Research School of Pacific Studies Australian National University, 1993), 228.

97 R.S. Browne, World Disarmament Movement, police reports, 12 November 1928, Papers of the Investigation Branch Victoria, NAA B741/3, V5323.

98 Eleanor M. Moore, *The Quest for Peace, as I Have Known It in Australia* (Melbourne: Wilkes & Co., 1949), 82.

99 R.S. Browne, World Disarmament Movement, police reports, 9 April 1930, Papers of the Investigation Branch Victoria, NAA B741/3, V5323.

100 Bobbie Oliver, *Peacemongers: Conscientious Objectors to Military Service in Australia, 1911–1945* (Fremantle, WA: Fremantle Arts Centre Press, 1997), 58.

101 Henry Bournes Higgins, *World Disarmament* (Melbourne: World Disarmament Movement, 1928), 2.

102 R.S. Browne, World Disarmament Movement, police reports, 27 July 1928, Papers of the Investigation Branch Victoria, NAA B741/3, V5323.

103 J.C. Rockwood Proud, *World Peace, the League and Australia* (Melbourne: Robertson & Mullens, 1936), 22.

104 Oliver, *Peacemongers*, 58.

105 R.S. Browne, World Disarmament Movement, police reports, 12 November 1928, Papers of the Investigation Branch Victoria, NAA B741/3, V5323.

106 Oliver, *Peacemongers*, 59.

107 Moore, *The Quest for Peace.*

108 Oliver, *Peacemongers*, 68.

109 R.S. Browne, World Disarmament Movement, police reports, 28 August 1929, Papers of the Investigation Branch Victoria, NAA B741/3, V5323.

110 R.S. Browne, World Disarmament Movement, police reports, 9 April 1930, Papers of the Investigation Branch Victoria, NAA B741/3, V5323.

111 A detailed discussion of Australian Communists and the Spanish Civil War can be found in Macintyre, *The Reds*, 297–303.

112 'Is Britain Preparing a Pacific War?', *WAR! What For?* 1, no. 8 (1934): 157.

113 *Ibid.*

114 Joyce Manton, *The Centenary Prepares War* (Melbourne: Starlight Press, 1934), 25.

115 'Red Army "Invades" Poland: Half of Poland Saved from Horrors of War', *World Peace* 4, no. 9 (1939): 112.

116 Rasmussen, *The Lesser Evil? Opposition to War and Fascism in Australia, 1920–1941*, 9.

117 Moore, *The Quest for Peace*, 81.

118 Malcolm Saunders and Ralph Summy, *The Australian Peace Movement: A Short History* (Canberra: Peace Research Centre Australian National University, 1986), 23.

119 *Ibid.*

120 See, for example, F.W. Eggleston, *Search for a Social Philosophy* (Melbourne: Melbourne University Press, 1941); W.K. Hancock, *Australia, The Modern World* (London: Ernest Benn, 1930).

121 William Morris Hughes, Armistice Day Speech, 11 November 1920, speech, Papers of William Morris Hughes, NLA MS 1538, Series 35 Subseries 2 Box 169 Folder 13.

122 *Ibid.*

123 Australia. House of Representatives 1921, Debates, vol. HR97, 5 October 1921, p. 11688.

124 Australia. House of Representatives 1924, Debates, vol. HR106, 3 April 1924, p. 339.

125 W.J. Hudson, *Australia and the League of Nations* (Sydney: Sydney University Press in association with the Australian Institute of International Affairs, 1980), 36.

126 Frederick Gisborne, *Democracy on Trial, and Other Essays* (London: Longman Green, 1928), 43.
127 Hudson, *Australia and the League of Nations*, 69.
128 Raymond Watt, ABC Broadcast, radio broadcast script, 1931, Papers of Raymond Watt, NLA MS 1923 Box 5.
129 E.M. Andrews, *Writing on the Wall: The British Commonwealth and Aggression in the East 1931–1935* (Sydney: Allen & Unwin, 1987), 98.
130 Raymond Watt, 'The League of Nations Has It Failed? What of Its Future?', *The Australian Quarterly* V, no. 4 (1933): 100.
131 *Ibid.*, 103.
132 William Morris Hughes, Speech to League of Nations Union, speech to League of Nations Union, Sydney, 5 July 1933, Papers of Raymond Watt, NLA, MS 1923 Box 3 Folder 36.
133 William Morris Hughes, *Australia and War to-Day: The Price of Peace* (Sydney: Angus & Robertson, 1935), 31.
134 *Ibid.*, 118.
135 United Australia Party, 'Australian Defence', *United Australia Party Monthly Bulletin*, no. 7 (1935): 99.
136 United Australia Party, 'Italo-Abyssinian Dispute—Australia Stands by the League of Nations', *United Australia Party Monthly Bulletin*, no. 5 (1935): 64.
137 McMullin, *The Light on the Hill*, 196.
138 Australia. House of Representatives 1935, Debates, vol. HR147, 23 September 1935, p. 37.
139 *Ibid.*, p. 41.
140 Australia. House of Representatives 1935, Debates, vol. HR147, 1 November 1935, p. 1258.
141 Australia. House of Representatives 1937–1938, Debates, vol. HR155, 1 December 1937, p. 59.
142 *Ibid.*, p. 60.
143 R.G. Menzies, Let there be peace, speech to Wesley Church Melbourne, November 1938, Papers of Robert G. Menzies, NLA MS 4936 Series 6 Box 251 Folder 5.
144 Ernest Bramsted, 'Apostles of Collective Security', *Australian Journal of Politics and History* 23, no. 3 (1967): 364.
145 A.G. Colley, 'Australia, Great Britain, and the League', *The Australian Quarterly* X, no. 2 (1938): 56.
146 Australia. House of Representatives 1938, Debates, vol. HR157, 5 October 1938, p. 400.
147 Australia. House of Representatives 1932, Debates, vol. HR136, 14 October 1932, p. 1290.

CHAPTER 8 **THE FAILURE OF AUSTRALIAN LEADERSHIP**

1 Archibald A. Montgomery-Massingberd to Maurice Hankey, letter, 30 January 1935, Papers of the Cabinet, Public Records Office (London), PRO CAB 21/397.
2 Harold Perkin, 'The Recruitment of Elites in British Society since 1800', *Journal of Social History* 12, no. 2 (1978): 222.
3 Vilfredo Pareto, *The Rise and Fall of Elites: An Application of Theoretical Sociology* (New Brunswick, New Jersey: Transaction Publishers, 1991), 36.
4 *Ibid.*, 60.
5 C. Wright Mills, *The Power Elite* (New York: Oxford University Press, 1956).
6 *Ibid.*, 4.
7 *Ibid.*, 9.
8 *Ibid.*, 3.
9 John Higley, Desley Deacon and Don Smart, *Elites in Australia* (London: Routledge & K. Paul, 1979).

10 G. Lowell Field and John Higley, *Elitism* (London: Routledge & Kegan Paul, 1980), 38.

11 Grant A. Fleming, Simon P. Ville and David Merrett, *The Big End of Town: Big Business and Corporate Leadership in Twentieth-Century Australia* (Melbourne: Cambridge University Press, 2004), 1.

12 Robert William Connell and Terence H. Irving, *Class Structure in Australian History: Documents, Narrative and Argument* (Melbourne: Longman Cheshire, 1980), 283.

13 *Ibid.*, 270.

14 Perkin, 'The Recruitment of Elites in British Society since 1800', 222.

15 For examples of the definitions of elites used by previous researchers see, for example, Field and Higley, *Elitism*; Higley, Deacon and Smart, *Elites in Australia*; John Higley and Gwen Moore, 'Elite Integration in the United States and Australia', *The American Political Science Review* 75, no. 3 (1981); C. Wright Mills, 'The American Business Elite: A Collective Portrait', in *Power, Politics and People: The Collected Essays of C. Wright Mills*, ed. Irving Louis Horowitz (New York: Oxford University Press, 1963); Mills, *The Power Elite*; Perkin, 'The Recruitment of Elites in British Society since 1800'; W.D. Rubinstein, 'Education and the Social Origins of British Elites 1880–1970', *Past and Present*, no. 112 (1986).

16 Ambrose Pratt and Edward Leeson, *The National Handbook of Australia's Industries* (Melbourne: Speciality Press, 1934).

18 *The Army List of the Australian Military Forces: Active List* (Melbourne: Government Publisher, 1924 and subsequent editions 1926, 1927, 1928, 1932, 1934, 1935, 1937, 1939) and as *The Staff and Regimental Lists of the Australian Military Forces* (Melbourne: Government Publisher, 1931).

19 *The Royal Australian Air Force List* (Melbourne: Government Publisher, 1927 and subsequent editions for 1928, 1929, 1930, 1933, 1934 and 1935).

20 *The Navy List* (Melbourne: Government Printer, 1920 and annual editions 1922–40).

21 Four members of the political elite were members of both the ALP and NAT–UAP inter-war elites, crossed the floor in 1931 and are counted in both parties.

22 Colin A. Hughes and B.D. Graham, *A Handbook of Australian Government and Politics, 1890–1964* (Canberra: Australian National University Press, 1968).

23 Joan Rydon, *A Biographical Register of the Commonwealth Parliament, 1901–1972* (Canberra: Australian National University Press, 1975).

24 See for example, Field and Higley, *Elitism*; Mills, *The Power Elite*; Perkin, 'The Recruitment of Elites in British Society since 1800'; Robert D. Putnam, *The Comparative Study of Political Elites, Contemporary Comparative Politics Series* (Englewood Cliffs, New Jersey: Prentice-Hall, 1976).

25 Robert Presthus, *Elites in the Policy Process* (London: Cambridge University Press, 1974), 47.

26 Putnam, *The Comparative Study of Political Elites*, 124.

27 Other factors have been discussed in the preceding chapters.

28 G.C. Peden, *British Rearmament and the Treasury, 1932–1939* (Edinburgh: Scottish Academic Press, 1979), 184.

29 Mills, *The Power Elite*, 47.

30 Putnam, *The Comparative Study of Political Elites*, 109.

31 Walter L. Arnstein, 'Wealth and the Wealthy in the Modern World', *Journal of Social History* 15, no. 4 (1982): 725.

32 Rubinstein, 'Education and the Social Origins of British Elites 1880–1970', 61.

33 John Scott, *Who Rules Britain?* (Oxford: Polity Press, 1991), 136.

34 J. Pierrepont Moffat, 'Australia and the Australians', in *Australia through American Eyes*, ed. P.G. Edwards (St Lucia: University of Queensland Press, 1979), 50.

35 James Belich, *Paradise Reforged: A History of the New Zealanders from the 1880s to the Year 2000* (Honolulu: University of Hawaii Press, 2001), 340–4.

36 Rubinstein, 'Education and the Social Origins of British Elites 1880–1970', 191.

38 Rydon, *A Federal Legislature*, 153.

39 Geoffrey Blainey and Norman H. Olver, *The University of Melbourne: A Centenary Portrait* (Melbourne: Melbourne University Press, 1956), 102.

40 Sabine Willis, 'The Formulation of Australian Attitudes Towards China: 1918–1941' (PhD diss., University of New South Wales, 1974), 264.

41 F.B. Smith, 'British History in Australia', *Melbourne Studies in Education* (1981): 42.

42 Blainey and Olver, *The University of Melbourne*, 102.

43 R.J.W. Selleck, *The Shop: The University of Melbourne 1850–1939* (Melbourne: Melbourne University Press, 2003), 188.

44 Janet McCalman, *Journeyings: The Biography of a Middle-Class Generation 1920–1990* (Melbourne: 1993), 124.

45 S.G. Firth, 'Social Values in the New South Wales Primary School 1880–1914: An Analysis of School Texts', *Melbourne Studies in Education* (1970): 133.

46 *Ibid.*, 132.

47 *Ibid.*, 129.

48 *Ibid.*, 131.

49 John Latham, *Australia and the British Commonwealth, The John Murtagh Macrossan Lectures; 1928* (London: Macmillan and Co., 1929).

50 McMullin, *The Light on the Hill*, 186.

51 Race Mathews, *Australia's First Fabians: Middle-Class Radicals, Labour Activists and the Early Labour Movement* (Melbourne: Cambridge University Press, 1993), 6.

52 *Ibid.*, 1.

53 Rohan Rivett, *Australian Citizen: Herbert Brookes, 1867–1963* (Melbourne: Melbourne University Press, 1965), 94.

54 Ken Buckley and E.L. Wheelwright, *False Paradise: Australian Capitalism Revisited, 1915–1955* (Melbourne: Oxford University Press, 1998), 63.

55 John Lack, 'Mckay, Hugh Victor', *Australian Dictionary of Biography* (Melbourne: Melbourne University Press, 1986).

56 Peter Cochrane, 'Dissident Capitalists: National Manufacturers in Conservative Politics, 1917–1934', in *Essays in the Political Economy of Australian Capitalism*, ed. E. L. Wheelwright and Ken Buckley (Sydney: Australia and New Zealand Book Co., 1980), 122.

57 Joan Rydon, *A Federal Legislature: The Australian Commonwealth Parliament, 1901–1980* (Melbourne: Oxford University Press, 1986), 46.

61 Oliver McKee, 'Political March of the Veterans', *The Commonweal: A Weekly Review of Literature, the Arts and Public Affairs* XIII, no. 2 (1930): 40.

62 *Ibid.*

63 *Ibid.*

64 *Ibid.*

65 Jennifer D. Keene, *Doughboys, the Great War, and the Remaking of America, War, Society, Culture.* (Baltimore: Johns Hopkins University Press, 2001), 210.

66 Richard Gardiner Casey, 'Australia in World Affairs', *International Affairs* 16, no. 5 (1937): 698.

67 *Ibid.*, 701.

68 Jay Pierrepont Moffat, diary entry, 12 September 1935, Diaries of Jay Pierrepont Moffat, US Consul-General to Australia, 1935–37, NLA MFM G7251.

69 W.J. Hudson, *Casey* (Melbourne: Oxford University Press, 1986), 49.

70 *Ibid.*, 119.

71 Solomon Encel, *Equality and Authority: A Study of Class, Status and Power in Australia* (Melbourne: Cheshire, 1970), 349.

72 Rivett, *Australian Citizen*, 84.

73 Papers of Herbert Brookes, NLA MS 1924 Series 19.

74 For examples of Brookes' anti-Catholicism see Papers of Herbert Brookes, NLA MS 1924 Series 20.

75 Political affiliation as reported in Joseph A. Alexander, *Who's Who in Australia 1938* (Melbourne: Herald Press, 1938); *Australian Dictionary of Biography*, 16 vols., vols. 7–16 (Melbourne: Melbourne University Press, 1979–2002); Christopher Cunneen, *Australian Dictionary of Biography: Supplement 1580–1980, with a Name Index to the Australian Dictionary of Biography to 1980* (Melbourne: Melbourne University Press, 2005); Baiba Beata Berzins Irving, The Nationalist Party, 1919–30: Organisation and Ideology (PhD, University of Sydney, 1972); Fred Johns,

Fred Johns's Annual (Melbourne: Sir Isaac Pitman & Sons, Ltd., 1914); Fred Johns, *Who's Who in Australia 1927–8* (Adelaide: The Hassell Press, 1927); Errol G. Knox, *Who's Who in Australia 1935* (Melbourne: Herald Press, 1935).

76 C.D. Coulthard-Clark, *Soldiers in Politics: The Impact of the Military on Australian Political Life and Institutions, Army Military History Series. Issues* (St Leonards, NSW: Allen & Unwin, 1996), 129.

77 'Message from People's Leaders: The Acting Prime Minister (Dr. Page)', *Argus*, 25 April 1935, p. 7.

78 '300,000 at the Dedication of the Shrine', *Argus*, 12 November 1934, p. 9.

79 Speeches made at Anzac Day Ceremonies are found in 'Armistice Day: How It Will Be Observed', *Argus*, 11 November 1925, p. 22; 'Honouring the Anzacs', *Argus*, 26 April 1922, p. 11; 'Lord Mayor's Message', *Argus*, 24 April 1934, p. 7; 'Message from People's Leaders: The Acting Prime Minister (Dr. Page)', *Argus*, 25 April 1935, p. 7; 'Reverent Remembrance', *Argus*, 25 April 1934, p. 9.

80 Carl Bridge, *Ranging Shots: New Directions in Australian Military History* (London: Sir Robert Menzies Centre for Australian Studies Institute of Commonwealth Studies University of London, 1998), 1.

81 L.F. Crisp and B.C. Atkinson, *Melbourne Punch Profiles, 1904–1929: A Chronological List* (Canberra: Australian National University, 1971).

82 'General Brudenell White', *Melbourne Punch*, 19 August 1926, p. 12; 'Sir John Monash', *Melbourne Punch*, 8 January 1920, p. 44.

83 Sir Leslie Wilson to Sir E. Harding who forwarded the letter on to Sir Maurice Hankey, letter, 20 January 1938, Papers of the Cabinet, Public Records Office (London), PRO CAB 21/2525.

84 For an example of the RAN's appearance in dress uniform see 'A Social Highlight', *Sun News Pictorial*, 6 November 1936, p. 22.

85 'Social Custom Revived: Naval and Military Ball', *Herald*, 1 November 1924, p. 13.

86 'New Flagship Arrives', *Herald*, 3 November 1928, p. 32.

87 'On Board the Flagship: "At Home" on the Australia Today', *Herald*, 5 November 1928, p. 12.

88 'Dancing Aboard Flagship', *Herald*, 7 November 1936, p. 25.

89 *Ibid.*

90 'Informal Pictures at Last Night's Navy League Ball', *Herald*, 5 November 1936, p. 34.

91 For examples of Navy League opinion see Libra, 'A Problem of National Defence: Aircraft as Cuckoo or Hawk?', *The Navy*, April 1935; E. George Marks, *Pacific Peril, or, Menace of Japan's Mandated Islands* (Sydney: Wynyard Book Arcade, 1933); Marks, *Watch the Pacific!: Defenceless Australia* (Sydney: Coles Book Arcade, 1924).

92 'Fleet Arrives', *Herald*, 2 November 1925, p. 19.

93 'Naval Men March in the City', *Herald*, 4 November 1936, p. 3.

94 'Polished Bayonets', *Sun News Pictorial*, 6 November 1936, p. 22.

95 *Centenary Naval Pageant* (Melbourne: Ramsay, 1934).

96 'History', *Herald*, 1 November 1934, p. 38.

97 Oswald Ziegler, *Victorian and Melbourne Centenary Celebrations* (Melbourne: Collins Court, 1934).

98 'The Fleet is Here: Happy Days for Sailors', *Herald*, 2 November 1931, p. 1.

99 'Australian Naval Squadron in Melbourne for the Cup', *Herald*, 2 November 1929, p. 32; 'Cup Carnival', *Herald*, 2 November 1933, p. 18.

100 'Naval Men Lose Pet Tortoise', *Herald*, 5 November 1936, p. 12.

101 'The Fleet is Here: Happy Days for Sailors', *Herald*, 2 November 1931', p. 1.

102 'Brilliant Ball at Australian Club', *Age*, 7 November 1936, p. 30.

103 'The Governor General's House Party for the Cup', *Herald*, 1 November 1927, p. 7.

104 C.D. Coulthard-Clark, *Duntroon, the Royal Military College of Australia, 1911–1986* (Sydney: Allen & Unwin, 1986), 134.

105 See for example, Thomas Blamey, 'The Sentinel', radio broadcast scripts, 1938–1939, AWM 3DRL/16643 Wallets 7/1-6.

106 Craig Wilcox, *For Hearths and Homes: Citizen Soldiering in Australia, 1854–1945* (St Leonards, NSW: Allen & Unwin, 1998), 88.
107 *Ibid.*, 88–9.
108 *Ibid.*, 89.
109 *Ibid.*
110 Major-General Sir Charles Rosenthal to Minister for Defence Harold Thorby, letter, 27 January 1938, Papers of Sir Frederick Shedden, NAA A5954/69, 906/3.
111 Minister for Defence, Harold Thorby to Major-General Sir Charles Rosenthal, letter, 21 April 1938, Papers of Sir Frederick Shedden, NAA A5954/69, 906/3.
112 A.J. Hill, 'Rosenthal, Sir Charles (1875–1954)', in *Australian Dictionary of Biography* (Melbourne: Melbourne University Press, 1988), 451–3.
113 Mark Clisby, *Guilty or Innocent?: The Gordon Bennett Case* (North Sydney: Allen & Unwin, 1992), 4.
114 Quoted in Frank Legg, *The Gordon Bennett Story* (Sydney: Angus and Robertson, 1965), 151.
115 Wilcox, *For Hearths and Homes*, 102.
116 Ziegler, *Victorian and Melbourne Centenary Celebrations.*
117 Ronald McNicoll, *Number 36 Collins Street, Melbourne Club 1838–1988* (Sydney: Allen & Unwin in conjunction with the Melbourne Club, 1988), 167.
118 It is the Club's 'Settled policy' that its archives 'not to be made available to any persons other than its own Archives Sub-Committee'.
119 Coulthard-Clark, *Duntroon, the Royal Military College of Australia, 1911–1986*, 102.
120 *Ibid.*, 123.
121 *Ibid.*, 128.
122 *Ibid.*, 275.
123 Ziegler, *Victorian and Melbourne Centenary Celebrations.*
124 C.D. Coulthard-Clark, *The Third Brother: The Royal Australian Air Force 1921–39* (North Sydney: Allen & Unwin, 1991), 152.
125 Jeffrey Grey, *A Military History of Australia* (Melbourne: Cambridge University Press, 1990), 130.
126 Coulthard-Clark, *The Third Brother*, 231.
127 George Jones, *From Private to Air Marshal: The Autobiography of Air Marshal Sir George Jones KB CB DFC* (Melbourne: Greenhouse, 1988), 36.
128 Alan Stephens, *The Royal Australian Air Force* (Melbourne: Oxford University Press, 2001), 45.
129 Coulthard-Clark, *The Third Brother*, 393.
130 *Ibid.*
131 *Ibid.*, 445.
132 *Ibid.*, 331.
133 Sir Edward Ellington, Ellington Report on Australian Air force and Air defence, report, 1938, Papers of Sir Frederick Shedden, NAA A5954/69, 2395/2.
134 Grey, *A Military History of Australia*, 130.
135 'Air Toll', *Canberra Times*, 17 May 1927, p. 1.
136 *Ibid.*
137 B.N. Primrose, 'Equipment and Naval Policy 1919–1942', *Australian Journal of Politics and History* 23, no. 2 (1977): 163.
138 Peter Cochrane, *Industrialization and Dependence: Australia's Road to Economic Development, 1870–1939* (St Lucia, Queensland.: University of Queensland Press, 1980), 116.
139 Herbert Gepp, *Democracy's Danger: Addresses on Various Occasions* (Sydney: Angus & Robertson, 1939), 15.
140 *Ibid.*, 23.
141 Herbert Gepp, Defence of Australia and its relation thereto Primary and Secondary Industries, speech, Gepp Papers, NLA MS 1584.
142 'Australia's Prosperity: Relation to World Position', *Argus*, 27 July 1935, p. 22.
143 'Dangers Ahead: Race Preservation', *Argus*, 26 July 1938, p. 21.
144 *Ibid.*

145 Herbert Gepp, 'Defence of Australia: What It Means to All', *Argus*, 10 November 1938, p. 4.
146 Herbert Gepp, 'Defence of Australia: How to Ensure Efficiency', *Argus*, 11 November 1938, p. 3.
147 Geoffrey Blainey, *The Steel Master: A Life of Essington Lewis* (Melbourne: Macmillan, 1971), 84.
148 *Ibid.*, 108.
149 *Ibid.*, 121.
150 *Ibid.*
151 Alan Trengove, *What's Good for Australia!: The Story of BHP* (Melbourne: Cassell, 1975), 166. The source of this quotation is not provided and a search of the indexes of the *Argus* and the *Sydney Morning Herald* did not provide the quotation.
152 *Ibid.*
153 *Ibid.*
154 Blainey, *The Steel Master*, 124.
155 *Ibid.*, 138.
156 Neither the *Argus* nor the *Sydney Morning Herald* indexes for the inter-war period had any entry for Essington Lewis until after the war had started.
157 Charles Denton Kemp, *Big Businessmen: Four Biographical Essays* (Melbourne: Institute of Public Affairs, 1964), 29.
158 Cochrane, *Industrialization and Dependence*, 77.
159 *Ibid.*, 91.
160 *Ibid.*, 2.
161 John Kennett, The Collins House Group (Master of Economics, Monash, 1982), 88.
162 *Ibid.*
163 *Ibid.*, 110.
164 Cochrane, *Industrialization and Dependence*, 91.
165 *Ibid.*, 2.
166 'Proposed Tour to Japan', *Monthly Journal of The Melbourne Chamber of Commerce* X, no. 4 (1933); 'Proposed Tour to Japan, Chosen (Korea) and Manchuria', *Monthly Journal of The Melbourne Chamber of Commerce* X, no. 3 (1933).
167 Sir Abe Bailey, 'The Abyssinian Crisis: Vital Interests of Britain and the British Empire', *Monthly Journal of The Melbourne Chamber of Commerce* XII, no. 4 (1935).
168 'Proposed Tour to Japan,' *Monthly Journal of The Melbourne Chamber of Commerce* X, no. 4 (1933): 63; 'Proposed Tour to Japan, Chosen (Korea) and Manchuria', *Monthly Journal of The Melbourne Chamber of Commerce* X, no. 3 (1933): 58.
169 Stanley Melbourne Bruce, 'Members' Luncheon to Honour Rt. Hon S.M. Bruce, C.H., P.C., M.C.', *Monthly Journal of The Melbourne Chamber of Commerce* IX, no. 12 (1932): 233–6.
170 Colin Forster, *Industrial Development in Australia 1920–1930* (Canberra: Australian National University, 1964), 128.
171 Ernst A. Boehm, *Twentieth Century Economic Development in Australia*, 2nd ed., *Topics on the Australian Economy* (Melbourne: Longman, 1979), 10.
172 Forster, *Industrial Development in Australia 1920–1930*, 128.
173 Cochrane, *Industrialization and Dependence*, 2.
174 Pat Brown and Helen Hughes, 'The Marketing Structure of Australian Manufacturing Industry, 1914 to 1963–4', in *Australian Economic Development in the Twentieth Century*, ed. Colin Forster and W.A. Sinclair (Sydney: George Allen & Unwin, 1970), 182.
175 *Ibid.*
176 Cochrane, *Industrialization and Dependence*, 77.
177 Kennett, The Collins House Group, 212.
178 *Ibid.*, 212–13.
179 *Ibid.*, 110.
180 Pat Brown, *Gatty: Prince of Navigators* (Hobart: Libra Books, 1997), 167.

181 'Australian Made Aeroplanes: The Activities of Tugan Air Craft Ltd.', *The Australasian Manufacturer: Special Industrial Annual*, 18 April 1936, 48–9, 134; 'Planning, Mapping, Surveying & Visualising: The Service New to Australia of Adastra Airways Ltd.', *The Australasian Manufacturer: Special Industrial Annual*, 18 April 1936, 75, 171.

182 Robert Conlon, *Wheels and Deals: The Automotive Industry in Twentieth Century Australia* (Sydney: Ashgate, 2001), 28.

183 Cochrane, *Industrialization and Dependence*, 116.

CHAPTER 9 **CONCLUSION**

1 The attacks on Australia are described in Erle Cox, *Fool's Harvest* (Melbourne: Robertson & Mullen, 1939), 42–50.

2 *Ibid.*, 53.

3 Mr John Curtin, Prime Minister, to Mr Winston Churchill, U.K. Prime Minister, Cablegram Johcu 21, 23 January 1942, in *Documents on Australian Foreign Policy 1937–49*, ed. W.J. Hudson *et al.*, vol. V, doc. 293 (Canberra: Australian Govt Publishing Service: 1982), p. 463.

4 C.D. Coulthard-Clark, *The Third Brother: The Royal Australian Air Force 1921–39* (North Sydney: Allen & Unwin, 1991), 180.

5 David Day, *The Politics of War* (Sydney: Harper Collins, 2003), 17.

6 David Day, 'The Horrors and Legacy of World War II', *Australian*, 15 August 2005, p. 8.

7 *Ibid.*

8 *Ibid.*

9 Day, *The Politics of War*, 49.

10 Day, 'The Horrors and Legacy of World War II', 8.

11 Ernle Chatfield, C.J. Deverell, E.L. Ellington, Appreciation of the Situation in the Far East, 1937, by the Chiefs of Staff Sub-Committee, appreciation, 14 June 1937, Papers of the Cabinet, Public Records Office (London), PRO CAB 16/182.

BIBLIOGRAPHY

The bibliography is divided into 'Primary sources' ('Manuscripts', 'Audio', and 'Published sources') and 'Secondary sources'. The 'Manuscripts' section lists the collections consulted—the abbreviation for each collection is given and in the case of National Archives of Australia and the National Library of Australia the Series number is also indicated.

Published material is cited in accordance with the Chicago Manual of Style 14th Edition or, for Australian sources, The Australian Government Style Manual with three exceptions: the date of parliamentary debates is included; material from the Digest of Decisions and Announcements and Important Speeches by the Prime Minister are cited by author, title of speech, title of digest, volume, issue number, place of publication, publisher, year; documents cited from Documents on Australian Foreign Policy 1937–49 include the document number and date of document in addition to the page number.

PRIMARY SOURCES

Manuscripts

Australian War Memorial (Canberra), AWM

Blamey Papers
General Collection

Churchill Archives Centre (Cambridge), CAC

Papers of Albert Victor Alexander, 1st Earl, AVAR
Papers of Sir Winston Leonard Spencer Churchill, CHAR
Papers of Alfred Duff Cooper, 1st Viscount, DUFC
Papers of Maurice Pascal Alers Hankey, 1st Baron, HNKY

Franklin D. Roosevelt Presidential Library (Hyde Park)

Robert Menzies Correspondence
Office of Social Entertainment—Lyons Visit
Papers of Sumner Welles

Imperial War Museum (London), IWM

Papers of Lieutenant General A.E. Percival CB DSO OBE MC

Liddell Hart Centre for Military Archives, King's College London

Papers of Engineer Cdr Sidney John Armstrong
Papers of Sir Henry Robert Moore Brooke-Popham
Papers of Field Marshall Sir John Dill
Papers of Capt Sir Basil Henry Liddell Hart
Papers of Charles Archibald Vlieland

National Archives of Australia (Canberra), NAA

Papers of Stanley Melbourne Bruce, Series M104
Papers of the Council of Defence, Series A9787
Papers of Dr J.S. Cumpston relating to Colonial and Imperial Conferences etc. Series A4640
Papers of the Department of Air, Series A1196
Papers of the Department of Defence, Series A664, Series A816, Series MP729/6, Series MP826/1
Papers of the Department of External Affairs, Series A981, A4640
Papers of the Navy Office, Series MP1185/8
Papers of Sir Frederick Shedden, Series A5954
War Cabinet Minutes, Series A2673

National Archives of Australia (Melbourne), NAA

Papers of Department of Defence, Series B197
Papers of the Investigation Branch Victoria, Series B741
Papers of J.K. Jensen, Series MP956/2
Papers of the Navy Office, Series MP1049/1

National Library of Australia Manuscripts Section (Canberra), NLA MS

Papers of the Australian Industries Protection League, NLA MS 756
Papers of Herbert Brookes, NLA MS 1924
Papers of Richard Gardiner Casey, NLA MS 2217
Papers of Herbert Gepp, NLA MS 390
Papers of William Morris Hughes, NLA MS 1538
Papers of E.A. Mann, NLA MS 1955
Papers of Robert G. Menzies, NLA MS 4936
Papers of Earle Page, NLA MS 1663
Papers of Archdale Parkhill, NLA MS 4742
Papers of George Foster Pearce, NLA MS 1827
Papers of E.L. Piesse, NLA MS 882
Papers of F.J. Riley, NLA MS 759
Papers of Raymond Watt, NLA MS 1923

National Library of Australia Microfilm Section (Canberra), NLA MFM

Papers of Jay Pierrepont Moffat, NLA MFM G7251

National Maritime Museum (Greenwich), NMM

Papers of Admiral of the Fleet Sir Ernle Chatfield, CHT
Papers of Admiral Sir Herbert Richmond, RIC

Public Record Office (London), PRO

Papers of the Admiralty, ADM
Papers of the Air Ministry, AIR
Papers of the Ministry of Aviation, AIR
Papers of the Cabinet, CAB
Papers of the Colonial Office, CO
Papers of the Dominion Office, DO
Papers of the Foreign Office, FO
Papers of the Prime Minister's Office, PREM
Papers of the War Office, WO

Audio

National Film and Sound Archive, NFSA

Joseph Lyons Broadcast, NFSA 244360

Published sources

'Achievement! Commonwealth Aircraft Corporations No.1 Wirraway Makes First Flight'. *The BHP Review* XVI, no. 3 (1939): 1–4.
Age (Melbourne), 1919–41.
'Alexander, Joseph A.', *Who's Who in Australia 1938*. Melbourne: Herald Press, 1938.
'All Eyes on the Pacific'. *World Peace* 2, no. 7 (1937): 99.
Angell, Norman. *The Defence of the Empire*. London: H. Hamilton, 1937.
Argus (Melbourne), 1919–41.
Armitage, C.G. 'Defence of Australia'. *Sydney Morning Herald*, 9 August 1933, p. 9.
Australia. House of Representatives 1919–42, 1992. Debates.
Australia. Senate 1919–42. Debates.
'Australia and the Czech Crisis'. In *Australian Commentaries: Select Articles from the 'Round Table' 1911–1942*. Edited by L.L. Robson. Melbourne: Melbourne University Press, 1975, pp. 179–82.
'Australia Demands Pacific Pact'. *World Peace* 4, no. 6 (1939): 62.
'Australian Made Aeroplanes: The Activities of Tugan Air Craft Ltd'. *The Australasian Manufacturer: Special Industrial Annual*, 18 April 1936: 48–9, 134.
Australian Worker (Sydney), 1919–41.
Bailey, Sir Abe. 'The Abyssinian Crisis: Vital Interests of Britain and the British Empire'. *Monthly Journal of The Melbourne Chamber of Commerce* XII, no. 4 (1935): 63–4.
Ball, W. Macmahon. 'Australian Press and World Affairs'. In *Press, Radio and World Affairs*. Edited by W. Macmahon Ball. Melbourne: Melbourne University Press, 1938, pp. 9–33.

Beasley, John. 'Need for Support for Australia'. *Digest of Decisions and Announcements and Important Speeches by the Prime Minister*, vol. 1, no. 16. Canberra: Commonwealth Government Printer, 1942.

Brigg, Solomon. 'Australia Must Be Neutral: Policy of War Resistance'. *Labor Daily*, 14 September 1935, p. 11.

Bruce, Stanley Melbourne. 'Members' Luncheon to Honour Rt. Hon S.M. Bruce, C.H., P.C., M.C'. *Monthly Journal of The Melbourne Chamber of Commerce* IX, no. 12 (1932): 233–6.

Burrell, Henry. *Mermaids Do Exist*. South Melbourne: Macmillan, 1986.

Campbell, General G.R. 'Australian Defence Policy'. In *Studies in Australian Affairs*. Melbourne: Macmillan, 1928, pp. 179–96.

Canberran. 'Pacific Chessboard'. *The Australian National Review* 5, no. 27 (1939): 10–20.

Casey, Richard Gardiner. 'America's Second Fight for Freedom'. In *Speeches in America*. Washington: 1940–41.

—— 'Australia and the War'. In *Speeches in America*. Washington: 1940–41.

—— 'Australia in World Affairs'. *International Affairs* 16, no. 5 (1937): 698–713.

—— *My Dear P.M.: R.G. Casey's Letters to S.M. Bruce, 1924–1929*. Edited by W.J. Hudson and J. North. Canberra: Australian Government Publishing Service, 1980.

—— 'Speech to Mid-Day Luncheon Club at Springfield Illinois'. In *Speeches in America*. Washington: 1940–41.

—— 'Speech to the Boston Chamber of Commerce'. In *Speeches in America*. Washington: 1940–*Caucus Minutes 1917–1931*. Edited by Patrick Weller. 3 vols. Vol. 2. Melbourne: Melbourne University Press, 1975.

Caucus Minutes 1932–1949. Edited by Patrick Weller. 3 vols. Vol. 3. Melbourne: Melbourne University Press, 1975.

Centenary Naval Pageant. Melbourne: Ramsay, 1934.

Churchill, Winston to Stanley Baldwin, 13 December 1924. Edited by Martin Gilbert. VIII vols. Vol. V Companion Part 1, *Winston S. Churchill: The Exchequer Years 1922–1929*. London: Heinemann, 1979.

Colley, A.G. 'Australia, Great Britain, and the League'. *The Australian Quarterly* X, no. 2 (1938): 49–56.

—— 'Australia's Enemies'. *The Australian Quarterly* IX, no. 4 (1937): 84–91.

Conference of Prime Ministers and Representatives of the United Kingdom, the Dominions, and India. London: J.J. Keliher & Co., 1921.

Cox, Erle. *Fool's Harvest*. Melbourne: Robertson & Mullen, 1939.

Crawford, J.G. 'Australia as a Pacific Power'. In *Australia's Foreign Policy*. Edited by W.G.K. Duncan, D.A.S. Campbell and Australian Institute of Political Science. Sydney: Angus & Robertson, 1938, pp. 69–122.

Curtin, John. 'Attack on Darwin'. *Digest of Decisions and Announcements and Important Speeches by the Prime Minister*, vol. 1, no. 19. Canberra: Commonwealth Government Printer, 1942.

—— 'Australian Defence'. *Digest of Decisions and Announcements and Important Speeches by the Prime Minister*, vol. 1, no. 11. Canberra: Commonwealth Government Printer, 1941.

—— 'Facing 1942'. *Digest of Decisions and Announcements and Important Speeches by the Prime Minister,* vol. 1, no. 13. Canberra: Commonwealth Government Printer, 1941.

—— 'Fall of Singapore'. *Digest of Decisions and Announcements and Important Speeches by the Prime Minister,* vol. 1, no. 19. Canberra: Commonwealth Government Printer, 1942.

—— 'Prime Minister's Broadcast'. *Digest of Decisions and Announcements and Important Speeches by the Prime Minister*, vol. 1, no. 16. Canberra: Commonwealth Government Printer, 1942.

—— 'Prime Minister's Speech'. *Digest of Decisions and Announcements and Important Speeches by the Prime Minister*, vol. 1, no. 18. Canberra: Commonwealth Government Printer, 1942.

—— 'Relations with America'. *Digest of Decisions and Announcements and Important Speeches by the Prime Minister*, vol. 1, no. 22. Canberra: Commonwealth Government Printer, 1942.

—— 'The Task Ahead'. *Herald*, 27 December 1941, 10.

—— *To Build and Defend a Happy and Self-Reliant Australia: Policy Speech of the Australian Labor Party*. Sydney, 1937.

Curtis, Lionel. *The Problem of the Commonwealth*. Toronto: Macmillan, 1916.

'The Decline of Americano-Mania'. *Bulletin*, 23 February 1922, p. 6.

Department of External Affairs. 'The Far East'. *Current Notes* VI (1939): 377–80.

Documents on Australian Foreign Policy, 1937–49. Edited by W.J. Hudson, P.G. Edwards, R.G. Neale, Wendy Way, H. Kenway, Pamela Andre, H.J.W. Stokes, M.E. Cook, Margaret Browne, Jane North and Ashton Robinson. 7 vols. Vols. 1–5. Canberra: Australian Government Publishing Service, 1975–82.

Eggleston, F.W. *Search for a Social Philosophy*. Melbourne: Melbourne University Press, 1941.

Eldershaw, M. Barnard. *My Australia*. London: Jarrolds, 1939.

Evatt, H.V. 'External Affairs Statement'. *Digest of Decisions and Announcements and Important Speeches by the Prime Minister*, vol. 1, no. 20. Canberra: Commonwealth Government Printer, 1942.

Fairbairn, J.V. 'Australia's Defence'. *The Australian National Review* 4, no. 23 (1938): 12–16.

Forde, Francis. 'Possibility of Invasion'. *Digest of Decisions and Announcements and Important Speeches by the Prime Minister*, vol. 1, no. 16. Canberra: Commonwealth Government Printer, 1942.

Fowler, J.M, *Australia's Perils: Real and Imaginary*. Melbourne: Brown, Prior & Company, 1926.

Gauss, Clarence. 'C.E. Gauss to the Secretary of State, 1 December 1940'. In *Australia through American Eye*. Edted by P.G. Edwards. St Lucia: University of Queensland Press, 1979, pp. 59–65.

Gepp, Herbert. *Democracy's Danger: Addresses on Various Occasions*. Sydney: Angus & Robertson, 1939.

Gisborne, Frederick. *Democracy on Trial, and Other Essays*. London: Longman Green, 1928.

Grattan, C. Hartley. *Introducing Australia*. New York: John Day, 1942.

Hancock, W.K. *Australia, The Modern World*. London: Ernest Benn, 1930.

Harris, H.L. *Australia's National Interests and National Policy*. Melbourne: Melbourne University Press, 1938.

Hartnett, Laurence, and John Veitch. *Big Wheels and Little Wheels*. Melbourne: Lansdowne, 1964.

Herald (Melbourne), 1919–41.

Higgins, Henry Bournes. *World Disarmament*. Melbourne: World Disarmament Movement, 1928.

Hornabrook, Rupert. *Japan and Ourselves: Humanity Cries for Peace*. Melbourne: Stillwell, 1939.

Hughes, William Morris. *Australia and War to-Day: The Price of Peace*. Sydney: Angus & Robertson, 1935.

—— 'Defence: A Policy for the Times'. *Sydney Morning Herald*, 7 August 1933, p. 8.

—— *The Splendid Adventure: A Review of Empire Relations within and without the Commonwealth of Britannic Nations*. London: Ernest Benn Limited, 1929.

'The Imperial Conference'. *The Round Table* XX, no. 80 (1930): 857–63.

'The Imperial Conference of 1923'. In *Colonial and Imperial Conferences from 1887–1937*. Edited by Maurice Olliver. Ottawa: Queen's Printer and Controller of Stationery, 1954.

Imperial Conference, 1923: Summary of Proceedings. Canberra: Commonwealth Government Printer, 1924.

Imperial Conference, 1926: Summary of Proceedings. Canberra: Commonwealth Government Printer, 1927.

Imperial Conference, 1937: Summary of Proceedings. Canberra: Commonwealth Government Printer, 1937.
International Peace Research Committee. *Crisis in the Pacific: The Coming Anglo-Japanese-American Conflict*. Melbourne: Ruskin Press, 1937.
'Is Britain Preparing a Pacific War?'. *WAR! What For?* 1, no. 8 (1934): 156–7.
Ishimaru, Tota. *Japan Must Fight Britain*. Translated by G.V. Rayment. London: Hurst & Blackett, 1936.
Jellicoe, John Rushworth. *The Jellicoe Papers: Selections from the Private and Official Correspondence of Admiral of the Fleet Earl Jellicoe of Scapa*. Edited by A. Temple Patterson and J.E.T. Harper. 2 vols. London: Spottiswoode Ballantyne for the Navy Records Society, 1966.
Johns, Fred. *Fred Johns's Annual*. Melbourne: Sir Isaac Pitman & Sons, Ltd., 1914.
—— *Who's Who in Australia 1927–8*. Adelaide: The Hassell Press, 1927.
Jones, Frederick. 'Defence of Australia'. *Sydney Morning Herald*, 10 August 1933, p. 4.
Jones, George. *From Private to Air Marshal: The Autobiography of Air Marshal Sir George Jones KB CB DFC*. Melbourne: Greenhouse, 1988.
King, H.F. 'Home Production'. *The BHP Review* XVI, no. 1 (1938): 8–9.
Knox, Errol G. *Who's Who in Australia 1935*. Melbourne: Herald Press, 1935.
Labor Anti-War Committee. *Labor's Case against War and Fascism*. Melbourne, 1935.
Labor Daily, 'Lyons Budget Does Not Give Anything to Anybody: Huge Defence Vote', 24 September 1935, p. 5.
Latham, John. *Australia and the British Commonwealth, The John Murtagh Macrossan Lectures: 1928*. London: Macmillan and Co., 1929.
—— *The Australian Eastern Mission, 1934: Report of the Rt. Hon. J.G. Latham, Leader of the Mission*. Canberra: Government Publisher, 1934.
Lavarack, J.D. 'The Defence of the British Empire with Special Reference to the Far East and Australia'. *Army Quarterly* XXV (1933): 207–17.
Libra. 'A Problem of National Defence: Aircraft as Cuckoo or Hawk?'. *The Navy*, April 1935, pp. 123–4.
Lyons, Enid Muriel. *So We Take Comfort*. London: Heinemann, 1965.
MacDonald, J. Ramsay. *National Defense*. London: George Allen, 1917.
MacNeil, Neil Harcourt. 'A Case for National Defence'. *The Australian Rhodes Review* 4 (1939): 50–4.
Mann, E.A. *Arrows in the Air: A Selection from Broadcasts by 'The Watchman'*. Melbourne: S. John Bacon, 1944.
Manton, Joyce. *The Centenary Prepares War*. Melbourne: Starlight Press, 1934.
Marks, E. George. *Pacific Peril, or, Menace of Japan's Mandated Islands*. Sydney: Wynyard Book Arcade, 1933.
—— *Watch the Pacific!: Defenceless Australia*. Sydney: Coles Book Arcade, 1924.
McCallum, J.A. 'The Economic Bases of Australian Politics'. In *Trends in Australian Politics*. Edited by Maurice Blackburn and W.G.K. Duncan. Sydney: Angus & Robertson in conjunction with the Australian Institute of Political Science, 1935, pp. 44–72.
McKee, Oliver. 'Political March of the Veterans'. *The Commonweal: A Weekly Review of Literature, the Arts and Public Affairs* XIII, no. 2 (1930): 40–2.
Melbourne Punch, 'General Brudenell White', 19 August 1926, p. 12.
Melbourne Punch, 'Sir John Monash', 8 January 1920, 44.
Menzies, Robert. *Australia's Place in the Empire*. Bungay, Suffolk: Richard Clay, 1935.
—— *Prime Minister on War Programme*. Canberra: Government Printer, 1940.
Menzies, Robert, and George Foster Pearce. 'International Situation-Ministerial Statement'. *Current Notes* III (1937): 208–12.
Moffat, J. Pierrepont. 'Australia and the Australians'. In *Australia through American Eyes*. Edited by P.G. Edwards, 45–58. St Lucia: University of Queensland Press, 1979.
—— *Moffat Papers: Selections from the Diplomatic Journals of Jay Pierrepont Moffat, 1919–1943*. Edited by Nancy Hooker. Cambridge: Harvard, 1956.
Moore, Eleanor M. *The Quest for Peace, as I Have Known It in Australia*. Melbourne: Wilkes & Co., 1949.
Observer. 'Australian Defence Policy'. *The Australian Quarterly* VII, no. 2 (1935): 65–74.

'Overseas Trade: Italy'. *Monthly Journal of The Melbourne Chamber of Commerce* XII, no. 7 (1935): 127–8.
Packer, Gerald. 'Demand for Defence'. *The Australian Quarterly* XI, no. 2 (1939): 97–101.
Parkhill, Archdale. *Statement of the Government's Policy Regarding the Defence of Australia.* Canberra: Commonwealth Government Printer, 1935.
Peabody, Frederick William, and Frederick E. Coe. *Honour or Dollars: A Critical Examination of the Moral Obligations of America to Her Former Allies.* Sydney: Angus & Robertson, 1929.
Pearce, George Foster. *Carpenter to Cabinet.* Melbourne: Hutchinson, 1951.
—— *Statement of the Government's Policy Regarding the Defence of Australia.* Melbourne: Department of Defence, 1933.
Piesse, E.L. 'Australia's Duty to Herself', *Austral–Asiatic Bulletin* 1, no. 2 (1937): 6–7.
—— 'Japan and Australia', *Foreign Affairs* IV, no. 3 (1926): 475–88.
—— *Japan and the Defence of Australia.* Melbourne: Robertson & Mullens, 1935.
—— 'Mr Wentworth's Demand for Defence'. *The Australian Quarterly* XI, no. 1 (1939): 54–61.
'Planning, Mapping, Surveying & Visualising: The Service New to Australia of Adastra Airways Ltd'. *The Australasian Manufacturer: Special Industrial Annual,* 18 April 1936, pp. 75, 171.
Pratt, Ambrose, and Edward Leeson. *The National Handbook of Australia's Industries.* Melbourne: Speciality Press, 1934.
Price, Willard. *Japan Reaches Out.* Sydney: Angus & Robertson, 1938.
'Proposed Tour to Japan'. *Monthly Journal of The Melbourne Chamber of Commerce* X, no. 4 (1933): 63.
'Proposed Tour to Japan, Chosen (Korea) and Manchuria', *Monthly Journal of The Melbourne Chamber of Commerce* X, no. 3 (1933): 58.
Proud, J.C. Rockwood. *World Peace, the League and Australia.* Melbourne: Robertson & Mullens, 1936.
'Red Army 'Invades' Poland: Half of Poland Saved from Horrors of War', *World Peace* 4, no. 9 (1939): 112.
Richmond, Herbert. 'Australia's Defences'. *Journal of the Royal United Service Institution* LXXXI, no. 521 (1936): 61–5.
—— 'An Outline of Imperial Defence'. *Army Quarterly* XX IV (1932): 260–79.
Robertson, Horace. *Defence of Australia.* Sydney: Smith & Lane, 1934.
Ross, Ian Clunies. 'Factors Influencing the Development of Australia's Trade with Japan'. In *Australia and the Far East.* Edited by I. Clunies Ross. Sydney: Angus & Robertson in conjunction with The Australian Institute of International Affairs, 1935, pp. 153–202.
Selby, A.R. 'The Association of the Dominions in the Direction of War'. *Army Quarterly* XI, no. 1 (1925): 24–32.
Sleeman, John H.C. *White China: An Austral-Asian Sensation.* Sydney: J.H.C. Sleeman, 1933.
Smith's Weekly, 'Mr. Bruce Faces Crisis of His Career: People's Mandate or Orders of the Moneybags?', 20 February 1926, p. 1.
Smith's Weekly, 'What Nationalists Spent on 15 Federal Candidates: Sensational Disclosures', 6 March 1926, p. 3.
Spinks, Charles Nelson. 'The Termination of the Anglo-Japanese Alliance'. *Pacific Historical Review* VI, no. 4 (1937): 321–40.
Stephensen, P.R. *Mental Rubbish from Overseas.* Sydney: Cultural Defence Committee, 1935.
Sydney Morning Herald (Sydney), 1919–41.
The Army List of the Australian Military Forces: Active List. Melbourne: Government Publisher, 1924, 1926–28, 1932, 1934–35, 1937, 1939.
The Navy List. Melbourne: Government Printer, 1920, 1922–40.
The Royal Australian Air Force List. Melbourne: Government Publisher, 1927–30, 1933–35.
The Staff and Regimental Lists of the Australian Military Forces. Melbourne: Government Publisher, 1931.

Times (London), 1919–26.
United Australia Party. 'Aircraft Manufacture'. *United Australia Party Monthly Bulletin* II, no. 2 (1937): 24–6.
—— 'Australian Defence'. *United Australia Party Monthly Bulletin*, no. 7 (1935): 98–101.
—— 'Britain's Defence Policy: Protection of Overseas Possessions'. *United Australia Party Monthly Bulletin* III, no. 2 (1938): 18.
—— 'Defence Policy'. *United Australia Party Monthly Bulletin*, no. 17 (1936): 245–7.
—— 'Defence—What the Lyons Government Has Done'. *United Australia Party Monthly Bulletin* III, no. 10 (1938): 142–7.
—— 'The European Crisis—Narration of Events'. *United Australia Party Monthly Bulletin* III, no. 8 (1938): 117–21.
—— 'Italo-Abyssinian Dispute—Australia Stands by the League of Nations'. *United Australia Party Monthly Bulletin*, no. 5 (1935): 63–4.
—— 'New Defence Programme: Increased Expenditure of Nearly 25 Millions'. *United Australia Party Monthly Bulletin* III, no. 2 (1938): 19–20.
United Kingdom. House of Commons 1919–42, Debates.
Vigilis, and Vera Shepel (trans.). 'Security in the Pacific Ocean'. *Izvestiya*, 21 May 1937.
Walser, Squadron Leader A.A. 'Aircraft and Imperial Defence'. *Army Quarterly* V, no. 1 (1922): 38–49.
Watt, Raymond. 'The League of Nations Has It Failed? What of Its Future?'. *The Australian Quarterly* V, no. 4 (1933): 99–107.
Wentworth, W.C. *Demand for Defence: Being a Plan to Keep Australia White and Free*. Sydney: W.C. Wentworth, 1939.
Wilcher, Lewis Charles. 'Australia and War to-Day (W.M. Hughes)'. *The Australian Rhodes Review* 2 (1936): 122–6.
Wynne, Cyrill. 'Cyrill Wynne to J. Pierrepont Moffat, 25 July 1936'. In *Australia through American Eyes*. Edited by P.G. Edwards. St Lucia: University of Queensland Press, 1979, pp. 37–40.
Wynter, H.D. 'The Strategical Inter-Relationship of the Navy, the Army, and the Air Force: An Australian View'. *Army Quarterly* XIV (1927): 15–34.
Ziegler, Oswald. *Victorian and Melbourne Centenary Celebrations*. Melbourne: Collins Court, 1934.

SECONDARY SOURCES

Addison, Paul. 'Menzies and Churchill at War'. *Journal of Imperial and Commonwealth History* 19, no. 1 (1991): 107–8.
Andrews, E.M. *Australia and China: The Ambiguous Relationship*. Melbourne: Melbourne University Press, 1985.
—— 'The Australian Government and Appeasement'. *Australian Journal of Politics and History* 13 (1967): 34–46.
—— 'Australian Labour and Foreign Policy 1935–1939'. *Labour History* 9 (1965): 22–33.
—— 'The Broken Promise C Britain's Failure to Consult Its Commonwealth on Defence in 1934, and the Implications for Australian Foreign and Defence Policy'. *The Australian Journal of Defence Studies* 2, no. 2 (1978): 102–13.
—— 'The Great Temptation: The Australian Government and the Sale of Arms to China During the Manchurian Crisis, 1931–33'. *Australian Journal of Politics and History* XXIII, no. 3 (1977): 346–59.
—— *Isolationism and Appeasement in Australia: Reactions to the European Crises, 1935–1939*. Canberra: Australian National University, 1970.
—— 'The 'Labor Daily's' Volte Face on the Abyssinian Crisis, 1935'. *Australian Outlook* 19, no. 2 (1965): 207–12.
—— *The Writing on the Wall: The British Commonwealth and Aggression in the East 1931–1935*. Sydney: Allen & Unwin, 1987.
Arnstein, Walter L. 'Wealth and the Wealthy in the Modern World'. *Journal of Social History* 15, no. 4 (1982): 723–5.

Atkinson, L.D. 'Australian Defence Policy: A Study of Empire and Nation (1897–1910)'. PhD diss., Australian National University, 1964.

Australian Dictionary of Biography. 16 vols. Vols. 7–16. Melbourne: Melbourne University Press, 1979–2002.

Bach, John. *The Australia Station: A History of the Royal Navy in the South West Pacific, 1821–1913*. Kensington, NSW: New South Wales University Press, 1986.

Barclay, Glen St James. 'Singapore Strategy: The Role of the United States in Imperial Defense'. *Military Affairs* 39, no. 2 (1975): 54–9.

Bartrop, Paul. *Bolt from the Blue: Australia, Britain and the Chanak Crisis*. Sydney: Halstead Press, 2002.

Beaumont, Joan. *Australian Defence: Sources and Statistics, The Australian Centenary History of Defence*. Melbourne: Oxford University Press, 2001.

Beazley Sr., Kim E. 'Labour and Foreign Policy', *Australian Outlook* 20, no. 2 (1966): 125–34.

Belich, James. *Paradise Reforged: A History of the New Zealanders from the 1880s to the Year 2000*. Honolulu: University of Hawaii Press, 2001.

Bell, Christopher. *The Royal Navy, Seapower and Strategy between the Wars*. London: Macmillan, 2000.

—— 'Winston Churchill, Pacific Security, and the Limits of British Power, 1921–1941'. In *Churchill and Strategic Dilemmas before the World Wars*. Edited by John H. Maurer. London: Frank Cass, 2003, pp. 51–87.

Bell, Philip and Roger J. Bell. *Implicated: The United States in Australia, Australian Retrospectives*. Melbourne: Oxford University Press, 1993.

Bender, Marylin and Selig Altschul. *The Chosen Instrument: Pan Am, Juan Trippe, the Rise and Fall of an American Entrepreneur*. New York: Simon and Schuster, 1982.

Best, Antony. *British Intelligence and the Japanese Challenge in Asia, 1914–1941*. Palgrave, 2002.

Bird, David Samuel. 'J.A. Lyons, the Tame Tasmanian: A Study in Australian Foreign and Defence Policy, 1932–39'. PhD diss., University of Melbourne, 2004.

Blainey, Geoffrey. *Jumping over the Wheel*. St Leonards, NSW: Allen & Unwin, 1993.

—— *The Steel Master: A Life of Essington Lewis*. Melbourne: Macmillan, 1971.

Blainey, Geoffrey and Norman H. Olver. *The University of Melbourne: A Centenary Portrait*. Melbourne: Melbourne University Press, 1956.

Blake, Robert. 'Churchill and His Promises', *Financial Times*, 6 August 1988.

Boehm, Ernst A. *Twentieth Century Economic Development in Australia*. 2nd ed. *Topics on the Australian Economy*. Melbourne: Longman, 1979.

Bramsted, Ernest. 'Apostles of Collective Security'. *Australian Journal of Politics and History* 23, no. 3 (1967): 347–64.

Brett, Judith. *The Australian Liberals and the Moral Middle Class: From Alfred Deakin to John Howard*. Port Melbourne: Cambridge University Press, 2003.

Bridge, Carl. 'Appeasement and After: Towards a Re-Assessment of the Lyons and Menzies Governments' Defence and Foreign Policies 1931–41'. *Australian Journal of Politics and History* 51, no. 3 (2005): 372–88.

—— 'Australia and the Italo-Abyssinian Crisis of 1935–6'. *Journal of the Royal Australian Historical Society* 92, no. 1 (2006): 1–14.

—— *Casey and the Americans: Australian War Propaganda in the United States, 1940–41*. London: Australian Studies Centre Institute of Commonwealth Studies, 1988.

—— 'Poland to Pearl Harbor'. In *Munich to Vietnam: Australia's Relations with Britain and the United States since the 1930s*. Edited by Carl Bridge. Melbourne: Melbourne University Press, 1991, pp. 38–51.

—— 'R.G. Casey, Australia's First Washington Legation, and the Origins of the Pacific War, 1940–42'. *Australian Journal of Politics and History* 28, no. 2 (1982): 181–9.

—— *Ranging Shots: New Directions in Australian Military History*. London: Sir Robert Menzies Centre for Australian Studies Institute of Commonwealth Studies University of London, 1998.

Brown, Bruce. *Gatty: Prince of Navigators*. Hobart: Libra Books, 1997.

Brown, Pat and Helen Hughes. 'The Marketing Structure of Australian Manufacturing Industry, 1914 to 1963–4'. In *Australian Economic Development in the Twentieth*

Century. Edited by Colin Forster and W.A. Sinclair. Sydney: George Allen & Unwin, 1970, pp. 169–208.

Buckley, Ken and E.L. Wheelwright. *False Paradise: Australian Capitalism Revisited, 1915–1955*. Melbourne: Oxford University Press, 1998.

Burns, Paul. *The Brisbane Line Controversy: Political Opportunism Versus National Security, 1942–45. Army Military History Series. Issues.* St Leonards, NSW: Allen & Unwin, 1998.

Butlin, Sydney James. *War Economy 1939–1942*. Canberra: Australian War Memorial, 1955.

Butt, Peter. 'Our Darkest Hour'. In *When the War came to Australia*, 55 min. Australia: ABC, 1991.

Carlton, David. 'The Dominions and British Policy in the Abyssinian Crisis'. *Journal of Imperial and Commonwealth History* I, no. 1 (1972): 59–77.

Carter, Gwendolen M. *The British Commonwealth and International Security: The Role of the Dominions, 1919–1939*. Toronto: Ryerson Press, 1947.

Churchward, L.G. *Australia & America, 1788–1972, an Alternative History*. Chippendale, NSW: Alternative Publishing, 1979.

Clark, Manning. *A Short History of Australia*. London: Heinemann, 1969.

Clisby, Mark. *Guilty or Innocent?: The Gordon Bennett Case*. North Sydney: Allen & Unwin, 1992.

Cochrane, Peter. 'Dissident Capitalists: National Manufacturers in Conservative Politics, 1917–1934'. In *Essays in the Political Economy of Australian Capitalism*. Edited by E.L. Wheelwright and Ken Buckley. Sydney: Australia and New Zealand Book Co., 1980, p. 210.

—— *Industrialization and Dependence: Australia's Road to Economic Development, 1870–1939*. St Lucia, Qld.: University of Queensland Press, 1980.

Conlon, Robert. *Wheels and Deals: The Automotive Industry in Twentieth Century Australia*. Sydney: Ashgate, 2001.

Connell, Robert William and Terence H. Irving. *Class Structure in Australian History: Documents, Narrative and Argument*. Melbourne: Longman Cheshire, 1980.

Connolly, Ray and Bob Wilson. *Cruel Britannia: Britannia Waives the Rules*. Belmont, NSW: R. Connolly and B. Wilson, 1994.

Costar, Brian and Peter Vlahos. 'Sir Earle Page'. In *Australian Prime Ministers*, 168–73. Sydney: New Holland, 2000.

Coulthard-Clark, C.D. *Breaking Free: Transforming Australia's Defence Industry*. Melbourne: Australian Scholarly Publishing, 1999.

—— *Duntroon, the Royal Military College of Australia, 1911–1986*. Sydney: Allen & Unwin, 1986.

—— 'Formation of the Australian Armed Services, 1901–1914'. In *Australia, Two Centuries of War & Peace*. Edited by Michael McKernan and Margaret Browne. Canberra, ACT: Australian War Memorial in association with Allen & Unwin Australia, 1988, pp. 121–46.

—— *Soldiers in Politics: The Impact of the Military on Australian Political Life and Institutions, Army Military History Series. Issues.* St Leonards, NSW: Allen & Unwin, 1996.

—— *The Third Brother: The Royal Australian Air Force 1921–39*. North Sydney: Allen & Unwin, 1991.

Crisp, L.F. *The Australian Federal Labour Party, 1901–1951*. Melbourne: Longmans, 1955.

Crisp, L.F. and B.C. Atkinson. *Melbourne Punch Profiles, 1904–1929: A Chronological List*. Canberra: Australian National University, 1971.

Cumpston, I.M. *Lord Bruce of Melbourne*. Melbourne: Longman, 1989.

Cunneen, Christopher. *Australian Dictionary of Biography: Supplement 1580–1980, with a Name Index to the Australian Dictionary of Biography to 1980*. Melbourne: Melbourne University Press, 2005.

Curran, James. *The Power of Speech: Australian Prime Ministers Defining the National Image*. Melbourne: Melbourne University Press, 2004.

Daley, Robert. *American Saga: Juan Trippe and His Pan Am Empire*. New York: Random House, 1980.

Darwin, John. 'Imperialism in Decline? Tendencies in British Imperial Policy between the Wars'. *The Historical Journal* 23, no. 3 (1980): 657–79.

—— 'A Third British Empire? The Dominion Idea in Imperial Politics'. In *The Twentieth Century*. Edited by William Roger Louis, Judith M. Brown and Alaine Low. Oxford: Oxford University Press, 1999, pp. 64–87.

Dawson, R. MacGregor. *The Development of Dominion Status, 1900–1936*. London: Frank Cass, 1965.

Day, David. *Claiming a Continent: A New History of Australia*. Pymble, NSW: Angus & Robertson, 1997.

—— *Conquest: A New History of the Modern World*. Pymble, NSW: HarperCollins Publishers, 2005.

—— 'Curtin Led us out of Dark Days into a Golden Age'. *Australian*, 5 July 2005, p. 13.

—— 'Farewell to the Old Country'. *Australian*, 15 August 2005.

—— *The Great Betrayal: Britain, Australia and the Onset of the Pacific War 1939–1942*. 1st ed. Sydney: Angus & Robertson, 1988.

—— *The Great Betrayal: Britain, Australia and the Onset of the Pacific War 1939–1942*. 2nd ed. Sydney: Angus & Robertson, 1992.

—— 'The Horrors and Legacy of World War II'. *Australian*, 15 August 2005, p. 8.

—— 'How the ALP Will Make Its Mark'. *Australian*, 2 December 2003, p. 13.

—— *John Curtin: A Life*. Pymble, NSW: Harper Collins, 1999.

—— 'Labor Must Be No Party to War Cry'. *Australian*, 4 October 2002, p. 11.

—— 'Menzies and Churchill at War'. *Courier-Mail*, 23 August 1986.

—— *Menzies and Churchill at War: A Controversial New Account of the 1941 Struggle for Power*. Sydney: Angus & Robertson, 1986.

—— 'Me-Too Gulf Adventurism Will Exact a Heavy Price'. *Australian*, 28 January 2003, p. 11.

—— *The Politics of War*. Sydney: Harper Collins, 2003.

—— 'The Politics of War'. *The Sydney Papers* 15, no. 1 (2003): 123–30.

—— *Reluctant Nation: Australia and the Allied Defeat of Japan 1942–45*. Melbourne: Oxford University Press, 1992.

—— 'Shooting at Shadows'. *Australian*, 26 April 2004, p. 9.

—— 'VP Day'. *Australian*, 16 August 2005, p. 13.

Dennis, Lionel. *Australia since 1890*. Melbourne: Addison, Wesley, and Longman, 1996.

Dennis, Peter. 'Australia and the Singapore Strategy'. In *Sixty Years On: The Fall of Singapore Revisited*. Edited by Brian Farrell and Sandy Hunter. Singapore: Eastern Universities Press, 2002, pp. 29–41.

Dennis, Peter, Jeffrey Grey, Ewan Morris, Robin Prior and John Connor. 'Citizen Military Forces (CMF)'. In *The Oxford Companion to Australian Military History*. Edited by Peter Dennis. Melbourne: Oxford University Press, 2008, pp. 146–50.

—— 'Imperial Defence'. In *The Oxford Companion to Australian Military History*. Edited by Peter Dennis. Melbourne: Oxford University Press, 2008, p. 307.

—— 'Singapore Strategy'. In *The Oxford Companion to Australian Military History*. Edited by Peter Dennis. Melbourne: Oxford University Press, 2008, pp. 549–50.

Edwards, John. *Curtin's Gift: Reinterpreting Australia's Greatest Prime Minister*. Crows Nest, NSW: Allen & Unwin, 2005.

Edwards, P.G. *Prime Ministers and Diplomats: The Making of Australian Foreign Policy, 1901–1949*. Melbourne: Oxford University Press in association with the Australian Institute of International Affairs, 1983.

Encel, Solomon. *Equality and Authority: A Study of Class, Status and Power in Australia*. Melbourne: Cheshire, 1970.

Esthus, Raymond. *From Enmity to Alliance: US–Australian Relations, 1931–1941*. Seattle: University of Washington Press, 1964.

Farrell, Brian. *The Defence and Fall of Singapore 1940–1942*. London: Tempus, 2005.

Field, G. Lowell and John Higley. *Elitism*. London: Routledge & Kegan Paul, 1980.

Firth, S.G. 'Social Values in the New South Wales Primary School 1880–1914: An Analysis of School Texts'. *Melbourne Studies in Education* (1970): 123–60.

Fitzhardinge, Laurence Frederic. *The Little Digger, 1914–1952: William Morris Hughes, a Political Biography*. 2 vols. Vol. 2. Sydney: Angus & Robertson, 1979.

Fleming, Grant A., Simon P. Ville and David Merrett. *The Big End of Town: Big Business and Corporate Leadership in Twentieth-Century Australia*. Melbourne: Cambridge University Press, 2004.

Forster, Colin. *Industrial Development in Australia 1920–1930*. Canberra: Australian National University, 1964.

Foster, Leonie. *High Hopes: The Men and Motives of the Australian Round Table*. Melbourne: Melbourne University Press, 1986.

Frame, Tom. *No Pleasure Cruise: The Story of the Royal Australian Navy*. Crows Nest, NSW: Allen & Unwin, 2004.

Frei, Henry. *Japan's Southward Advance and Australia: From Sixteenth Century to World War II*. Honolulu: University of Hawaii Press, 1991.

Freudenberg, Graham. *Churchill and Australia*. Pan Macmillan Australia: Sydney, 2008.

Galbraith, John S. 'The Imperial Conference of 1921 and the Washington Conference'. *The Canadian Historical Review* XXIX, no. 2 (1948): 143–52.

Geeves, Philip and Oam Frahs. *The Dawn of Australia's Radio Broadcasting*. Alexandria: Electronics Australia, 1993.

Gillison, Douglas. *Royal Australian Air Force, 1939–42*. 4 vols. Vol. 1. *Australia in the War of 1939–1945: Series 3, Air*. Canberra: Australian War Memorial, 1954.

Gooch, John. 'The Politics of Strategy: Great Britain, Australia and the War against Japan, 1939–1945'. *War in History* 10, no. 4 (2003): 424–47.

Gordon, Donald C. *The Dominion Partnership in Imperial Defense, 1870–1914*. Baltimore: Johns Hopkins Press, 1965.

Gow, Neil. 'Australian Army Strategic Planning 1919–1939'. *Australian Journal of Politics and History* 23, no. 2 (1977): 169–72.

Greenwood, Gordon. 'Development in the Twenties, 1919–29'. In *Australia: A Social and Political History*. Edited by Gordon Greenwood. Sydney: Angus & Robertson, 1974, pp. 287–343.

Grey, Jeffrey. *The Australian Army*. Melbourne: Oxford University Press, 2001.

—— *A Military History of Australia*. Melbourne: Cambridge University Press, 1990.

Grose, Peter. *A Very Rude Awakening: The Night the Japanese Midget Subs Came to Sydney Harbour*. Sydney: Allen & Unwin, 2007.

Hack, Karl and Kevin Blackburn. *Did Singapore Have to Fall? Churchill and the Impregnable Fortress*. London: Routledge Curzon, 2003.

Haenke, Kathy. 'The Boomerang Story'. Edited by John Haenke. Nomad Television Productions, 1994.

Haggie, Paul. *Britannia at Bay: The Defence of the British Empire against Japan 1931–1941*. Oxford: Clarendon Press, 1981.

Hamill, Ian. 'An Australian Defence Policy?: The Singapore Strategy and the Defence of Australia'. *Australian National University Historical Journal* 10–11 (1973–1974): 10–20.

—— *The Strategic Illusion: The Singapore Strategy and the Defence of Australia and New Zealand, 1919–1942*. Singapore: Singapore University Press, 1981.

Harper, Norman. *A Great and Powerful Friend: A Study of Australian American Relations between 1900 and 1975*. St Lucia: University of Queensland Press, 1987.

Hart, Philip. 'J.A. Lyons: A Political Biography'. PhD diss., Australian National University, 1967.

—— 'The Piper and the Tune'. In *Australian Conservatism: Essays in Twentieth Century Political History*. Edited by Cameron Hazlehurst. Canberra: Australian National University Press, 1979, pp. 111–48.

Hasluck, Paul. *The Government and the People, 1939–1941*. 2 vols. Vol. 1. *Australia in the War of 1939–1945. Series 4, Civil*. Canberra: Australian War Memorial, 1952.

Hastings, Peter. 'Britain's Great Betrayal'. *Sydney Morning Herald*, 25 April 1988, p. 9.

Hazlehurst, Cameron. 'David Day, Menzies and Churchill at War'. *Politics: Journal of the Australasian Political Studies Association* 22, no. 2 (1987): 130–1.

Higley, John, Desley Deacon and Don Smart. *Elites in Australia*. London: Routledge & K. Paul, 1979.

Higley, John and Gwen Moore. 'Elite Integration in the United States and Australia'. *The American Political Science Review* 75, no. 3 (1981): 581–97.
Hill, A.J. 'Rosenthal, Sir Charles (1875–1954)'. In *Australian Dictionary of Biography*. Melbourne: Melbourne University Press, 1988, pp. 451–3.
Hilmer, Norman. 'The Foreign Office, the Dominions and the Diplomatic Unity of the Empire, 1925–29'. In *Retreat from Power: Studies in Britain's Foreign Policy of the Twentieth Century*. Edited by David Dilks. London: Macmillan, 1981, pp. 64–77.
Horner, David. 'Australian Army Strategic Planning between the Wars'. In *Serving Vital Interests: Australia's Strategic Planning in Peace and War: Proceedings of the Australian Army History Conference Held at the Australian War Memorial, 30 September 1996*. Edited by Peter Dennis and Jeffrey Grey. Canberra: Australian Defence Force Academy, 1996, pp. 75–101.
—— 'Australian Estimates of the Japanese Threat, 1905–1941'. In *Estimating Foreign Military Power*. Edited by Philip Towle. London: Croom Helm, 1982, pp. 139–71.
—— *Blamey: Commander in Chief*. Sydney: Allen & Unwin, 1998.
—— *Defence Supremo: Sir Frederick Shedden and the Making of Australian Defence Policy*. Sydney: Allen & Unwin, 2000.
—— *High Command: Australia and Allied Strategy, 1939–1945*. Canberra: Australian War Memorial, 1982.
—— *The Gunners: A History of Australian Artillery*. St Leonards, NSW: Allen & Unwin, 1995.
Howard, Michael. 'British Military Preparations for the Second World War'. In *Retreat from Power: Studies in Britain's Foreign Policy of the Twentieth Century*. Edited by David Dilks. London: Macmillan, 1981, pp. 102–17.
Howarth, Stephen. *Morning Glory: A History of the Imperial Japanese Navy*. London: Arrow, 1985.
Hudson, W.J. *Australia and the League of Nations*. Sydney: Sydney University Press in association with the Australian Institute of International Affairs, 1980.
—— *Casey*. Melbourne: Oxford University Press, 1986.
Hudson, W.J. and M.P. Sharp. *Australian Independence: Colony to Reluctant Kingdom*. Melbourne: Melbourne University Press, 1988.
Hughes, Colin A. and B.D. Graham. *A Handbook of Australian Government and Politics, 1890–1964*. Canberra: Australian National University Press, 1968.
Hyslop, Robert. *Australian Naval Administration 1900–1939*. Melbourne: Hawthorn Press, 1973.
Inglis, Amirah. *Australians in the Spanish Civil War*. Sydney: Allen & Unwin, 1987.
Inglis, K.S. and Jan Brazier. *This is the ABC: The Australian Broadcasting Commission, 1932–1983*. Melbourne: Melbourne University Press, 1983.
Irving, Baiba Beata Berzins. 'The Nationalist Party, 1919–1930: Organisation and Ideology'. PhD diss., University of Sydney, 1972.
Johnson, Douglas. 'Kangeroo Shadow-Boxing' [*sic*]. *History Today* 37, no. 5 (1987): 56.
Johnson, Franklyn A. *Defence by Committee: The British Committee of Imperial Defence*. London: Oxford University Press, 1960.
Johnson, Lesley. *The Unseen Voice: A Cultural Study of Early Australian Radio*. London: Routledge, 1988.
Jones, Paul. 'Trading in a "Fool's Paradise"? White Australia and the Trade Diversion Dispute of 1936'. In *Relationships: Japan and Australia 1870s–1950s*. Edited by Vera C. Mackie and Paul Anthony Francis Jones. Melbourne: History Department University of Melbourne, 2001, pp. 133–63.
Keating, Paul. 'Foreword'. In *Reluctant Nation: Australia and the Allied Defeat of Japan 1942–45*. Melbourne: Oxford University Press, 1992, pp. iii–iv.
—— *Paul Keating, Prime Minister: Major Speeches of the First Year*. Canberra: Australian Labor Party, 1993.
Keene, Jennifer D. *Doughboys, the Great War, and the Remaking of America, War, Society, Culture*. Baltimore: Johns Hopkins University Press, 2001.
Kemp, Charles Denton. *Big Businessmen: Four Biographical Essays*. Melbourne: Institute of Public Affairs, 1964.

Kennett, John. 'The Collins House Group'. MEcon, Monash, 1982.
Kneipp, Pauline. A Comparative Study of American and Australian Catholic Reaction to European Diplomatic Crises: 1935 to 1939. PhD diss., University of Sydney, 1974.
—— 'Australian Catholics and the Abyssinian War'. *The Journal of Religious History* 10, no. 4 (1979): 417–30.
Knightley, Phillip. 'Victim of the Colonial Mentality'. *The Sunday Times*, 17 July 1988.
Kristianson, G.L. *The Politics of Patriotism: The Pressure Group Activities of the Returned Servicemen's League*. Canberra: Australian National University Press, 1966.
Lack, John. 'McKay, Hugh Victor'. In *Australian Dictionary of Biography*. Melbourne: Melbourne University Press, 1986, pp. 291–4.
Lee, Bradford A. *Britain and the Sino-Japanese War, 1937–1939: A Study in the Dilemmas of British Decline*. Stanford: Stanford University Press, 1973.
Legg, Frank. *The Gordon Bennett Story*. Sydney: Angus & Robertson, 1965.
Lloyd, C.J. 'The Development and Organisation of the Federal Parliamentary Press Gallery, 1901–1978'. MA, Australian National University, 1979.
—— 'The Formation and Development of the United Australia Party, 1929–37', PhD diss., Australian National University, 1984.
—— 'The Rise and Fall of the United Australia Party'. In *Liberalism and the Australian Federation*. Edited by J.R. Nethercote. Annandale, NSW: Federation Press, 2001, pp. 134–62.
Lloyd, Lorna. 'Loosening the Apron Strings: The Dominions and Britain in the Interwar Years'. *The Round Table*, no. 369 (2003): 279–303.
Lodge, A.B. *Lavarack: Rival General*. Sydney: Allen & Unwin, 1998.
Long, Gavin. *The Six Years War: A Concise History of Australia in the 1939–45 War*. Canberra: Australian War Memorial and the Australian Government Publishing Service, 1973.
—— *To Benghazi*. 7 vols. Vol. 1. *Australia in the War of 1939–1945. Series 1, Army*. Canberra: Australian War Memorial, 1952.
Macintyre, Stuart. 'Annihilation of the Annals'. *Australian*, 20 May 2005, p. 15.
—— *The Reds: The Communist Party of Australia from Origins to Illegality*. Sydney: Allen & Unwin, 1998.
Massie, Robert K. *Dreadnought: Britain, Germany, and the Coming of the Great War*. New York: Random House, 1991.
Mathews, Race. *Australia's First Fabians: Middle-Class Radicals, Labour Activists and the Early Labour Movement*. Melbourne: Cambridge University Press, 1993.
Matthews, Jill Julius. 'Which America'. In *Americanization and Australia*. Edited by Roger J. Bell and Philip Bell. Sydney: University of New South Wales Press, 1998, pp. 15–31.
May, Andrew. 'Fortress Australia'. In *Between Empire and Nation: Australia's External Relations from Federation to the Second World War*. Edited by Carl Bridge and Bernard Attard. Melbourne: Australian Scholarly Publishing, 2000, pp. 205–29.
Mayer, Henry. 'Pressure Groups in Australia'. In *Australian Politics: A Reader*. Edited by Kurt Mayer. Melbourne: Cheshire, 1966, pp. 181–223.
McCalman, Janet. *Journeyings: The Biography of a Middle-Class Generation 1920–1990*. Melbourne, 1993.
McCarthy, Dudley. *South-West Pacific Area – First Year: Kokoda to Wau*. Canberra: Australian War Memorial, 1959.
McCarthy, John Malcolm. *Australia and Imperial Defence 1918–39: A Study in Air and Sea Power*. St Lucia: University of Queensland Press, 1976.
—— 'Australia and Imperial Defence: Co-Operation and Conflict 1918–1939'. *Australian Journal of Politics and History* XVII, no. 1 (1971): 19–32.
—— 'The 'Great Betrayal' Reconsidered: An Australian Perspective'. *Australian Journal of International Affairs* 48, no. 1 (1994): 54–62.
—— 'The Imperial Commitment 1939–41'. *Australian Journal of Politics and History* 23, no. 2 (1977): 178–81.
McGibbon, Ian. *Blue-Water Rationale: The Naval Defence of New Zealand 1914–1942*. Wellington: Government Printer, 1981.

McIntyre, William David. *The Rise and Fall of the Singapore Naval Base, 1919–1942.* Hamden, Ct.: Archon Books, 1979.
McMullin, Ross. *The Light on the Hill: The Australian Labor Party, 1891–1991.* Melbourne: Oxford University Press, 1992.
McNicoll, Ronald. *Number 36 Collins Street, Melbourne Club 1838–1988.* Sydney: Allen & Unwin in conjunction with the Melbourne Club, 1988.
Meaney, Neville. 'Australia and the World'. In *Under New Heavens: Cultural Transmission and the Making of Australia.* Edited by Neville Meaney. Melbourne: Heinemann Educational, 1989, pp. 381–450.
—— *Fears & Phobias: E.L. Piesse and the Problem of Japan.* Canberra: National Library of Australia, 1996.
—— *The Search for Security in the Pacific, 1901–14.* Sydney: Sydney University Press, 1976.
Megaw, Ruth. 'Australia and the Anglo-American Trade Agreement, 1938'. *Journal of Imperial and Commonwealth History* III, no. 2 (1975): 191–211.
—— 'The Australian Goodwill Mission to the Far East in 1934 and the Evolution of Australian Foreign Policy'. *Journal of Royal Australian Historical Society* 59, no. 4 (1973): 247–63.
—— 'The Scramble for the Pacific Anglo-United States Rivalry in the 1930s'. *Historical Studies* 17, no. 69 (1977): 438–73.
—— 'Undiplomatic Channels: Australian Representation in the United States, 1919–1939'. *Historical Studies* 15, no. 60 (1973): 610–30.
Millar, T.B. *Australia in Peace and War.* Canberra: Australian National University Press, 1991.
Miller, Edward. *War Plan Orange: The U.S. Strategy to Defeat Japan, 1897–1945.* Annapolis: Naval Institute Press, 1991.
Mills, C. Wright. 'The American Business Elite: A Collective Portrait'. In *Power, Politics and People: The Collected Essays of C. Wright Mills.* Edited by Irving Louis Horowitz. New York: Oxford University Press, 1963, pp. 110–40.
—— *The Power Elite.* New York: Oxford University Press, 1956.
Moore, Eleanor M. *The Quest for Peace, as I Have Known It in Australia.* Melbourne: Wilkes & Co., 1949.
Mordike, John Leonard. *We Should Do This Thing Quietly: Japan and the Great Deception in Australian Defence Policy 1911–1914.* Canberra: Aerospace Centre, 2002.
Morrow, John Howard. *The Great War: An Imperial History.* London: Routledge, 2004.
Murfett, Malcolm. 'Living in the Past: A Critical Re-examination of the Singapore Naval Strategy, 1918–1941'. *War & Society* 11, no. 1 (1993): 73–103.
—— . 'The Singapore Strategy'. In *Between Empire and Nation: Australia's External Relations from Federation to the Second World War.* Edited by Carl Bridge and Bernard Attard. Melbourne: Australian Scholarly Publishing, 2000, pp. 230–50.
Murfett, Malcolm H., John N. Miksic, Brian P. Farrell and Ming Shun Chiang. *Between Two Oceans: A Military History of Singapore From First Settlement to Final British Withdrawal.* Singapore: Marshall Cavendish Academic, 2004.
Murray, Jacqui. *Watching the Sun Rise: Australian Reporting of Japan, 1931 to the Fall of Singapore.* New York: Lexington Books, 2004.
Nairn, Bede. *The 'Big Fella': Jack Lang and the Australian Labor Party 1891–1949.* Melbourne: Melbourne University Press, 1986.
Neidpath, James. *The Singapore Naval Base and the Defence of Britain's Eastern Empire, 1919–1941.* Oxford: Oxford University Press, 1981.
Nish, Ian. 'Relations with Japan'. In *Between Empire and Nation: Australia's External Relations from Federation to the Second World War.* Edited by Carl Bridge and Bernard Attard. Melbourne: Australian Scholarly Publishing, 2000, pp. 159–71.
O'Brien, John. 'Empire V. National Interests in Australian-British Relations During the 1930s'. *Historical Studies* 22, no. 89 (1987): 569–86.
O'Brien, Phillips Payson. *British and American Naval Power: Politics and Policy, 1900–1936.* Westport, CT.: Praeger, 1998.
Oliver, Bobbie. *Peacemongers: Conscientious Objectors to Military Service in Australia, 1911–1945.* Fremantle, WA: Fremantle Arts Centre Press, 1997.

Osmond, Warren. *Frederic Eggleston: An Intellectual in Australian Politics*. Sydney: George Allen & Unwin, 1985.
Ovendale, Ritchie. *'Appeasement' and the English Speaking World: Britain, the United States, the Dominions, and the Policy of 'Appeasement' 1937–1939*. Cardiff: University of Wales Press, 1975.
Palazzo, Albert. *The Australian Army: A History of Its Organisation 1901–2001. Australian Army History Series.* South Melbourne: Oxford University Press, 2001.
Pareto, Vilfredo. *The Rise and Fall of Elites: An Application of Theoretical Sociology*. New Brunswick, New Jersey: Transaction Publishers, 1991.
Parker, R.S. 'Group Interests and the Non-Labour Parties since 1930'. In *Readings in Australian Government*. Edited by Colin A. Hughes. St Lucia: University of Queensland Press, 1968, pp. 380–91.
Partridge, P.H. 'Depression and War, 1929–1950'. In *Australia: A Social and Political History*. Edited by Gordon Greenwood. Sydney: Angus & Robertson, 1974, pp. 344–417.
Peden, G.C. *British Rearmament and the Treasury, 1932–1939*. Edinburgh: Scottish Academic Press, 1979.
—— . 'The Burden of Imperial Defence and the Continental Commitment Reconsidered'. *The Historical Journal* 27, no. 2 (1984): 405–23.
Perkin, Harold. 'The Recruitment of Elites in British Society since 1800'. *Journal of Social History* 12, no. 2 (1978): 222–34.
Perry, Warren. 'The Late Sir Frederick Shedden: An Appreciation'. *Victorian Historical Magazine* 42, no. 3 (1971): 633–7.
—— . 'Lieutenant General Henry Douglas Wynter: An Officer of the Australian Staff Corps'. *Victorian Historical Magazine* 43, no. 1 (1972): 837–72.
—— . 'Wynter, Henry Douglas'. In *Australian Dictionary of Biography*. Melbourne: Melbourne University Press, 2002, pp. 599–600.
Presthus, Robert. *Elites in the Policy Process*. London: Cambridge University Press, 1974.
Primrose, B.N. 'Equipment and Naval Policy 1919–1942'. *Australian Journal of Politics and History* 23, no. 2 (1977): 163–8.
Putnam, Robert D. *The Comparative Study of Political Elites, Contemporary Comparative Politics Series*. Englewood Cliffs, New Jersey: Prentice-Hall, 1976.
Quinault, Roland. 'Churchill and Australia: The Military Relationship, 1899–1945'. *War & Society* 6, no. 1 (1988): 41–64.
Rasmussen, Carolyn. *The Lesser Evil? Opposition to War and Fascism in Australia, 1920–1941, Melbourne University History Monographs: No. 15*. Melbourne: History Department University of Melbourne, 1992.
Rayner, Robert. *The Darwin Detachment*. Wollongong: Rudder Press, 2002.
'Recent Books on International Relations'. *Foreign Affairs* 68, no. 3 (1989): 176.
Reynolds, David. *The Creation of the Anglo-American Alliance, 1937–41: A Study in Competitive Co-Operation*. Chapel Hill: University of North Carolina Press, 1982.
Rhodes, Benjamin. 'The Image of Britain in the United States, 1919–1929'. In *Anglo-American Relations in the 1920's: The Struggle for Supremacy*. Edited by B.J.C. McKercher. Houndmills, Basingstoke, Hampshire: Macmillan, 1991, pp. 187–207.
Rivett, Rohan. *Australian Citizen: Herbert Brookes, 1867–1963*. Melbourne: Melbourne University Press, 1965.
Robertson, Horace. *Defence of Australia*. Sydney: Smith & Lane, 1934.
Robertson, John. *Australia at War 1939–1945*. Melbourne: Heinemann, 1981.
—— *J.H. Scullin: A Political Biography*. Nedlands, WA: University of Western Australia Press, 1974.
Ross, Andrew. *Armed and Ready: The Industrial Development & Defence of Australia, 1900–1945*. Sydney: Turton & Armstrong, 1995.
—— 'The Arming of Australia: The Politics and Administration of Australia's Self Containment Strategy for Munitions Supply 1901–1945'. PhD diss., University of New South Wales, Australian Defence Forces Academy, 1986.

—— 'The Rise of Australian Defence Industry and Science 1901–1945'. In *Arming the Nation*. Edited by Frank Cain. Canberra: Australian Defence Studies Centre, 1999, pp. 23–38.
Rubinstein, W.D. 'Education and the Social Origins of British Elites 1880–1970'. *Past and Present*, no. 112 (1986): 163–207.
Rydon, Joan. *A Biographical Register of the Commonwealth Parliament, 1901–1972*. Canberra: Australian National University Press, 1975.
—— 'The Conservative Electoral Ascendancy between the Wars'. In *Australian Conservatism: Essays in Twentieth Century Political History*. Edited by Cameron Hazlehurst. Canberra: Australian National University Press, 1979, pp. 51–70.
—— *A Federal Legislature: The Australian Commonwealth Parliament, 1901–1980*. Melbourne: Oxford University Press, 1986.
Sales, Peter M. 'W.M. Hughes and the Chanak Crisis of 1922'. *The Australian Journal of Politics and History* XVII, no. 3 (1971): 392–405.
Saunders, Malcolm. *Quiet Dissenter: The Life and Thought of an Australian Pacifist: Eleanor May Moore 1875–1949, Monograph/Peace Research Centre, No. 12*. Canberra: Peace Research Centre Research School of Pacific Studies Australian National University, 1993.
Saunders, Malcolm, and Ralph Summy. *The Australian Peace Movement: A Short History*. Canberra: Peace Research Centre Australian National University, 1986.
Sawer, Geoffrey. *Australian Federal Politics and Law, 1929–1949*. Melbourne: Melbourne University Press, 1963.
Scott, Ernest, and Herbert Burton. *A Short History of Australia*. 7th ed. Melbourne: Oxford University Press, 1947.
Scott, John. *Who Rules Britain?* Oxford: Polity Press, 1991.
Sears, Jason. '1929–1939: Depression and Rearmament'. In *The Royal Australian Navy*. Edited by David Stevens. Oxford: Oxford University Press, 2001, pp. 81–101.
Selleck, R.J.W. *The Shop: The University of Melbourne 1850–1939*. Melbourne: Melbourne University Press, 2003.
Serle, Geoffrey. *From Deserts the Prophets Come: The Creative Spirit in Australia 1788–1972*. Melbourne: Heinemann, 1973.
—— 'Great Britain and Australia, 1919–39', DPhil, Oxford, 1949.
Shaw, A.G.L. *The Story of Australia*. 2nd ed. *Faber Paper Covered Editions*. London: Faber and Faber, 1962.
Sissons, D.C.S. 'Manchester V. Japan: The Imperial Background to the Australian Trade Diversion Dispute with Japan, 1936'. *Australian Outlook* 30, no. 3 (1976): 480–502.
Smith, F.B. 'British History in Australia'. *Melbourne studies in Education* (1981): 42–59.
Stanley, Peter. "He's (not) Coming South': 'The Invasion That Wasn't', *Wartime*, Issue 19, July 2002, pp. 7–8.
—— 'Who Won the War in 1944?: Nationalism and Australian Historians of the Second World War'. In *Ranging Shots: New Directions in Australian Military History*. Edited by Carl Bridge. London: Sir Robert Menzies Centre for Australian Studies Institute of Commonwealth Studies University of London, 1998, pp. 67–79.
Stephens, Alan. *The Royal Australian Air Force*. Melbourne: Oxford University Press, 2001.
Thomas, Alan. *Broadcast and Be Damned: The ABC's First Two Decades*. Melbourne: Melbourne University Press, 1980.
—— 'Political Pressure in the ABC'. In *Stay Tuned: An Australian Broadcasting Reader*. Edited by Albert Moran. Sydney: Allen & Unwin, 1992, pp. 66–70.
Thomson, Alistair. *Anzac Memories: Living with the Legend*. Melbourne: Oxford University Press, 1994.
Thorne, Christopher. 'Book Reviews'. *The Journal of Imperial and Commonwealth History* 17, no. 3 (1989): 474–5.
Thornton, Robert. 'Australia and the Abrogation of the Anglo-Japanese Alliance'. MA, University of Melbourne, 1975.

Trainor, Luke. *British Imperialism and Australian Nationalism: Manipulation, Conflict, and Compromise in the Late Nineteenth Century, Studies in Australian History.* Melbourne: Cambridge University Press, 1994.

Trengove, Alan. *What's Good for Australia!: The Story of BHP*. Melbourne: Cassell, 1975.

Tsokhas, Kosmas. *Making a Nation State: Cultural Identity, Economic Nationalism and Sexuality in Australian History*. Melbourne: Melbourne University Press, 2001.

Walder, David. *The Chanak Affair*. London: Hutchinson, 1969.

Walker, David. *Anxious Nation: Australia and the Rise of Asia 1850–1939*. St Lucia: University of Queensland, 1999.

Waters, Christopher. *The Empire Fractures: Anglo-Australian Conflict in the 1940s*. Melbourne: Australian Scholarly Publishing, 1995.

Watson, Lex. 'The United Australia Party and Its Sponsors'. In *Australian Conservatism: Essays in Twentieth Century Political History*. Edited by Cameron Hazlehurst. Canberra: Australian National University Press, 1979, pp. 71–109.

Wigmore, Lionel. *The Japanese Thrust*. 7 vols. Vol. 4. *Australia in the War of 1939–1945. Series 1, Army*. Canberra: Australian War Memorial, 1957.

Wilcox, Craig. *For Hearths and Homes: Citizen Soldiering in Australia, 1854–1945*. St Leonards, NSW: Allen & Unwin, 1998.

Willis, Sabine. 'The Formulation of Australian Attitudes Towards China: 1918–1941'. PhD diss., University of New South Wales, 1974.

Wilson, Stewart. 'Glory Days: Australian Aircraft Production in WWII'. *Aero Australia*, January–March 2004: 36–43.

Winter, Captain P.D. 'Comparing the 'Singapore Strategy' and 'Fortress Australia': Concepts for Australia's Defence in the 1930s'. *Defence Force Journal*, no. 65 (1987): 29–39.

Wurth, Bob. *1942: Australia's Greatest Peril.* Sydney: Pan Macmillan, 2008.

INDEX